GĪTĀ FOR SUCCESS IN MODERN LIFE

This book discusses and explains the implications of certain parts of Bhagavad-Gītā insofar as they affect the daily life of a reasonably well-placed person. The text written in simple language is particularly aimed at the forever-busy and on the move folk. Contrary to popular belief that the Gītā is for the aged, the scripture is useful at all stages of one's life. As they say, if Big Ben has time, the Tower of Pisa has the inclination. So also, if the modern man has the time, the Gītā is designed to help him realise his objectives in life. In short, the Gītā implies fruitful living and this book is a modest attempt to establish this fact.

Gītā for Success in Modern Life

From Basement to Boardroom

R.S. Garg

New Age Books

ISBN: 81-7822-125-x

Second Revised Edition: Delhi, 2004

First Edition: Delhi, 2003

Published by

NEW AGE BOOKS

A-44 Naraina Phase-I

New Delhi-110 028 (INDIA)

Email: nab@vsnl.in

Website: www.newagebooksindia.com

Printed in India

at Shri Jainendra Press

A-45 Naraina Phase-I, New Delhi-110 028

To
all men and women
of action
who seek Peace and Happiness
in the troubled world
of today.

Preface to the Second Revised Edition

In the preface to the first edition, I had said that my endeavor was to attempt this book in a way which is simple in language and presentation so that readers feel that the Gītā is for them and for their benefit. Since I believe that agents of change are young people, I tried to make the book acceptable and enjoyable to them particularly, though not exclusively. The young is out in the world to rise, succeed in life and make money. Business and Corporate World are important hubs of activities for them. Therefore, I have focussed on these elements in society. If the youth, business and corporate world will follow the right value system, every one would rise and succeed. One can succeed with righteous means and right values. Dishonesty is a slippery ladder. The great epic—the Gītā—shows the way as to how. I have only tried to interpret "as to how" in a slightly different but scientific manner.

Link between body and mind: Peace and Productivity: Stress and Slow-down needs to be understood. Similarly, incorrect life-style and ill-health are also interlinked. Getting tired too soon may lead to getting retired and fired. Health is a precious resource. Let nobody waste it.

I would use this opportunity of writing preface to this improved edition for removing some misconception about morality and success. Morality does not flow from rituals inside or outside temples but through following right values at home, school, office, farm and factory. Success lies in growing market share, satisfied employees and committed customers. Instead of worshipping, live Gītā. Let it enrich and brighten our lives.

My grateful thanks to past and prospective readers.

R. S. Garg

Preface

It is not easy to justify yet another book on the Gītā. All the same, as I see the social scenario all around, the need for the book is perhaps more than justified Firstly, for good practical reasons, the Gitā needs to be taken off the shelf and its religious wrappings removed. It need not be worshipped as a religious object or as a daily ritual, but adopted in real life. It must be clearly understood that practice of its injunctions in life, not its worship, is going to deliver man from the causes of his unhappiness and make his life a peaceful, happy and enjoyable experience. In the modern age, the Gītā is not beneficial for those who merely respect or revere it, but it does greatly benefit those who adopt its teachings in their day-to-day life. Respect for the Gītā not fully comprehended is a poor substitute for following its teachings. Adoption of its teachings must manifest itself in one's changed or improved approach to life or better value-systems.

As with medication, same with the teachings of the Gītā. Unless used in proper prescribed manner, no amount of praise of medicine will cure a malady.

The moral, spritual and cultural decay in society, despite the growing graph of deity worshippers, inside the temple and in households, is indicative of the wide gap between appearance and reality or what man professes and his practice. There are many reasons which have contributed to the prevailing situation wherein a normal human being would not change his usual course of behavior in favor of truthfulness or righteous action.

First, it is a wrong belief that worshipping or at best reading of the Gītā (or other scriptures for that matter) would suffice *per se*. The truth of the contrary is not emphasized or highlighted. Such a wrong belief might be generated either out of ignorance, or as a result of vested interests of those on whom society generally relies for interpretation of scriptures. It may also be due to the bent of mind of the majority of men and women who are in favor of shortcuts and easy ways. For example, a large majority of people whose words and actions do not match are not aware nor made aware by others that every action, good or bad, must produce a corresponding result (effect) and that there is absolutely no escape from the cycle of cause and effect.

Secondly, I believe that since the Gītā is for me it should be available to me in a language I can comprehend and in style that makes it easy for me to relate its teachings to my life. Behind this is the approach that rules, law etc. should be made simple and comprehensible for those for whom they are meant. In the beginning of my career with the Government of India, I did a stint with Personnel Adminisitration. I realized that rules which are simple and written in a simple language ensure better compliance and fewer violations. The same logic should apply to the Gītā. Emphasis should be on those parts of the Gītā, which affect one's life directly and for that reason, one would be inclined to read, understand and imbibe the teachings contained in it. Otherwise, one may find it drab and get put off in those parts in particular

In this book, my endeavor has not been to particularly address religious or other scholar. I have neither the intention nor do I presume the capability to do that. My objective has been to make this great scripture of knowledge a book of Everyman's life. Everyone is interested in his or her own life and in making it peaceful, happy and enjoyable. If I am convinced that the Gītā shows the way, the Gītā is for me. Conviction should flow from onés own understanding of the logic behind the teachings, and this book is an attempt to view this immense religious tome from a commoner's angle. Simplicity of language and presentation has been kept in mind so that the reader feels that the Gītā is for him and for his benefit. He is going to be the net gainer for all the expense of time and effort. All men of action, businessmen (owners and workers alike), professionals, corporate executives, students, at whatever station in life or at whatever stage in the journey of life they may be, are, finally, benefeciaries. I am fully conscious that while they will not follow the Gītā in blind faith, equally they cannot undertake an elaborate study of the Gītā, in its entirety. Teachings must be explained as result-oriented techniques. It is beyond question that the teachings of the Gītā bring peace, composure and happiness to man and at the very least he would certainly be better equipped to cope with various situations he encounters without stress.

Hypocrisy, or the gap between creed and conduct, would be naturally reduced if one is convinced that reliance on untruth and hypocrisy is not only not necessary but could positively be harmful. One should be convinced that truth and honesty would not fail him. They are his true friends even in worldly terms for profit, productivity, prosperity all around. This is exactly what I have tried to bring out and logically establish. As they say, if Big Ben has time, the Tower of Pisa has inclination. In the same way, if modern man has the time, the Gītā is designed to help him realise his objectives in life.

The immediate inspiration behind this undertaking to write a simplified and logical analysis of the different strands of thoughts expounded in the Gītā came from an old college friend, Professor Ram Lal, a retired college teacher in the Department of English, Delhi University.

He has been interested in Hindu scriptures, particularly the Gītā, right from his college days . He has collected an enormous mass of books and commentaries on the subject which he placed at my disposal. Otherwise also he has been of immense help to me in the course of writing this book.

My grateful thanks to him for his invaluable assistance no less than for his constant encouragement.

My desire and my friend's efforts would be fully rewarded if this book helps even in a small degree in moving the Gītā from the high pedestal of respect to the boardrooms of the corporations and into the hands of men and women who would not only mould thier own destinies but that of the nations across the globe, by understanding its practical, meaningful teachings and adopting them in their corporate and individual lives.

R. S. Garg

Contents

बन्धुर् आत्मात्मनस् तस्य येनात्मैवात्मना जितः।
अनात्मनस् तु शत्रुत्वे वर्तेतात्मैव शत्रुवत् ॥ B.G. VI (6)

Meaning: One's mind is a friend of those who have control over it but for those who have no control over it, mind may act like an enemy.

Apart from many other messages contained in the above Verse No. 6 of Chapter VI of the Gītā, the verse brings out duality in nature. The very same mind can be one's friend or foe. In other words, one does not have to look for either friend or foe externally. Both are present internally. Similarly, energy has dual uses. In the present nuclear age, we quite often read about dual-use fuel, materials and technologies—for helping the mankind with power generation etc. as also for destroying it large-scale with nuclear weapons. The user decides as to what use to put the resources. Let us start with making our minds our friends and making positive use of this great asset.

Introduction

Bhagavad-Gītā—the song celestial, literally meaning song in praise of the Lord, is an episode of the famous Indian epic Mahābhārata. The episode runs into seven hundred verses. An attempt has been made in this book to discuss and explain the implications of certain parts of Bhagavad-Gītā insofar as they affect the daily life of a reasonably well-placed person. He or she is educated and may even be in the decision-making position as an executive in a government department or in a corporate division or he may be a professional committed to implementation of certain policies for the country or society. In any case, he or she has to make decisions about his or her life also, as a student, a youth, a householder or in some other capacity. He or she is busy, modern in outlook and has a scientific temperament. Rituals, dogmas and conformism do not make much sense to him or her.

Such a person simultaneously lives in a highly competitive society. Like everybody else, he too, willingly or unwillingly, has joined the mad race of life, in pursuit of material success for profit and pelf. To come out a winner he has turned his back on principles and scruples. To him these are only hurdles in his pursuit of the one-up approach. A value-based approach has been replaced by profit motivation.

Such a person believes, rightly or wrongly, that he is too busy with his vocation or profession, because advancement in one's own profession or occupation and maximization of profit have become the main objectives of his life for various reasons. He has a busy schedule of work which sometimes he finds difficult to manage. He is always on the move with or without any idea about the direction in which he is moving. He has no time to sit back and relax and know whether or not he is moving in the right direction to realize the true goal of life. His concept of relaxation leads to jumbling of priorities and thus creates more problems or, at best, leads to postponement of solutions and accumulation of problems. In the process of making a good living, he tends to forget life itself and its true essence. In such a situation, how can he afford to set time aside for things called 'religious' or 'spiritual'? At times, he has even to take a posture of being anti-religious to escape being considered conservative or dogmatic. After all, he is a modern man living in a scientifically advanced age and wishes to be reckoned as such.

If the modern busy man with a scientific temperament, concentrates simply on different aspects and requisites of *Karma Yoga* (Yoga of action) alone, leaving out *Jñāna Yoga* (yoga of knowledge), *Bhakti Yoga* (yoga of devotion) and *Karma-Saṃnyāsa Yoga* (yoga of renunciation) as well as metaphysical aspects of the Gītā, it would appear as if the Gītā has been written for him and for this modern age. As opposed to some misconceived notions, the Gītā is for action and activity and definitely against inaction and passivity. It seeks to stop exodus of good persons from the field of activity lest the field fall into the hands of undesirable persons. Lord Kṛṣṇa uses all pleas to make Arjuna fight the war (of Kurukṣetra), overcoming his despondency and confusion of mind because it is the war of righteousness against evil. Lord Kṛṣṇa tries to argue on worldly attraction of kingdom on success and fear of worldly condemnation on failure. When these do not work, the Lord goes into the true nature of birth, death and immortality of soul and eventually focuses Arjuna's obligation to fight. Therefore, by no stretch of imagination can anyone say that the Gītā takes one to a life of renunciation, or that of an ascetic or a recluse. Even devotion to God or study of scriptures as a full-time pursuit is not insisted upon. The battle of Kurukṣetra is the battle in everybody's life and Arjuna's despondency and confusion is shared by everyone.

Lord Kṛṣṇa gives his own personal example. He says that he

does not have to engage in any activity for his own sake but he does it for the sake of preserving the good in the world. For the same reason, he advises, rather mandates, those who are well-off or self-realized, not interested in undertaking action, to act for the welfare of society.

With due respect and without any intention of raising any controversy and encouraged by the fact that in the Gītā, Lord Kṛṣṇa has discoursed on his own personal example, one may look into some other aspects of his life. His childhood pranks are full of enjoyment. He plays tricks with village folk, goes about merrily sporting with friends, teasing girls and even helping himself and friends with free milk, butter etc. He enjoyed his childhood thoroughly and would naturally expect us also to do likewise. In youth, he enjoyed the company of young women, played music and danced with them making their heart throb for him. The same Kṛṣṇa acted rather responsibly to save his village from a deluge. The Gītā enjoins us to participate in life like him albeit in moderation and to rise to face responsibilities and work towards social causes. When the time comes, Lord Kṛṣṇa acts as a guide and philosopher for the Pāṇḍavas (representing good) against the Kauravas (representing evil).

In the events that precede Mahābhārata war, the personā of Kṛṣṇa even makes clever use of untruth, when needed, to help the good win over evil. In as much, the Gītā's message is also a political treatise. Prior to the beginning of Mahābhārata war, Kṛṣṇa pretended to be asleep, when Duryodhana (a Kaurava prince) approached him for support. He woke up when Arjuna (a Pāṇḍava prince) arrived with a similar request. Cleverly, he managed to be on the side of Arjuna because this meant siding with the good. There is another example of truth spoken by Yudhiṣṭhira (the Pāṇḍava prince who would never speak an untruth) being made to have the effect of untruth. The message is clear for all. The good must win and we must work to make it win. The other very important message is that in times of difficulty there is a tendency even among noble persons to gravitate towards evil rather than side with the good. One example is the attempt to disrobe Draupadī, sole, common wife of the Pāṇḍava brothers, in the court in the presence of numerous princes and *gurus.* There was no opposition or walkout even by the *gurus,* the so-called learned and pious persons who seemed to have lost their nerve on the occasion. The other example is provided by the fact that at the time of fighting the war, the Kauravas had eleven army divisions on their side, while the Pāṇḍavas had seven. In making the Pāṇḍavas win decisively, the message of the Gītā is that God is active; He is on the side of the righteous even when they are no match for the foe. HE will eventually ensure victory by working HIMSELF and engaging you to work overtime.

Our modern busy man, for whom this book is mainly meant is young; he has taken the plunge or is about to take a plunge in life. He is modern in outlook, has a scientific mind and is open to fresh ideas which may help him score better and faster. Let the fresh idea, for a change be that the Gītā does not encourage blind faith. It more than satisfies the scientific temper, only if one makes an attempt to read it. Rather than encouraging an other-worldly attitude, it reconstructs one's life here itself. It does not promise miracles but takes one towards self-improvement step-by-step. A person may be middle aged or even in advanced age, caught up in cross-currents, midstream, straddling, struggling and trying to charter his course of life. He is worried and confused, unable to find answers to questions which baffle him. Turning to Gita's perennial philosophy often rescues him.

The general belief that the age for reading scriptures e.g. the Gītā is towards the latter part of life is not true. Recoursing to the value-system as ordained in the Gītā only towards the end of life is like repairing the building from the top while the foundation is weak.

The emphasis, contrary to the general belief, is on the youth who are on the threshold of life, those who have to make their own important decisions in life. A scientific mind, such as they generally have, does not require that it should be devoid of religion, only if a narrow interpretation is not placed on religion. Moreover, the Gītā does not talk of any religion at all. There is no mention of religion even at a single place or in a single śloka (verse). It lays emphasis, instead, on one's own *Dharma* (DUTY) implying that it cannot be the same for everyone. The '*Dharma*' of the Gītā is not a steamrolling agency. In any case, religion (in the right sense) and science should be seen to be complementing, not competing with each other. Their findings should be blended, like the left and right eyes, combining to provide a full picture/view of the object. One may perhaps say, without bias, that while *science is the lens for correcting the near vision, religion (rather spiritualism) is the lens for correcting and enhancing the distance vision.*

Even if one concedes that mind becomes sharper and more penetrating as the years pass, postponement of adoption of a healthy value-system is not desirable. Starting late can at best be an exercise in damage control. It is like trying to win a game by scoring disproportionately high towards the end only or ignoring the studies for the major part of the year and cramming up the stuff only towards the final examination.

The right way is to have a simple strong foundation and start building upwards as early in life as feasible. Early is desirable but late is never too late.

To make it easy for assimilation and adoption in daily life, thoughts or messages from the Gītā are presented, in this book, in a rather simple and easily comprehensible manner. No religious regimen is included in this book.

This book written in simple language is particularly aimed at the forever busy and on-the-move folk who suffer from the notion of real or assumed constraint of time. It is intended to help germinate and grow the seed of goodness which is lying embedded for fear of being destroyed by evil forces of life.

The grain of goodness is lying embedded somewhere in every man. It needs help in some form to germinate. Let the Gītā do it for you. Psychologists inform us that early influences like those of childhood and youth are far more lasting. Let the Gītā provide these right influences. Even those who are late in receiving and imbibing the Gītā's messages are not too late. In his Gītāñjalī, poet philospher Rabindra Nath Tagore had sung, "*Je nodi maru pathey haralo dhara/Jaani hey Jaani tao hoy ni hara ...*" (The river that lost its course in a desert / I know, isn't lost forever, I know". The very fact that the modern young person too is desirous of finding answers to baffling questions in life makes him a truth-seeker of sorts. He is not made of stone or wood but of the same flesh and blood as the other. Besides, he has feelings and emotion. He is not a recluse. He needs and cares for company. Therefore, he wants to acquire friends and family and is willing to make certain contributions to that end because this process is sure to give him a sense of belonging and identity.

To give him the benefit of doubt, he may have joined the mad and unscrupulous race for money and success not out of his own choice but as a victim of circumstances engendered by a declining value system. More and more people are coming to believe that means are not important so long as one can achieve one's goal. This mentality is fraught with dangerous contradictions. How can one rise or improve in life by adopting falling standards? It is self-defeating and deceptive. One is seemingly climbing up the ladder but the ladder itself is slipping. The ladder and, with the ladder, the climber too is going to fall flat.

In any case, the aim of his life has, rightly or wrongly, become success as he understands it. He might have adopted undesirable means to achieve his brand of success only because not doing so would mean being left out or falling by the wayside. But success through foul means is like a widely spread rumour that can only do ill. After material success, his target shifts to recognition and fame. Here, at least family and society at large start figuring in his mind. He needs a seal of recognition and an identity for himself. Otherwise, success in not all that sweet.

Luckily, for all of us, the present times are witnessing a shift, though slow, towards ethics and a value-system. In western countries, the Indian family structure is being respected more and more. Corporates as well other social groups (apart from church) are talking of family values. Like yoga, and now the ancient Indian system of medicine Āyurveda (science of life), the Indian value-based approach to life in general is acquiring more and more adherents.

Following a value-based life is profitable and beneficial even in material terms. Just to cite an example: Indians are now preferred as employees by big corporations in U.S.A. etc. The reason discovered was that Indians' contribution was more, as their minds were free from suspicions and tension because of mutual trust between husband and wife. In other cases sometimes, both husband and wife are known to be spying on each other due to lack of mutual trust. So much so that a new invention 'Fidelity Test Kit' is slated to be in the market soon. It will enable one to stealthily use it on the undergarments etc. of one's spouse and find out about his or her misdemeanors. The message is loud and clear: ***honesty and integrity in married life as in other aspects of life are of paramount importance.*** There is an interesting story about the life of a married person and that of a single person. The boss asked his junior who was single to do some overtime in the office because he did not have any wife who would be waiting for him at home. The junior replied that he (the boss) had somebody at home to relax and enjoy himself with but he (the junior) had to find one and hence his inability to stay late in the office. Marriage provides a person with a settled life which in turn provides a peaceful mind. A steady and stable relationship with family and friends is a saver of precious resources viz. time, energy and finances.

It is inconceivable that a person can be partly sincere and partly not. It is not possible that one can cheat a friend, her or his spouse, but not the corporation he works for. Cheating in a card game, jumping a traffic light etc. go into making one's character. In some countries, the number of traffic tickets given by police go into the personal record of trainee-executives to inculcate in them respect for law and right behavior. Dishonesty of character can show in different forms and can gradually assume a bigger and bigger dimension. Good and bad emotions are also an important part of one's character. That is why, now there is an emphasis on this new found ingredient of character. Emotional Quotient (EQ) is the new test the young executives have to go through. 'Personal' and 'public' are not considered separate water-tight compartments any longer.

Unlike the past medical and psychological approaches of looking at the physical body and the mind as separate entities, a holistic approach is gaining fresh ground in the West also. A human being is looked at as an individual who has a right to will. He is more than a mere sum total of physical body, mind and spirit. This, in turn, has brought into greater and sharper focus the importance of peace of mind. This is the most sought-after commodity. This is where one's value-system becomes still more relevant and important.

"*Karma Yoga*" (or Yoga of action) essentially means action (as against inaction) with the right mental attitude (joining the body with the mind i.e. the two acting in harmony) towards life in general and one's profession or occupation, in particular. Happiness in life and achievement in one's profession are the twin goals. In fact, these are interlinked and happiness eventually becomes the main aim or goal of life.

Parables and metaphors in the Gītā have been used as in other ancient scriptures and literature to explain the subtle meanings in a simple manner to the reader. For example, mind has been compared to a boat rocked in a stormy sea or ignorance with dust covering the mirror (knowledge). The best metaphor is that of the chariot driven by horses where reins are held by the charioteer Lord Kṛṣṇa. It symbolizes the complex body—mind—intellect mechanism of the command system.

Right mental attitude is essential for generating right actions. Mind has to function before the body acts, hence the emphasis on the mind. The ingredients for the right mental attitude are many. Some of these are: 'peace of mind'; 'concentration'; 'selflessness'; 'self or sense-control'; 'faith'; 'fearlessness'; 'no-doership'; 'sense of duty'; 'no-undue concern for result'. Separate chapters have been devoted to these different ingredients of *Karma Yoga*.

A perusal of the relevant chapters would make it clear to the reader and convince him or her of the efficacy of different concepts of the Gītā. These, not only make a person a happy person but also help his or her productivity in all fields of activity. As for time, one would save enough time lost due to lack of peace; lack of concentration; too much worry for result; bouts of anger etc. In this age of recycling of waste by-products, one should try to recycle wasted mental and physical energy into fresh and positive results. With a peaceful and composed mind, one would not need to unwind because there is no winding in the first place. Problems would not disappear but the attitude towards problems would definitely undergo a change. A problem-free life is a life without challenges, not worthwhile at all. But the problems will not give one nightmares nor would these cause stress.

Interestingly enough, the Gītā, the world famous scripture on spiritualism; metaphysics, cosmos; cosmic energy; universe, universal unity etc. also deals with seemingly mundane subjects such as food and sleep. This shows that the Gītā is for the physical body too, in addition to mind and spirit. The significance of lifestyle in all its aspects e.g. the matter of over-eating and over-sleeping included, has been discussed in the Gītā in detail to bring out their relationship *inter-se* as well as the difference it can make on the body, mind and the thought process. Body chemistry cannot be independent of body-intake. To avoid diseases of body and mind, the key message of the Gītā is moderation. What food is to the body, thoughts are to the mind.

It is not in vain that medical institutions of repute are referring some of their patients to meditation centers, yoga centers and Prāṇic healing centres. Even corporations have started providing facilities for meditation centers alongside gymnasia on their premises. They are well aware that illness means lost man-hours and mounting medical bills. Corporate culture in India and abroad is undergoing a change. Spiritual seminars, retreats; spiritual workshops are well-meaning facilities to increase productivity. Problems arise in mind and have to be tackled there. Even the best situation gives rise to problems albeit of a different nature. A peaceful mind is not devoid of problems but it solves them in a far better manner. Thus, problems do not linger on and do not have an unsettling effect on mind.

Therefore, the present provides the best environment for reassessing our attitudes towards different facets of life, developing business or professional ethics which are constructive and helpful, instead of destructive or couldn't careless attitude.

No religious regimen or visits to holy men or holy places is mandated. The values recommended in the Gītā have to be gradually imbibed in one's thought process and then reflected in one's actions. It will not hurt one's pride, self-respect or erase one's identity. The preceding brief discussion seems to suggest that quite independent of one's faith or belief in the Gītā, adopting the simple messages of the Gītā even as a policy can prove very beneficial in real life. It has been said that honesty is the best policy. So, even as a policy, values like honesty, integrity, composure, control, concentration steadfastness, equanimity etc. are worth assimilating in life. These are full of potential to deliver peace of mind, profit and overall progress without conflict, tension and stress. Thus a value-based attitude in daily life fits in the theory of reward and punishment as well.

Spiritual and social sides of a person go together. Tagore has compared Gītā with a silk-shot, a fabric which reflects different colors depending upon the angle of light falling on it. Gītā has the wonderful quality of simplicity as well as depth. It is useful for persons of all walks of life, all strata of society with different mental capabilities. And, thus, a choice of different yogas e.g. *Jñāna Yoga; Karma Yoga*, *Bhakti Yoga* etc. is offered. It is particularly useful for *Karma yogīs*—that being the largest category in the society because so long as there is human body one has to engage in some minimum action (*Karma*). All the same, all yogīs are seekers in one way or the other.

If life can be described as a workshop, the Gītā provides the tools. If the world is an edifice, the Gītā is the ladder to get to the top. Though, the view from the top is always the best what is more important and pragmatically useful, for, us ordinary folk, is to commence the journey. If vastness signifies universe, the Gītā refines and sharpens the mind to grasp it.

In computer terms, a value-system is perhaps comparable to software. For desired results, a good software in a suitable hardware is necessary, more so to ward off the dangers of corruption by unscrupulous hackers. Positive values need to be acquired, kept safe inside the mind by warding off the dangers of negativity from outside.

In this age of electronics and computers the way spiritualism works could be better understood and appreciated. Spiritualism is about making use of the latent energies of body and mind rightfully. Thoughts are also forms of energy which flow in all directions. Thus, logically thoughts have been accepted now to be entities. Your thoughts are not your property alone. Persons with the right equipment (mental or material) can receive, read and record these.

At the end, may it be said that this presentation may be gone through in just one go? But a second reading or a leisurely persual may be useful because in that process one may find different meanings, different interpretations of one's own ideas and surely a deeper thought will emerge in the reader's mind. Naturally, to different readers it might appear to mean a different message. However in reality it would only mean giving better meaning to life itself, through step-by-step self-growth.

There is a word of caution before embarking upon the study of the Gītā. There is an abundant use of the word 'I' & 'ME' in the Gītā by Lord Kṛṣṇa, in various verses. He also asks us, the followers, to have faith in HIM; concentrate exclusively on HIM, surrender unto HIM and so on. Lord Kṛṣṇa who is teaching control of ego and arrogance, to the readers of the Gītā, could not by any stretch of imagination be egoistic or arrogant, himself. These pronouns are not to be taken to mean Lord Kṛṣṇa as being in the embodied physical form, only like any ordinary mortal. HE represents the supreme Consciousness or Energy. The body form of the formless. 'I', 'ME' and 'MINE'; 'HE', 'HIM' and 'HIS' all point to the single unifying force of the cosmos —understood by the spiritualists and sought to be explained in a single theory of energy by the scientists.

Wishing you happy reading and
happy surfing on thought waves.

CHAPTER 1

Contemporary Relevance of the Gītā

Bhagavad-Gītā is the earliest but still the most comprehensive enunciation of the principles of human life in micro and macro-form. It tackles the problems of this world and the world beyond. It deals both with practical life and ideal life—life as it is and life as it should be. Its messages relate to ethics as well as to metaphysics. It is also an excellent synthesis of different approaches emanating from different ancient scriptures (e.g. the Vedas, the Upaniṣads and the Sūtras) and schools of thought, religious as well as philosophical.

The Gītā embodies knowledge derived from various branches of science which condition and shape human life like genetics, biology, body-chemistry, and inter-connectedness between body, mind, spirit and universe. It has been woven in a subtle and imperceptible manner in the *Bhagavad-Gītā* as in no other comparable book of antiquity. The principles and concepts expounded in the Gītā stand amply vindicated by modern science.

Fortunately, such well-founded concepts have been handed down to mankind in general and to Indian people in particular, from generation to generation.

By common observation, visible religious practices and religious discourses by men of God have increased particularly in urban India. The number of Hindu temples and religious places of all other denominations continue to increase and funds for the purpose continue to pour in. Popularity of deities symbolizing victory of good over evil has increased manifold. Inspite of these obvious positive indicators there is a near-total collapse of ethical values in society. Corruption of all types—moral, social, economic and political is all-pervasive. It has crept into the life of the individual, family, society, nation, and the entire human race. The reason is not too difficult to find. It is the ever-widening gap between precept and practice, between man's word and his deed. Like bad effect, its cause is also present everywhere and in all persons. People have come to believe, of course wrongly, that mere words are a good enough substitute for right action. Thus, the significance of right action as enjoined in the Gītā has been completely eroded. Religion has been reduced to an external label rather than an inner virtue. It has become a profession and as corrupt as any other. Instead of being a source of knowledge, wisdom, a way of ascendancy, a movement from lower to higher consciousness or an inspiration for value-based life, it has been misappropriated by unscrupulous people who are using it as a mask and an instrument of exploitation. Holy men of all sorts offer gimmicks and quickfixes and shortcuts to material gains without so much as even a suggestion in favor of right action or fulfilling one's duty as enjoined in the Gītā or elsewhere in other holy books. Holy places offer entry into heaven or escape from hell for wrongdoing, for a price. Instead, society needs to be informed by holy men and others that cause and effect are inseparable. Good actions produce good rewards although the Gītā preaches the gospel of selfless action. Conversely, a dip in the holy river, a free meal to the *sādhus*, a mere ritual of worship etc., cannot save man unless he changes course and realizes the essence of right action.

The only currency God accepts is the currency of good deeds. Do not try to deceive Him by using counterfeit. You will end up deceiving yourself. External religiousness will not remove internal chaos and confusion. A righteous mind conquering greed, attachment and anger, engaged in selfless action as duty, will attain the clarity of thought and peace that surpasses understanding. Let us, then, bridge the gap between our words and our deeds and shed hypocrisy of all sorts and we will discover that the Gītā—the song celestial—has a path to offer to everyone to get out of his worldly trammels. Generally speaking, for our purpose, the Gītā deals essentially with three paths of yogas. These are: Path of Knowledge (*Jñāna Yoga*), Path of Action (*Karma Yoga*) and Path of Devotion (*Bhakti Yoga*) the last being easily accessible to the generality of people constituting the work-a-day world. We have purposely left out the Path of Renunciation (*Saṃnyāsa Yoga*)—it being not desirable from the angle of society. Different persons have different inclinations, different aptitudes, different capacities and different capabilities of body and mind. For this reason the same path may not be suitable for all. This may be further explained by the analogy of a good doctor who uses a different approach and line of treatment for different patients though their ailments may be apparently similar. The Gītā offers the various above-mentioned paths to help men arrive at the same goal. To some, the path of knowledge is more appealing and suitable, while to others it may be the path of devotion. For obvious reasons, the path of work or action (*Karma Yoga*) falls to the lot of the great majority of people, because barring exceptions, all are engaged in work or action whether out of choice or necessity.

Exceptions are where men have taken recourse to renunciation. They have opted out of active world. It may be good for them but it cannot serve as an ideal for society in general or the world they renounce.

Moreover, human body is the vehicle for existence as much for the follower of the Path of Renunciation (*Saṃnyāsa Yoga*) as for the follower of the Path of Knowledge (*Jñāna Yoga*) or for the follower of the Path of Devotion (*Bhakti Yoga*) or for the follower of the Path of Action (*Karma Yoga*).

If one looks closely at the matter, a *Karma Yogī* (follower of the path of action) needs to imbibe *Jñāna* (knowledge) also to some degree because thought being the seed for any action, right thought is necessary. Thus, a Karma Yogī is essentially a Jñāna yogī also, if his actions are to be desirable.

The large number of members of society and the inevitability of their engaging in some form of action—either of their own choice or as a result of circumstances in which they find themselves at different stages of life would justify that Path of Work (*Karma Yoga*) should receive maximum attention in any discussion of the Gītā.

This vast tribe of men of action is represented by Arjuna in the Gītā. The battlefield of Kurukṣetra is the field of action (*Karma Bhūmi*) around us. Arjuna's dilemma and indecisiveness as to what is wrong and what is right is the dilemma of everyone who has to engage in some form of activity.

To understand the purpose of the Gītā, one needs to refer to its beginning and the end. In the beginning, Arjuna (at the time of commencement of the war), after surveying armies on both sides—the side of Kauravas, the enemy, and his own side, becomes doubtful as to whether the outcome of the war, which was to ensue, would at all justify the cost involved viz. killing of near and dear ones, destruction of families, destruction of spirituality and impiety corrupting the women.

In verses 32, 33 and 34 of chapter I of the Gītā, Arjuna expresses his doubts and mental confusion.

In verse 32 of Chapter I, Gītā says:

Arjuna says:

> *na kāṅkṣe vijayaṃ kṛṣna na ca rājyaṃ sukhāni ca*
> *kiṃ no rājyena govinda kiṃ bhogair jīvitena vā*

Meaning: I do not long for victory, O Kṛṣṇa, nor kingdom nor pleasures. Of what use is kingdom to us, O Kṛṣṇa or enjoyment (pleasures) or even life?

In verse 33 of Chapter I, Gītā says:

Arjuna says:

> *yeṣām arthe kāṅkṣitaṃ no rājyaṃ bhogāḥ sukhāni ca*
> *ta ime'vasthitā yuddhe prāṇāṃs tyakatvā dhanāni ca*

Meaning: Those for whose sake we desire kingdom,

न काङ्क्षे विजयं कृष्ण न च राज्यं सुखानि च।
किं नो राज्येन गोविन्द किं भोगैर् जीवितेन वा॥ I (32)

येषाम् अर्थे काङ्क्षितं नो राज्यं भोगाः सुखानि च।
त इमेऽवस्थिता युद्धे प्राणांस् त्यकत्वा धनानि च॥ I (33)

enjoyment, and pleasures, stand here in battle, renouncing their lives and wealth.

Verse 34 of Chapter I of the Gītā says:

Arjuna continues:

ācāryāḥ pitaraḥ putrās tathaiva ca pitāmahāḥ
mātulāḥ śvaśurāḥ pautrāḥ śyālāḥ sambandhinas tathā

Meaning: Teachers (gurus), fathers, sons and also grandfathers; uncles and fathers-in-law, grand-sons and brothers-in-law and other relations.

The above verses indicate Arjuna's inclination to renunciation. In moments of great sorrow, men are generally tempted to adopt the method of renunciation. The commentary on the Gītā, by Dr. S. Radhakrishnan, mentions that at the time of the composition of the Gītā, certain sects, were dominated by the ideal of withdrawal from activity and retreat from the world. Such an influence exercised and dominated the mind of Arjuna. He did not want to fight and advanced his own reasons which were incorrect in terms of value-system and inappropriate at the particular moment. It was absenteeism from duty, cowardice, false fear, wrong precepts that dominated Arjuna's mind. The purpose of the Gītā was to change that mind-set and to ready Arjuna to fight the righteous war. Non-violence is not an unconditional virtue. *Maintaining silence in the face of untruth amounts to speaking the untruth.* This is a part of the law of evidence in India even today. The method adopted for the purpose of conveying the message was the dialogue between Lord Kṛṣṇa and Arjuna. The dialogue covers life in its various aspects in this world as well as the world beyond—physical, ethical and metaphysical. Lord Kṛṣṇa, transports Arjuna, or the reader of the Gītā, to different planes of consciousness during the dialogue.

Verse 73 of the last chapter XVIII of the Gītā says:

आचार्याः पितरः पुत्रास् तथैव च पितामहाः।
मातुला श्वशुराः पौत्राः श्यालाः सम्बन्धिनस् तथा॥ I (34)

Arjuna Uvāca:

naṣto mohaḥ smṛtir labdhā tvatprasādān mayā cyuta
sthito'smi gatasaṃdehaḥ kariṣye vacanaṃ tava

Meaning: Destroyed is my delusion and recognition has been gained by me through thy grace, O Acyuta (Kṛṣṇa). I stand firm with my doubts dispelled. I shall act according to thy word.

Evidently, the high purpose of the Gītā was achieved, through Arjuna, for all of us. Therefore, Lord Kṛṣṇa's advice to Arjuna holds (good) for all of us.

There is no escape from action but what kind of action should be performed and what kind should be avoided is a matter for decision. Such a decision, however, would depend upon the individual doer himself. Because every action follows as an outcome of certain thoughts, the significance of right thoughts occupying the mind at the time of action cannot be overemphasized. This brings us to the question of right thought followed by right action.

Emphasis is on right action rather than on inaction. Imagine for a moment that good people finding no purpose or real meaning in life decide to renounce the world and retire to some retreat in the Himālayas or another such solitary abode. Gradually, it would lead to a decline in the number of good people and a corresponding increase in that of evil people in the world. It will be a case of *bad currency chasing out good currency* in the spiritual economics. Evil people love power. If power flows from the barrel of a gun, they would wield the gun. If corruption gives them the leverage, they would gladly resort to corruption of all hues and strands. Lesser actors in the field of action-world would gravitate to the center of power.

We are aware of the concern of western social scientists about aging population as a result of a declining birth rate and increasing longevity of human life due to the advancement of medical science. If both the trends continue, the western

---

अर्जुन उवाच
नष्टो मोहः स्मृतिर् लब्धा त्वत्प्रसादान् मयाऽच्युत।
स्थितोऽस्मि गतसंदेहः करिश्ये वचनं तव॥ XVIII (73)

countries will be laden with non-working population disproportionate to the working population, leading to the decay of society. The phenomenon, of good people resorting to inaction while the opposite type continue to engage in action, as discussed in the Gītā, is somewhat similar and with similar dangerous portents for society. Lord Kṛṣṇa clearly advises the knowledgeable to act, particularly because the ignorant, in any case, would continue to act. *Society needs world-savers, not world-escapists.* Society needs good currency in sufficient quantity to stay in circulation. When a big quantity of bad currency gets into circulation, not only does it endanger the economy, but it also unduly exercises the minds of the people because they are always worried lest they should be affected personally for holding bad currency mistakenly. As bad currency can wreck the economic health of a country, so can evil damage and destroy the moral and spiritual health of an individual, a society or a country.

The reader would perhaps agree that this is what is actually happening in society right now. Evil is driving out good from all spheres of life. Therefore, an Arjuna of today as of the Mahābhārata times, cannot be allowed to lay down arms. He cannot be allowed to evade action and thereby leave the field open for evil doers. In this difficult and dangerous situation, the Gītā shows the way. It offers a value-system, a practical philosophy of life which aims at meeting an individual's needs as an individual, as a householder and as a social being. A large number of Hindus and others, both in India and abroad, believe in the Gītā as a matter of personal faith. There are others who practise its teachings as a matter of policy in the same way as most person in the modern world practise honesty not so much as a matter of faith but as a pattern beneficial in the long run.

Most eastern religions advocate retreat from the active world. In India, Hinduism, Buddhism and Jainism emphasise curbing of needs and even neglect of physical body. One of the aims of the Gītā is to check this shift of focus in society from active worldly life to renunciation, from action to inaction. The 'other worldly' approach is not the solution. Instead, one should live in this very world, but in the right way.

Such a mind-set of inaction had overtaken Arjuna too. He refused to act when action was needed in the interest of a just and healthy society. Running away from the battlefield would have amounted to surrender to injustice. Society at the time was passing through a phase of severe chaos and conflict. Kauravas—the opponents of Pāṇḍavas—had rejected the most reasonable terms for settlement of their respective claims to the kingdom of Hastināpur (in North India). Devious and deceitful methods were employed by the Kauravas to deprive the Pāṇḍavas of their rightful share in the kingdom and usurp it entirely. An analogous situation prevails in India and elsewhere today. Confused and distressed people are not able to stand steadfast and persevere in any pursuit with honesty but are forced either into passivity or to join the swelling ranks of the corrupt. Therefore, the Gītā is essentially a mandate for action as against inaction much more urgently today than in the past. It enjoins upon its reader the imperative need to sustain and save the world by living in it and not by running away from it.

One may argue that in the present times, there is no inaction. Nobody is renouncing the world or running away from it which might have been the case at the time the Gītā was composed. Unlike Arjuna not many are hesistant to kill their cousins or rivals or get them killed or harmed, only if there be a chance to enhance their prospects in business or politics or in getting a bigger share of profit or property. Rivals in business and politics are out to destroy one another. They engage in competition with a killer instinct. They want to wipe out the competition if not the competitor. Thus, there is no dearth of action. On the contrary, there is too much action. Nobody is bothered about losing a good reputation as an individual, as a family, as a businessman or as a business house. One does not need Lord Kṛṣṇa's pep talk or sermon to fight. One is already at it and all the time. He is so much dedicated to fight the 'enemy' that he is working overtime with less and less sleep and relaxation. He has devised methods in the form of medicines, beverages etc. to reduce body fatigue and to make do with minimum hours of sleep. He must be awake and be with the world with different time zones most of the day and night. He has also reduced the time spent on food, family, friends and, of course, the time for sleep. How can the Gītā be relevant to the already hard-working and overbusy man of today?

And yes, the Gītā is very much relevant today, even more so than at the time when it was composed around 25th Century B.C. It applies to the modern busy man as it was to the ancient man of history. For the modern man, and busy executives, stakes are rather high in reference to his own time frame. Their entire life is at stake in terms — not of economics but in terms of peace of mind and mental and physical health. No doubt, he is acting all the time but often with a wrong state of mind generating wrong action. He is ever fighting but often the wrong or non-existent enemy. He creates the enemy out of his own imagination, attacks the enemy of his imagination but injures himself in the process. The famous Spanish fiction writer Cervantes in his work 'Adventures of Don Quixote' has a character by this name who is an adventurer of sorts. He is accompanied by his squire called Sancho Panza. Don Quixote undertakes several adventures in the plains of Spain. Once, he sees, from a distance thirty to forty windmills. Due to distance and mist in the air, he mistakes them to be ghosts with long arms. Despite warning from Sancho Panza about their true identity he does not change his belief that these were indeed ghosts. In his spirit of adventure, he attacks them with his lance. In the process, he loses control of the horse he was riding on, falls on the ground, injures himself and also breaks his lance. At this point, Sancho Panzo, the squire of the knight Don Quixote says that nobody could mistake windmills for ghosts unless he had windmills in the brain. The modern man is wielding his sword against the non-existent enemy in the outside world—ghosts of his own wrong imagination or creation of his ignorance as the Gītā would have it. He is fighting ceaselessly and injuring himself in the process of falling from the horse, meaning losing control of the horse, or losing sense and self-control because like the knight's brain his mind too has windmills in it. That is to say, his mind is not peaceful. The real multi-faceted enemy is within oneself. The Gītā teaches us as to how to tackle and conquer the enemy within, through exercising sense-control or self-control while doing action. The Gītā is not only meant to check the flight of wise and good people in the present and in the future from the world of activity. It is equally, rather more importantly, relevant also to check the rot in the present day society. It aims to check the fall and descent of man and help him to rise and ascend. One needs to remember that the fall can be free and fast whereas the rise is gradual and needs effort.

The Gītā helps all—those who care to learn the art of right living as a *Karma Yogī*—staying and working in the world. The Gītā for a *Karma Yogī* is about self-improvement, self-growth, reconstructing this very life, harmonizing the action with body-mind-intellect apparatus, provided by nature. Staying in the world and working therein is desirable rather than quitting in despair and letting the social decay creep in. Act righteously and be a hero and a trendsetter to others. 'Live, not Leave' is the message of the Gītā. One can do that only while living in the world and not from outside. A renunciate can be a hero to other renunciates of the present and of the future but not to *Karma Yogīs*. The latter need their own hero—modern yet steadfast and rooted in faith; busy yet free for doing their various duties, enjoying pleasures of life always in moderation and not in excess. There is no self-denial. Only self-restraint has a place in the life of a modern hero. If one can control and even promote one's business, enhancing productivity, by right actions with a right state of mind, without having to abandon one's modernity, worldly duties and enjoyment of pleasures, what more can one ask for? It is the most cost-effective method of living well.

Most, if not all the requisites relate to the state of mind (not so much to the physique) behind the action. Selflessness, sense of duty, sense of sacrifice, unconcern for the outcome and sense of no-doership make all the difference, in the attitude of the performer of action. Right attitude takes away the stress and makes the mind peaceful and harmonious both upstream and downstream i.e. internally in the mind and externally in the outside world.

In the modern world of the modern man, cost or economics is an important factor in any decision-making. As anyone can figure out, the transformation or reconstruction of life as per the teachings of the Gītā is cost-free. It is said that the best things of life e.g. light, sunshine, air, water are provided free by nature. That is, probably, why spirituality has been dug out of the archives of history, so to say, and given a place of honor even in the board-rooms of big corporations, worldwide. It may not be too wrong to say that Indian companies are adopting spirituality as a part of corporate culture, unfortunately not as leaders but as followers of the West. In any case, its contemporary relevance is not questioned or doubted any more. If spirituality works, why not try and take benefit? Spirituality does make sound business sense!

The view pioneered by Āyurveda (science of life) that lifestyle has a lot to do with one's health is now accepted by all systems of medicines. Smoking, drinking, eating in excess or sleeping in excess affect the body currents or bio-rhythms. Yoga helps a person to relieve himself of stress and tensions caused by the so-called modern but wrong lifestyle. One must distinguish between the modern world and the modern lifestyle. Modern world should imply the world wherein the scientific and technological development has been put to use for the good of the human being in various fields e.g. communication, information, medicine etc. But to call a wrong lifestyle, a modern lifestyle, is a mistake.

A wrong lifestyle devoid of moderation in food, sleep and other habits leads to ill-health. Stressful life is often the result of irregular habits and life—in the matter of eating, drinking, sleeping etc. The beginning of ill-health can be a simple headache or indigestion, but it can lead to the onslaught of serious diseases or conditions such as overweight, hypertension, diabetes, ulcers, heart trouble and so on. The big corporations have to pay fat medical bills and higher insurance premia. In the bargain, work hours or workdays are lost. The stressful and overworked mind of an individual will manifest itself in some sort of imbalance in the body chemistry. It leads to anger and makes the person temperamental. The family suffers. Strained family relations, arguments, sometimes lead to divorce which is a grave social problem. Divorce, broken homes, spoiled or neglected children from such homes become a serious social problem. Generally speaking, juvenile crime can be traced to broken homes. A sense of belonging is just not available to the children of parents who decide to acquire new life partners.

In a majority of divorce cases, the custody of children becomes a knotty emotional issue. When the parents split up, one of the parent needs the court's permission to visit his/her own child—his or her own blood. It does not need a psychologist to analyse the effect on the children of the circumstances which lead to and follow a divorce. The cause of divorce may be lack of adjustment or lack of fidelity etc. But the effect in terms of loss, of a companion, of an outlet for emotions, loneliness, and loss of peace of mind shows up in many forms for the individual. To the business house, the changed, sometimes unpredictable behavior of the employee means immense loss of self-image as well as productivity. Divorces do divide the families but cannot extinguish the emotion of love for children or divide it. Periodical visits with fixed hours are a poor substitute for parental love and in no way promote family values even in the new relationships or in the newly acquired families.

Spirituality could have prevented such a scenario. In this age of hard and aggressive selling, the corporate world is spending increasingly on different kinds of spiritual activities or spirituality sessions to release tension of their executives and enhance their self-confidence and concentration and hence productivity. It is one example of 'back to the future'.

Yoga and meditation are other major attractions to the open-minded and the well–informed. Techniques for both are a part of the Gītā. The beauty of *Yogic* exercises is that these relax and energise a person without tiring him or her, physically or mentally. The word '*yoga*' means 'joining' or 'yoking' together. Therefore, by definition itself, it pre-supposes joining of at least two things or two entities. These two are mind and body. Yoga aligns the two, establishes harmony between the two and brings about relaxation of both. It is harnessing the energy through control of prāṇa or bio-rhythms. Waste of energy is checked and the energy is ploughed back in the right direction, passing through various energy centres (Cakras). In more and more western cities, *yoga* and meditation centres are coming up. In India even public parks are full of people of all ages engaged in yogic practices collectively under the guidance of a teacher (*guru*). Guidance of a teacher is almost a necessity particularly in the early stages. Yogic exercises serve as a preventive against as well as a cure for common diseases.

Meditation, in particular, has found a place of honor in the corporate world and elsewhere. The Gītā goes into much detail, regarding the practice of meditation in Chapter VI. It recommends a quiet place where one can experience and enjoy solitude, free from external noises to the extent possible so that one's inner voice becomes audible. The type of seat is also discussed but in the world of today it can be any comfortable seat on the ground where one should sit cross-legged in an erect posture. A straight spine aligns the central channel of the spine and all the Cakras so that energy flows smoothly and calms the mind. With eyes closed the mind turned inward for even five minutes helps relaxation and concentration. Different methods, such as concentrating on a candle flame, an idol or on the flow of breath are available and are equally effective. It is believed, and sensibly enough, that meditation produces physiological changes. In turn, it means reduction in heart beat, blood pressure and regulation of breathing. The body and mind are greatly relaxed. Dr. Herbert Bension, a Harvard cardiologist calls this "the relaxation response" and this response counteracts negative thoughts leading to fear, anger etc. which the Gītā calls enemies of man. Obviously, the technique of meditation will be more useful to those who adopt it after abandoning the wrong lifestyle and switching over to a life of moderation.

Corporate work culture is undergoing a change in another way too. The employees are made to feel that they are working with the corporation rather than for the corporation. They are encouraged to have a feeling of togetherness instead of aloofness. The author of the book, 'Fifth Generation Management', Mr. Charles M. Savage, President Knowledge Era Enterprises Inc. has this to say on the change in the corporate outlook :

> "Lot of IT folks overlook the importance of the human element, and yet without this element, IT can never come alive. The industrial era taught us to leave our thoughts, feelings and visions at the factory gates. Yet, it is precisely these elements that drive our economy. It has only been in the last five years that we have started appreciating emotional intelligence (or emotional quotient). Emotions are one of the biggest drivers of business."

For the employees, work (action) has to be a purposeful, and, further, a human and humane one instead of being an experience of their victimization or exploitation due to the circumstances they are in.

The Gītā teaches that action may be made not only a purposeful exercise but an exercise for a higher purpose. Probably that is why some corporations now-a-days, encourage their employees to participate occasionally in community welfare activities.

The Gītā has won universal respect of the scientists for its understanding of the principles of metaphysical and cosmic world. It also contains a detailed study of human behavior. It is evidence enough of the sharpness, capacity and depth of human mind. Scientists, physiologists spiritualists *et al* placed the Gītā on a high pedestal. On the worldly plane, the Gītā brought out the linkage between one's lifestyle, and his physical and mental health. The relation *inter se* of food, sleep, indigestion, anger, memory, anxiety, blood pressure, stress etc. has been understood and appreciated by medical science. This aspect of the Gītā has endeared it to *Karma Yogīs* in different walks of life, young executives and corporations alike.

Confining itself to the human behavior, the Gītā not only deals with human behavior, more importantly it teaches one how to improve that by reconstructing one's life. The same building blocs can be used differently for a better and happier life. After all, happiness is the goal of everyone's life. The Gītā is a great source of strength for those who face distress and dejection and also suffer from a fear of failure. Mahatma Gandhi wrote :

> "When disappointment stares me in the face and all alone I see not a ray of light, I go back to Bhagavad-Gītā. I find a verse here and a verse there and I immediately begin to smile in the midst of overwhelming tragedies."

Some observers want us to believe that interest in the study of religion is on the increase. Harper Collins has brought out a 'Dictionary of Religion.' Hinduism is one of the longest entries. The authors saw the dictionary as a reference tool for teachers and students. But it turns out to be for anyone from the academic to the curious. In any case, this is yet another piece of evidence of the contemporary relevance of the Gītā.

The Gītā is for all and for all times.

CHAPTER 2

The Gītā's Philosophy as a Practical Policy

To the modern man, the word policy sounds more familiar and acceptable than faith. It is much harder to develop faith in any ideology or philosophy than accepting a policy and an action plan. The false notion, spread by some, that the Gītā teaches renunciation of and withdrawal from worldly life needs to be removed. The message of the Gītā is a clear-cut mandate for action. It is a command against inactivity or inaction. This aspect (i.e. action) in a modern man's life is not a subject of dispute or discussion. It is a settled issue that everyone irrespective of his or her role in society must engage in action. It includes workers using brain, brawn or mind, muscle or both. Arjuna is chided by Lord Kṛṣṇa for despondency against fighting tendency (struggling). To have been born in this world necessarily means that there is no running away from action. Policy and action plan are laid down in keeping with one's aims and objectives. The aims and objectives may relate to an individual, a family, a business firm, a corporate body or a country. In the ultimate analysis, however, it is the individuals who will prepare the ground for any structure—family or corporate in nature. What is the aim of one's life? **Perhaps happiness! Nothing less, nothing more**.

Dalai Lama said:

> "The wish to get free of suffering is the legitimate goal of every human being. It is the corollary of our wish to be happy. Thus it is entirely appropriate that we seek the causes of our unhappiness and do whatever we can to alleviate our problems..."

To an average man what brings happiness is a problem-free healthy body, a reasonably profitable job, business or profession, a happy family, and respect in society. Let us see how the Gītā can help the busy man of today in attaining these without him having to renounce or abandon his business or professional pursuits.

Let us begin with general health of both body and mind. We have all known the phrase, 'a sound mind in a sound body'. Definitely, there is a link between the two—body and mind. These do not exist in isolation or to the exclusion of each other. To body and mind has been added, spirit. This has given rise to what is called *holistic approach*. Doctors today no longer treat body alone. Further, the human body is not mere flesh and bones. It is not even a sum total of body, mind and spirit. It is further than that. For the present, the intention is to introduce the phrase—*body chemistry* which changes with the *type of food, drink, emotions* and even the *mood* people have. Hence, the significance of food and drink in the functioning of body chemistry. In the Gītā, there is a discussion about food as well. *Sāttvika food* is recommended over *rājasika* and *tāmasika* types. In simple words, it is the balanced diet which will be wholesome, mild on the palate, easy on the stomach.

The Gītā deals with science of life as with philosophy of life. It recommends moderation of habits even in the matter of food and sleep. One must neither eat too much nor too little. One must neither sleep too much nor too little.

Verse 8 of Chapter XVII of the Gītā says:

> *āyuḥ sattva balārogya-sukha prīti vivardhanāḥ*
> *rasyāḥ snigdhāḥ sthirā hṛdyā āhārāḥ sāttvikapriyāḥ*

आयुःसत्त्वबलारोग्य-सुखप्रीतिविवर्धनाः ।
रस्याः स्निग्धाः स्थिरा हृद्या आहाराः सात्त्विकप्रियाः ॥ XVII (8)

Meaning: The foods that promote life, (not only increase longevity but improve it in general as well i.e. promote both physical and mental health) vitality, strength, health, happiness, joy, are sweet, soft (mild and juicy) nourishing (wholesome) and agreeable (to the system i.e. stomach, intestines etc.) are dear to the 'good' i.e. virtuous person.

The above verse details the various purposes food is meant to serve and what type of food it should be to serve the intended purposes for a virtuous or good person. In other words, good food would make a person good. The opposite is equally true.

The Gītā also mentions the importance of the time, posture, mode and mood for taking food. Again, in practical terms, it means that one has to find time for a proper meal. It must be enjoyed so that right digestive juices in right quantities are available for the food and the body chemistry is properly conducted and plays its role in the human body. Swallowing junk food is not eating. Mixing hot and cold stuff is not enjoying the food. Now-a-days one might notice people eating, drinking while walking, talking and even driving.

It is against common sense, leave aside, medical considerations, to drive while drinking coffee or munching food, with a newspaper in the lap (to be read at traffic lights) and a cellular phone tucked between the shoulder and the ear. Indeed, it is *egoistic demonstration of being busy by a modern man.* He is always on the move and always short of time.

Let us not forget that a human being is not like a cow which can eat fast and store food to chew it later. Nor is he like a camel which can store water for many days.

Man must eat and drink at regular intervals at a slow pace. If one can do these essential acts, for maintaining the body and mind in good health, in a sitting posture with a calm mind, as advised in the Gītā the result would be definitely more satisfying. Again, on the advice of the Gītā one may perform the act of eating with an attitude of gratitude, accepting food as a gift from the creator not as something resulting from one's own sweat and toil.

This simple change in attitude will make the person less egoistic and more modest. The mere act of realizing God's creation all around you, will remind you of your own cosmic existence as opposed to self-importance. You are converted into a grateful receiver from an egoistic demander.

The modern man often helps himself with grub. Occasionally, he has a five or even seven-course dinner generally at the expense of the corporation, outside his home. He does not settle down for food, often it is food that 'settles' in him instead of getting digested. Neither the entry (dry food being pushed down with gaseous drinks) nor the exit is smooth. Indigestion and constipation are the result compelling him to resort to medicine, initially once in a while and later on regularly. Irregular food has led to a regular difficulty in digestion and evacuation. Food has become a foe and medicine a friend. It is a curious fact in the life of the modern man that generally he spends less time at the table eating food than evacuating in the toilet, so much so that he resorts to reading newspaper and small books while seated on the commode. The Gītā is not against enjoying life. Enjoy it to the full—the right way. Enjoy life and enjoy food too. Try, you will find time. Availability of real time for an act is relative to the value you have for that act in your mind.

The next important thing for a healthy body-mind is adequate sleep. Sleep is nature's way of resting and refreshing the body, and rejuvenating the body and mind. Again, oversleep is as bad as undersleep. Unfortunately, modern man considers sleeping a waste of time. The so-called corporate culture takes pride in denying to its executives this basic body need. In the West, it is often referred as a mark of status that the executives of a business house have no time for sleep. They fly from one continent to another, shave and shower at the airport and are off straight to the office. This drill is repeated rather often in different directions with the result that the body clock cannot keep pace with the various time zones.

Demands on body and mind increase, allowing less and less time for catching up on sleep. First, we do not have time for sleep, later even when we do have time, we cannot sleep. In brief, unregulated lifestyle results in anxiety, stress and stress-related problems like loss or lack of sleep, lack of appetite, stomach disorders, ulcers, high-blood pressure and diabetes. Starting with popping pills for simple symptoms such as headache, one gets into the clutches of serious ailments like diabetes. The metabolism of the body is progressively disturbed. Knowing well enough that stress developed by modern lifestyle is the root cause, we do not try enough, if at all, to change this.

Careers with a fast and steep rise are cut short. Hope turns into frustration, agitation and anger. According to the Gītā, these are the results of unquenched desires. Control these desires and remove reasons which lead to these desires. A right value-system and a right state of mind will help. The Gītā is not against action or activity nor is it against enjoyment of life. Enjoy it by all means. But we have to evolve the right concept of enjoyment. While aiming at enjoyment, let us not damage or destroy the vehicle of enjoyment which is the human body. Activity or enjoyment cannot mean chipping it away.

In this context the famous story of the celebrated Russian writer Leo Tolstoy, "How much land does a man need?" comes to mind. Tempted by the offer that Pahom (the main character in the story)—a poor farmer—will get as much land as he could encircle or enclose by walking or running from sunrise to sunset, he commences to walk as the sun rises. His endeavor was to maximize the circumference of the circle or enclosure by the time of the sunset so that he could get maximum land. But near the time he was about to complete the circle, he falls dead—occupying land just enough for the burial of his body.

There is a big lesson in this short story. This story is as much about controlling desires as is the teaching of the Gitā in this regard. To the modern busy man, time comes as a handy scapegoat. He believes, of course wrongly, that, but for lack of time at his disposal, he would have set his life right. Strangely enough, the same modern man finds time for socializing, attending clubs and long-drawn-out parties continuing through the night. One wonders what sort of 'unwinding' or relaxation such parties offer. Menfolk are busy finding out each other's status, progress and financial worth. Women may be more busy looking at each other's dresses, jewellery and assessing the quality and brand of perfume. They also discuss affairs and scandals of all sorts—marriages, divorces and living together in the social group. At one party, they talk about the next. During one holiday they discuss the next holiday, new hotels and new resorts. Big parties with rich food and alcohol are followed by days of junk food. A sleepless night followed by over-sleeping the next morning has become part of a modern man's life. The game of Snakes and ladder has overtaken what the Gītā calls moderation and steadfastness in life.

All this is agitating and not pacifying the body and mind. It is all about memories and hopes—nostalgia concerning the past and hopes for the future. According to the Gītā it means egos and desires, not the much-needed peace and poise. It is a case of values and priorities gone astray. There is a rather amusing (atleast to the Indian reader) social or community service being evolved in the West. To avoid drunken driving on festive days like New Years Day, social groups offer rides to those who have consumed too much alcohol and are overdrunk. Such drunk persons are picked up from clubs and restaurants and dropped at their respective homes. Some social cause to espouse! Let them drink but not drive. It is a perfect example of putting the cart before the horse.

For a healthy body, modern man needs to adopt sports or some other form of physical exercise. Yogic exercises are better suited for toning up the body-mind system and recharging the batteries or the energy centres of the body on a daily basis. Yogic exercises and sports have their own respective positive aspects. They can be undertaken within the house without any equipment and without others' participation. They are smooth, steady, non-tiring and non-strenuous. The effect is holistic and soothing overall. Sports and other physical exercises may be relatively jerky and liable to overuse the body in parts. On the positive side, sports help single-mindedness and orientation towards goal.

In any case, for any type of physical exercise, the modern man must find time. Under-used body runs as much of a health risk as does the overused body. Moderation is the key word—in the matter of food, in the matter of sleep and in the matter of physical exercise. Physical exercise complements the function of eating and sleeping. Food gets easily digested by the rejuvenated body without digestive aids and sleep is induced naturally without resort to sleeping pills.

Corporate bodies have realized the importance of the good health of their employees. Illness of the employees means lost workdays, fat medical bills, higher insurance premia, in addition to family and social cost.

In pure worldly wisdom, corporates have increasingly started providing gymnasium facilities in or near the work place, and paying membership of sports clubs. The most important ingredient in the lifestyle of the modern man for a sound body-mind system should be meditation. The word meditation may have many meanings and connotations. But, for the purpose of the busy modern man, it should simply mean sitting preferably cross-legged on the ground by himself for a few minutes. During this period he tries to withdraw from external activities (physical acts) and internal mental activities (i.e. thoughts and distractions) and to enjoy the resultant mental purity and energy.

It has been said that problems arise in the mind and that is where solutions lie. An agitated mind gives rise to problems whereas a calm mind dissolves them. Therefore, the aim of meditation is to take away all the pressure off the mind and make it light and tranquil. One empties the mind, so to say. All contradictions and negativities are barred entry into the mind. In that state of NOTHINGNESS of the mind, one realizes one's essential nature HAPPINESS AND BLISS. *Meditation is the safest and most effective tranquilizer without side-effects.*

To appreciate the negative force of senses (i.e. attachment to sense objects), the following verses (66) and (67) of chapter II of the Gītā are relevant.

The verse 67 of Chapter II, Gītā says:

indriyāṇāṃ hi caratāṃ yan mano'nuvidhīyate
tadasya harati prajñāṃ vāyur nāvam ivāmbhasi

Meaning: The wind turns a ship from its course upon the waters : The wandering winds of the sense cast man's mind adrift and turn his better judgement from its course.

इन्द्रियाणां हि चरतां यन् मनोऽनुविधीयते ।
तदस्य हरति प्रज्ञां वायुर् नावम् इवाम्भसि ॥ II (67)

The verse 66 Chapter II, Gītā says :

nāsti buddhir ayuktasya na cāyuktasya bhāvanā
na cābhāvayataḥ śāntir aśāntasya kutaḥ sukham

Meaning: The uncontrolled mind does not have the intelligence (knowledge of Atma): How can it concentrate (meditate)? Without concentration (meditation) where is peace? Without peace, where is happiness?

A mental vacuum is not in the realm of the possible at least for an ordinary person. What is possible and achievable, however, is that one unseats and ousts selfish and negative thoughts from the mind and replaces them with unselfish and positive ones. Thereafter, as happens in the game of musical chairs, even the positive thoughts are removed one by one and only one chair to seat the supreme is left. In this state, he is the sole occupant worthy of our concentration during meditation.

It is not for nothing that more and more meditation centres are opening up in India and in the western countries. Forms and techniques used in such centres may vary but the essential purpose is that the modern busy man, instead of using the false plea of alibi for spare time, must make a positive effort to find time for meditation—whatever its form or technique—whereby he may be able to concentrate on some higher purpose in life, forgetting worldly woes, even though for a short span of time. Corporate leaders themselves are turning away from psychology and psychiatry and moving towards *"philosophy counselling"*. Books like "If Aristotle Ran General Motors : The New Soul of Business" have appeared in the West. Businessmen are using philosophy successfully both in private as well as in professional life. Recently, yoga and meditation have caught up with politicians too. It is a very healthy development, indeed. The Chief Minister of Andhra Pradesh, N. Chandra Babu Naidu, known for his love for high technology, laid out an interesting daily regimen for his party (Telgu Desam Party) workers. Political training camps were organised at party headquarters in November

---

नास्ति बुद्धिर् अयुक्तस्य न चायुक्तस्य भावना ।
न चाभावयतः शान्तिर् अशान्तस्य कुतः सुखम् ॥ II (66)

2001 which included daily rigorous morning walk, followed by classes in *Yoga*; health check, guidance on diet regulation etc. The object was to introduce the idea of preventive medicine through yoga and meditation, rather than depending on curative medicine alone. He termed the senior party workers 'agents of change' and proposed that *'Stress leads to complication at work.'* He seems to understand the Gītā profoundly and that it is useful for the modern, high-tech man or any other man in any profession.

The state of mind is the springboard which gives rise to thoughts and actions. Right thoughts and right actions are not likely to cause agitation and stress in the mind. If one can manage the mind one can manage stress. In fact, *stress management is nothing if not self-management.* Certainly, the modern man does not need a psychiatrist or a psychologist for self-management. He needs himself with the right state of mind and right attitude. The two are not different. The skills for achieving the goal of HAPPINESS are provided for in PHILOSOPHY, NOT IN ECONOMICS. The Gītā is a brilliant practical example if this.

After health, comes the business or profession or vocation as a source of financial income. All those engaged in some sort of activity— mental or manual or both, are *Karma Yogīs* i.e. they have decided not to renounce the life of activity. They have also decided not to solely or mainly engage in contemplation in their quest for the supreme knowledge. By definition, barring a rather small number, all are *Karma Yogīs* in their respective fields of action and hence the greater importance of *Karma Yoga* in comparison to other forms of *Yogas*. The significance of *Karma Yoga* may also be seen with profit in social and historical background. There has been an allegation, so to say, against philosophy of inaction and renunciation in life. All activity was considered a source of bondage. A different but more practical concept known as *Karma Yoga* or *Yoga* of Action was evolved. Yoga with righteous action was elevated to the same high level as other yogas. Thus *Karma Yoga* would also ensures the goal of happiness with similar efficacy as other *Yogas*.

We might take up the point of religion here. Christianity and Islam have helped the concept of human brotherhood more. Vedāntic approach as much as Buddhism and Jainism encouraged Indians to insulate themselves, withdrawing from society and social activity in pursuit of Nirvāṇa though for different reasons. The result has been that Indians became passive, everyman getting closer to God than to his neighbor. Duty towards society in terms of protecting the good against evil, the weak against the strong and providing for the less privileged was not emphasized enough. To check the decay resulting from the progressive desertion of society by the good and wise leaving the field open to the opposite type, the Gītā reintroduced and reinforced the concept of duty towards society. Even those who do not need to or are not inclined to engage in action for its own sake due to their material or spiritual level of achievement, must undertake action for the welfare of society, nation and mankind. They are the more important benefactors of society. They include businessmen-turned philanthropists, philosophers, spiritualists, social reformers, educationists, artists etc.

But for the moves of such altruistically minded members of the society, the world would still have been poorer spiritually, materially and scientifically. Man would have been struggling with his life for his bare needs spending far more time and energy leaving no or little time for subtler things of life. The creative writers, philosophers, poets, scientists and researchers in the past lived a life of poverty or owed their existence to state patronage. There is no argument that the present generation of this class, lives and works in far better circumstances, thanks largely to the funding by Karma Yogīs who espouse and work for a higher purpose in their lives. Let us see how we too may grow and graduate to that level.

Every individual, he or she, student, professional, businessman, or a corporate executive, does have to have an *objective or goal,* howsoever, trivial or important, atleast in the short-term or both in the short-term as well as in the long-term. In the Gītā, Arjuna comes to the battlefield of Kurukṣetra with the objective of fighting against the Kauravas, attaining victory over them to receive what is his and his brothers' righteous victory in the war that had a higher purpose —to subdue evil.

At this stage, however, Arjuna under the influence of factors like attachment, unfounded fears, concern for the outcome of the war, becomes unsure and wavering in his mind as to the correctness of his objective. He becomes despondent and *resiles* from his duty to fight.

What follows in the Gītā (Chapters II to XVIII) is the dialogue between Lord Kṛṣṇa and Arjuna intended to educate Arjuna in the perennial philosophy of life in all its aspects with a view to ridding him of his doubts, confusions and overcoming emotional impediments in the bettlefield such as attachment, fear, ego, results of action in the way of goal and fighting i.e. working with a view to achieving it. The philosophical content of Lord Kṛṣṇa's sermon is at times perplexing, repetitive and even contradictory though the essential messages are not too difficult to comprehend and to put into actual practice in day-to-day life. These may serve as *Secrets of Success* in the worldly life as well as in the spiritual life.

In the concluding Chapter-XVIII of the Gītā, as a result of the discourse wonderfully and convincingly argued by Lord Kṛṣṇa, Arjuna's delusion as to his objective was dispelled. He identified his objective. His doubts having been removed, he was firm and ready to undertake action.

All of us are contemporary Arjunas. At times we are not clear about our objectives. We are confused whether to do this or that or nothing at all, wanting just to run away from the scene of life itself in the face of unforseen powers. The battlefield of Mahābhārata (Kurukṣetra) is both within oneself and in the outside world. In fact, the struggle or *battle outside is an extension of the battle within*. Since, the dilemma that Arjuna faced is common to all of us, the Gītā's message for resolution of the dilemma is also valid for all of us.

The teachings of the Gītā are useful not merely for identifying the goal or one's objective in life, but are also helpful in achieving the same. Teachings are really a technique scientifically developed by sages and seers, knowing man's essential nature—the weaknesses and strengths of his body, mind and intellect.

We often hear and read about the business corporations and companies preparing and declaring their memorandum of objectives and their policies, strategies and action plan. Individuals also have to have objectives, policies and action plans although not as elaborate as those of corporations. Now-a-days we are hearing more than ever before that living is an art. Living should include business aspects of life too. If we agree (which we should) it implies that this art must be learnt. It does not come to us automatically, without effort. For almost all walks of life, professionals (doctors, engineers, teachers, lawyers etc.) commercial and domestic, learning and training is must or atleast desirable. So it is axiomatic that the art of right living too needs training in terms of learning and practice. Mere existence and survival is not living. It is far more than that. We may call it right living and the technique needed, the art of right living.

While embarking on the course of training, let us understand the essentials of body and mind for our purpose. The human body has five sense-organs (*Jñānendriyas*)—Eyes (Sight), Ears (Sound), Nose (Smell), Tongue (Taste), Skin (Touch) all over the body. Then, there is mind which is higher than the senses. Senses perceive and interact with the objects in the external world and transmit the stimuli to the mind. Higher than the mind is intellect. Reaction or response generated to the stimuli received, is in the form of command to organs of action *'Karmendriyas'*.

Organs of action generate actions in the external world in obedience to the commands received from the mind. Thus, the mind is linked with the sense-organs on one hand and the intellect on the other. The former is on the lower plane while the latter is on the higher plane.

The role required of the intellect is to rein in the mind, to oversee and guide the activities of the mind.

In the Gītā, this has been figuratively explained through the picture of the *Chariot* driven by Lord Kṛṣṇa. The horses represent the senses, reins, (through which the Chariot driver or the charioteer controls the horses senses), symbolise the mind. The Charioteer symbolises the intellect which, with the help of the reins, controls the senses or desires. It is worth taking note of that three—senses, mind and intellect—intellect is the highest and seated firmly in the chariot, symbolic of human body.

Mind is ever restless. It is mercurial in nature, unsteady in the extreme. Hundreds and thousands of thoughts cross the mind every moment. Thoughts are the products of desires—desires of any type, good, not so good, bad or not so bad. Since sense-organs working in the external world have given rise to desires in the past and continue to do so in the present, the mind is getting continuously fed with desires. Therefore, the job of the intellect is to control the mind on a continuing basis. Intellect has to sift good from bad and as a responsible custodian guarding the mind allows only good visitors inside it. A wiseman prays that his intellect may never leave his mind unguarded lest the mind should give command to the body to perform actions which are patently or potentially harmful in the short-term or in the long-term.

An Urdu Poet Mohd. Iqabal, however, pleads for the heart to have occasional freedom to do its own bidding. He says :

> *"Lazim Hai Dil Ke Pass, Rahe Pasbane Akal*
> *Lekin, Kabhi Kabhi ise Tanha Bhi Chhorde"*
>
> (It is essential that the intellect stand guard over the mind but sometimes the mind should be left free (unguarded) to act on its own.)

The implication is quite clear. Free or unguarded mind is capable of indulgence sought by desires but not vouchsafed as correct by the intellect. The poet is asking for occasional permissiveness even though he appreciates the role of the intellect as a sentinel.

To restrain the sense-organs and their appetite, in the form of endless desires, is the job of the mind-intellect team. While mind can be influenced by desires, feelings, emotions, egos, intellect relies on logic, experience and even intuition which is even higher than intellect.

Having recognised the importance of the role of the mind, we also should accept that the state of mind is also of paramount significance. It is so for a corporate leader, executive, professional or even a student. Even an individual and every organization big or small is entitled to grow, expand, increase productivity and profitability. The Gītā is all for this and definitely not against such an approach. The right state of mind will ensure that your activities are not injurious to you individually, or to the organization you are associated with and also not harmful to society.

One important part of training is to keep your cool. Environment is one factor which may help you keep cool or prevent losing your cool. Though, mental environment is more important than the physical environment, the latter also has a role to play or a contribution to make. Basic cleanliness and hygienic conditions must be maintained in the office or workplace. Adequate light and flow of fresh air are useful aids to efficiency. Entering the work place with a cheerful rather than a tense, taut face is quite likely to spread the cheer all around. Peace and harmony of the mind and peace and harmony in the workplace complement each other. Drawing up action plans and their execution proceed smoothly in harmonious environment, increasing efficiency and productivity at all levels. Even politicians agree that peace and prosperity are inseparable. In the language of *Reiki* and *Prāṇic* healing, negative energy i.e. stress leaves the body and mind and positive energy enters body and mind in a smooth manner without hindrance or resistance. Talking of physical environment, even pictures, paintings, objects of art play a role. The picture of your favorite deity may give you his/her blessings, strength and also keep you on course. Pictures of elders, family and dear ones may serve to deepen your vision and help discover a wider purpose in life. The Gītā tells us to engage in action but with several qualifications. One such qualification is that the action should be selfless. The moment the action becomes selfless i.e. crosses the barrier of selfish desire such an action has moved to a higher plane. It has acquired a higher purpose. Engaging in action for the family (even if we ignore for the time being society, nation and mankind) is the first step towards recognising your duty to some others besides yourself. Similarly, pictures of high personages depicting serenity and peace in their demeanor will make you aspire for a nobler purpose in life and a positive approach to problems. On the other hand, nudes, females in skimpy dresses are likely to derail your mind unless you are actually in the category of emancipated artists. Pictures of a raging bull, an attacking tiger, hunting dogs and the like may sharpen the killer instinct but cannot enhance you or your image. Paintings and pictures of lofty mountain peaks, vast oceans, forests and flora will keep reminding you of your insignificance in nature's scheme of things, and thereby help dissolve or even conquer your ego, on one hand and expose the mind to newer heights and wider horizons on the other. May be it will make you a nature lover in the bargain. Unconsciously, you are already following the Gītā which asks you to control your ego and move to a higher purpose in life and a higher level of consciousness.

Though physical and external environment is important in its own way, the most important is the mental environment. Peace of mind determines the state of mind. For right thoughts, right decisions, and right actions, a right state of mind is essential. In the modern business management and elsewhere, the attitude towards colleagues and all aspects of your dealings with them is of paramount significance. Only a peaceful person can be purposeful, efficient and effective. One must remember that only a peaceful person can achieve the above and succeed even in the most material sense. Therefore, one must check against disturbing elements till such time that a peaceful attitude becomes a part of habit. It does not come easy, even all your money cannot buy it. The peace of mind does not come to the highest bidder. On the other hand, a realization that an agitated mind is like an overheated engine or an inflated tyre which can go bust any time is more likely to help you to keep your cool. In order to carry your team alongwith you, certain techniques have to be followed. Now-a-days, one is to act as a LEADER AND NOT AS A BOSS. There is no point shouting orders. The same thing can be said in a better manner by way of a suggestion or a bit of advice. The persons on the lower rungs understand it perfectly well that a suggestion or a piece of advice from the senior is, in fact, an order politely worded. Similarly, a proposal from a junior should not meet with a flat NO. It would only show an attitude of ego of the boss. The Gītā teaches us to control ego and not to feed it nor allow if to be fed by others nor demonstrate it in office, workplace or elsewhere. Rebuff is not a substitute for advice. *"The ruler whose government is calm and unobtrusive, his people are upright and honest"*, said, Lao Tzu. A polite disagreement would convey the same message. It is also necessary that the person in your organization whom you are talking to does not feel unwanted or useless. Such an attitude of generating inferiority complex in others makes such other persons less productive and perhaps hostile. Hearing out a person is as good as removing his grievances by half. Being a leader of the team, you must understand the psychology of those around you. Anyone in distress wants to open up to someone. You may be the one to whom your junior wants to speak out and give vent to his suppressed feelings. Give him a chance. It will not harm you but it will help the other person. We, so often, see the wise politicians giving their opposition a chance to shout hoarse but never agreeing to their grievances. Thus, hearing out the other person, needs patience but such an attitude even if as a mere policy has its rewards. Avoiding argument with people around you is another art. Argument pushes the other person up to your own level or conversely, in the process, you are bringing yourself to his level. Neither is your objective.

One's working environment can be a breeding ground for rumours. This again is human weakness, particularly for certain types who enjoy fabricating stories and circulating them in the office. The best way to take care of such an environment is not to lend ear to rumours. One should not be available for listening to rumours. It causes disturbance of the mind and anger as a result. It is better to be slow in reacting to such rumours. We may keep in mind that our worst enemy works through our own mind. Therefore, the mind has to be kept under constant watch and guarded like a computer is against the virus and corruption by hackers.

Faith, Trust and Loyalty are not one-way street. As a team leader, you must have faith and trust in your team members. Faith and trust are the factors which contribute to the efficiency of the team. In fact, these are virtues in any meaningful relationship. Only when you have faith in your team will the team have faith in you. The same applies to loyalty which is a two-way street, the leader has to be loyal to the team members and vice versa. An attitude of loyalty naturally would include an attitude of caring and sharing. Your business activities should not only aim at self-satisfaction. Those who are helping you in running the organization and generating profits should be able to hope for their betterment as well. It does not, however, mean that this betterment will be of the same level or to the same extent for all the persons involved in the effort. But some reasonable semblance of sharing the fruits of labour should be there and visible too. There is a beautiful Hindi couplet by Kabir which reads as follows :

"Baḍe huay to kyā huay, jaise peḍa khajūr
Pañchī ko chāyā nahin, phala lāge ati dūra".

(How does it matter if one grows tall like the tree of a date-palm because there is no shade for the bird and the fruit is out of reach.)

The message is simple but very meaningful. Your own prosperity and rise should benefit you but also others. When the business grows, the growth should bring the benefits and cool shade of security to all concerned. If one celebrates and rejoices over success but does not share the benefits with others, it is doubly harmful. Therefore, the Gītā's practical advice is not to show off or rejoice unduly over success. Stick to moderation both in enjoying and sharing the fruit of success.

In the Gītā, sharing has been emphasized in more than one chapter. The following two verses from Chapter III are relevant.

Verse 12 of Chapter III, Gītā says:

iṣṭān bhogān hi vo devā dāsyante yajñabhāvitāḥ
tair dattān apradāyaibhyo yo bhuṅkte stena eva saḥ

Meaning: The Devas nourished by the sacrifice, will give you the desired objects. Indeed he who enjoys objects, given by the Devas, without offering (in return) to them, is verily a thief.

Verse 13 of Chapter III, Gītā says:

yajñāśiṣṭāśinaḥ santo mucyante sarva kilbiṣaiḥ
bhuñjate te tv aghaṃ pāpā ye pacantyātmakāraṇāt

Meaning: The Righteous, who eat the remnants of the sacrifices are freed from all sins; but those sinful ones; who cook food, only for their own sake, verily eat but sin.

Without having to go into the literal meaning or interpretation, the message relevant to the modern times is loud and clear. The

---

इष्टान् भोगान् हि वो देवा दास्यन्ते यज्ञभाविताः ।
तैर दत्तान् अप्रदायैभ्यो यो भुङ्क्ते स्तेन एव सः ॥ III (12)

यज्ञाशिष्टाशिनः सन्तो मुच्यन्ते सर्वकिल्बिषैः ।
भुञ्जते ते त्व् अघं पापा ये पचन्त्यात्मकारणात् ॥ III (13)

Gītā's mandate is that nobody should usurp the entire benefit of his activities. Instead, we should partake of only a reasonable part of the benefit. It is presumed in the message that no single person is capable of producing benefit by his efforts alone. In numerous ways, visible and invisible, God, Nature and God's creation has helped him to generate the benefits. Therefore, the injunction is against not sharing even a small part of benefits with others. *These noble ideas are livable in the real life. Such a living does not limit the potential of a person in any way. It only enhances his personality and raises him to a higher level of consciousness.* Other religions viz. Christianity and Islam have also similarly ordained sharing of fruit of labor with others, so much so that even a person, who has not contributed or is incapable of contribution to the benefit-producing activity needs, to be looked after and helped as necessary.

In India, the joint family system which prevailed in Hindu society till recently is a perfect example. Granting, that all members of the family cannot be equally capable, mentally or physically, they cannot add to the family kitty in equal measure. But their needs should be met all the same, ignoring their respective level of contribution. One who may have contributed less might get more as per his or her respective needs and not according to their respective contribution. Communism, in fact, is rooted in joint family system of India. Its motto is: *"From, each according to his ability. To, each according to his need".*

The joint family system is the practical application of communism or of the concept of a welfare state. The difference, is that both in the case of a communist/socialist or welfare state, the faceless and emotionless state replaces a loving and caring family.

We have noted that profit is the goal of any business or professional activity. There is absolutely nothing wrong ethically or otherwise with such a goal. All the same, it is a short-term goal, the long-term goal being one's reputation. Both are important from the practical view point as a business strategy. Any organization needs profitability but without losing on the other more important front i.e. reputation. The image or reputation of an individual or an organization is rather important. A lot of resources are spent on image building. Apart from financial resources spent on advertising etc., in-house practices, honesty, fairness in giving dividends to shareholders, healthy employer-employee relationship contribute to creating and sustaining a healthy image. In the business world, particularly, an image has enormous advantages e.g. securing credit from financial institutions, successfully bringing out public issues or marketing the products. A reputed company has easy access to private and public funding because its creditworthiness is rated high naturally based on track record and the reputation enjoyed. Similarly, products get associated with the company. Certain industrial companies find it far easier as compared to others in the same field to sell their products. This helps boost the sales figures and profitability which remains the major goal. That is how a brand equity is built by scrupulous and sound manufacturer's practices as envisaged by international organisations such as UNO. No doubt, a healthy reputation encompassing various healthy practices will take the individual or the organization to higher and international levels through linkages and joint ventures with peers and leaders in the field. We have taken care of profit as well as reputation—the twin goals of a normal individual or business organization without resort to any malpractices. Having once tasted the sweetness of the fruits of honesty and other good values, chances are that you or your employees will not tread the self-destructive path of dishonesty and selfishness. As the saying goes : *"A well fed pet dog will not look into public dustbins for its food."*

Last, but not the least, is the family and home of our modern man. Unfortunately home has lost its meaning and also its usefulness. In England home was referred to as "SWEET HOME" and "FAMILY HEARTH" was the place where family members would sit, eat and chat, around the 'fire' Modernization has changed all that and taken away the sweetness of home and the warmth of the hearth. In India, home had a special meaning in everybody's life. It was not only a place for just living together in a joint family but a sacrosanct place, vibrating with activity, full of love and emotion where one grows imbibing cultural and other values passed on from generation to generation. In brief, different members learn at home the art of living, discharging their duties to elders, posterity, society and the nation.

This concept has taken a severe knocking, diminishing its importance and role in life. *The poor probably have a home but need a house to put the home in. The rich have a house but do not have a home.* A structure, its walls with all the modern gadgetry and equipment do not make a home. Carpets, draperies, paintings, wall-hangings, objects-of art, fail to provide much needed comfort, peace and happiness to those who dwell there. The family table is a poor substitute for family hearth, more so if it becomes debating table for exchange of arguments and placing their respective demands by members of the family. Even so, one meal daily together at the table, which has become rare, is welcome in modern times. It may be observed here that the Gītā like most Indian scriptures lays emphasis on one's duty rather than right. Everyone has a set of duties to someone whose right it becomes. (Due to overemphasis on rights in the modern age, some countries have citizens' duties enshrined in their constitution alongwith rights).

Modern man, short of time as he is, visits the home rather than live there. To make one's home a source of happiness this has to change. All the members of the family including the rather-busy modern man should look forward to coming home at the end of a day's work. All the roads should lead to home and not to a club or other destination. On returning home, do not use it as a place to empty out your woes. It is not a garbage dump to be stuffed with waste and unwanted stuff. Instead, a home should be like a flower-vase giving out to all sweet fragrances of love and compassion. It is not a place for argument and picking on one another's faults. Relax and unwind by all means but not by swearing nor by punching bags. These are expressions of hatred. The object of hatred may be your rival, your boss, or your teacher, or a classmate you do not like or even a family member. For a happy family, kissing, hugging, sharing a joke or experiences of children at school are some of the positive channels available. The family, basically, implies, to a certain extent, merger of identities to make a bigger, better, and a nobler whole viz. family. Nature has given basic energy to all human beings. How we use it i.e. whether for a positive purpose or negative purpose is left to us. That is the message given by the Gītā in Verse 5 of Chapter VI.

It says:

> *uddhared ātmanātmānaṃ nātmānam avasādayet*
> *ātmaiva hyātmano bandhur ātmaiva ripur ātmanaḥ*

Meaning: Let a man lift himself by his own self alone, and let him not lower himself; for, this self alone is the friend of oneself, and this self is the enemy of oneself.

The above verse means that one can be one's own friend or one's own foe, depending upon how one uses one's own energy. The same principle applies to the family. It can be an asset providing strength, succour and a source of happiness. On the contrary, it may become a liability, a mill-stone around the neck, slowing down your pace, negating your efforts, filling life with boredom and unhappiness. Each one must elevate not degrade oneself. The amount of time spent together with an attitude of caring and sharing can make all the difference. The goals of individual members of the family should become the single goal of the entire family—*Happiness of all.* Money cannot buy all this. But a positive attitude can ensure this. Paying to the tutor is not the same thing as taking consistent interest in the progress of the child.

Beyond the family, there is society and beyond your own individual angle, there is a social angle. The Gītā brings in this concept of *Lokasaṃgraha* many times, in different chapters underlining its importance. Its universal application is of immense use to the society. The emphasis is on the basic value-system that one does not act for oneself alone or live for one-self only. Instead, he acts for others atleast in part. Lord Kṛṣṇa has observed that action is a must for everyone. Even Load Kṛṣṇa engaged himself in action although, as is obvious, He (Lord Kṛṣṇa) did not have the need for himself to engage in action. The explanation lies in the social angle i.e. responsibility towards society. Indirectly, it is a directive to engage in action for the sake of others, even when one himself does not need to. That is how a society or a nation becomes strong.

उद्धरेद् आत्मनात्मानं नात्मानम् अवसादयेत् ।
आत्मैव ह्यात्मनो बन्धुर् आत्मैव रिपुर् आत्मनः ॥ VI (5)

At Harvard Business School in U.S.A., the first lesson they give to the students is on the objective or purpose of business. Students are told that it is to make money. Lessons that follow inform the students, interestingly enough, that business has a purpose, other than making money, also. Students are taught that they have to nurture the needs of the society they live and do business in. As a result, they will have a sense of belonging, a sense or feeling of well-being and a higher degree of self-esteem.

According to the Gītā the 'other' purpose is higher than the normal purpose. It is the social angle or purpose, called *Lokasaṃgraha*. Sharing the fruit of one's action with others (particularly the less fortunate) helps one grow in self-esteem or, in the words of the Gītā helps one's self-growth. A right mix of business and spiritualism is the practical need of the man of today.

Philanthropy is another form of helping the society. However, a word of caution must be added. While philanthropy is praiseworthy, the philanthropist must also work to eliminate causes like economic injustice which make philanthropy a social need. It is no use to be contributing to the causes of poverty and misery on one hand and then claiming credit for a little charity from this ill-gotten money on the other.

Status and growth in society of a successful person—businessman, executive or a professional, is reflected in the overall balancesheet, comprising of him as an individual, as a businessman, as an executive and also as a father, mother, son, daughter and a husband, wife.

The Gītā helps to show the way to happiness in all aspects of life. However, it only shows the way by providing a guide map, providing a philosophy, rather than chartering the course for all aspects of life. But the walking has to be done by individuals (you and me) themselves, staying steady on course without losing the way or going astray.

The Gītā helps reconstruct life to make one a complete and a happy person.

CHAPTER 3

Peace and Harmony

Verse 64 of Chapter II of the Gītā says:

rāga dveṣa viyuktais tu viṣayān indriyaiścaran
ātmavaśyair vidheyātmā prasādam adhigacchati

Meaning: But the self-controlled man, moving among objects, with his senses under restraint and free from both attraction and repulsion (love and hate) attains peace.

Further, verse 65 of Chapter II of the Gītā says:

prasāde sarva duḥkhānāṃ hānir asyo'pajāyate
prasannacetaso hyāśu buddhiḥ paryavatiṣṭhate

Meaning: In that peace all sorrows are destroyed because the intellect of the peaceful (person) soon becomes steady.

If we examine the first verse, quoted above we can discern therein that both physical and non-physical i.e. mind-intellect aspects of the human body have been discussed. Firstly, the verse presumes that man is 'moving among objects'. It does not make it a condition,

---

रागद्वेषवियुक्तैस्तु विषयान् इन्द्रियैश्चरन्।
आत्मवश्यैर् विधेयात्मा प्रसादम् अधिगच्छिति॥ II (64)

प्रसादे सर्वदुखानां हानिर् अस्योपजायते।
प्रसन्नचेतसो ह्याशु बुद्धिः पर्यवतिष्ठते॥ II (65)

precedent or a prerequisite, that man should be physically separated from the sense-objects. As a part of worldly life, he has to interact with sense-objects. There is no escape from them in absolute terms. The physical apparatus i.e. the five sense-organs (eyes, ears, nose, tongue and skin) will ceaselessly continue to perceive the physical world. But the receiving end (mind-intellect) is not tuned and switched on or receptive, to the transmitted physical stimulus . They are not being registered by the mind at all or are being registered only partly. Almost all of us have some experiences of such situations.

One can be so busy mentally in one's studies or some other pursuit that another person may come or go or sit by his side unnoticed. One may even forget other engagements. Even hunger and sleep get postponed without any effort. One has to be reminded to eat or to go to sleep. It is a case of seeing the tree and missing the forest. What it means is that physical body and mind-intellect are on different planes. We often hear that 'his mind is somewhere else'. His mind is not available for perception of sense-objects at least temporarily. He is only 'moving among the sense-objects' but not influenced or affected by them. This is possible for a man whose senses are under restraint and who is equanimous i.e. neither attracted nor repelled by physical objects. *Physical Stuff is not his Mind Stuff.* Such a person is called a self-controlled one. 'Channel Select' monitor is under his control. For such a person the unnecessary or undesirable stuff does not exist, so to say. He is automatically led to peace.

The reward, as a result of 'moving among objects with sense-control, equanimity of mind by the self-controlled one and attaining peace is declared in the next verse viz. verse no. 65. It is not merely attaining peace momentarily, just as a brief experience, as if with the help of a tranquiliser. The reward of peace stays with such a person in that state of mind in a stable and steady manner.

All troubles or sorrows get dissolved in that bliss of peace. Troubles or sorrows are the outcome of disturbance or turbulence. When, with control leading to self-control, all the disturbances and turbulence have settled down on an even level or keel, peace and happiness which is the essential nature of man is discovered. These essential attributes (peace and happiness) did not leave man nor did they disappear into nowhere but got covered by a veil. Having discovered his true nature, such a person becomes steady-minded. The logical need for steadiness of mind is further explained in verse 66, which Gītā says:

> *nāsti buddhir ayuktasya na cāyuktasya bhāvanā*
> *na cābhāvayataḥ śāntir aśāntasya kutaḥ sukham*

> **Meaning:** There is not knowledge to the unsteady (uncontrolled) and to the unsteady no meditation (power of concentration), and to the unmeditative no peace, to the peaceless how can there be happiness.

By paraphrasing the above verse, the chain of logic which emerges is like this. Having become steady (of mind) proceed to gain knowledge of the self (as opposed to information or academic knowledge) and meditation, so that the peace and happiness are yours.

These three verses (64, 65 and 66) are a narration of cause and effect. One cause leading to one effect and that effect becoming the cause of another effect. Sense-restraint leads to self-control; self-control leads to mental immunity to the physical world; mental immunity to physical world leads to peace; peace leads to dissolution of disturbances (including jubilation); dissolution of disturbance leads to steadiness and stability viz. abiding happiness—one's essential nature.

Therefore, the key word or the starting point is sense-restraint. The Gītā is not for torturing the body or sense-organs as some ascetics practise and preach. The Gītā is for restraint and hence the phrase 'moving among the objects'. The Gītā does not preach running away from life but living life in a restrained or regulated manner. It is the victory of the inner self over external objects. It makes life an art. Life can be a curse or a blessing, depending on how one conducts oneself. Nature's playfield can be as much a man's playfield also.

नास्ति बुद्धिर् अयुक्तस्य न चायुक्तस्य भावना।
न चाभा वयतः शान्तिर् अशान्तस्य कुतः सुखम्॥ II (66)

For ordinary mortals, businessmen and corporate executives, it may not be a good idea to throw or accept challenges and test one's internal peace and strength, particularly in the initial stage. There are various types of entertainment shows, movies etc. where the commercial value depends on their provocative content. These are not conducive to happiness even as an external environment. It is better to be considered meek and devoid of courage than to be indulging in drugs or sex etc. Mahatma Gandhi narrates in his autobiography 'My Experiments with Truth' an incident of his life. He went to the house of a prostitute. Unable to make up his mind further he was thrown out of the prostitute's house. Mahatma Gandhi writes, had he not been thrown out of that door then, he might have been deprived of many better opportunities in life.

Sometimes, we hear of people going away for holidays—after much preparation to have peace of mind. Generally, one goes to mountains, pastoral areas, seaside etc. in search of peace. Change from routine and some extra time for oneself and one's family during holidays is welcome. It also gives one time for repair of the body and keep it disease free. A diseased body has more cravings than a healthy body. One wants to escape the noise of life. But the searcher for peace need not be an escapist. Whether on duty or on holiday, for peace one needs to turn inwardly.

While 'moving among the sense-objects one is not necessarily affected or influenced by the objects, objects *per se* can not do any harm to a disciplined or a self-controlled person. He is like a passerby in the market place probably because his route homewards lies that way but he is not a buyer or a shopper. Take the case of a businessman, bureaucrat or an executive. Sycophants would wait upon and try to approach him only if he has a reputation of liking sycophants. On the contrary, if he has a reputation of disliking sycophants, he will be spared attention by them. Similarly, a peaceful, steady person, whose mind-intellect apparatus is in control of his senses and who is his own master, will not be distracted or disturbed by desires. Unnecessary harmful desires will drop off one by one. Even the beneficial ones will stay as per one's own choice and for as long as one wants. Here, one needs to appreciate that all desires good or bad are limited in time and space.

Certain desires may be good at times but not so forever. Only peace and happiness are good for all times. Peace and happiness are one's essential nature and these are everybody's goal. Mix-up occurs because we do not know the right abode of peace or happiness. These lie within everyone of us while we search for these in physical objects, in certain physical conditions and in certain time-frame.

Sometimes, we seek peace in family, sometimes among friends sometime at home, at other times in office and eventually we find peace neither here nor there. Probably, we then believe, that a club, away from both office and home, may be the hiding place for the all-elusive peace.

The feeling of being incomplete, lacking in something, is always there with man, particularly, when he is alone and alone he is in the final analysis. Ordinary people are baffled more by this feeling as they are not able to tune up with themselves. An ordinary person wishes to be eternally busy. He creates business even when it is not necessary. He wants to forget, run away from something and get to something else but does not know what it is and where it is. Generally our search is in wrong places. We search for it in external objects where it is not but do not try to get it within where it is. Modern science and modern technology has made life more and more comfortable physically but not peaceful mentally. No amount of physical comfort can bring about peace of mind. On the contrary it has caused more disturbance in the man's mind because more and more spare time needs to be 'utilised' as less and less time is needed for survival. Interestingly enough once at the family dinner table, the discussion veered around to the topic as to the effect on society of modern life of automation. A young member of the family at the table said that income levels will go up in the sense that with less and less time or hours per week or per month spent, one would be able to make enough money for a reasonable living. As a result, he would have more spare time which would imply more and more leisure time. Thus, in socio-economic terms it would mean expansion of entertainment industry in all its facets—travel, tour etc. Another member at the table said that some members of the society with a different bent of mind would probably enter the crime world and therefore police force by whatever name one may call it would need to be increased. Both the predictions have come true. Entertainment industry including tour, travel, hotel industry, and restaurant industry have grown sharply. Police forces in all countries have been increased to control crimes of different natures including the cyber crimes.

What about additional spare time attracting a greater number of new adherents to man's search or quest of self. One likes to think that now this field too has more researchers—scientists or saints—working to know our cosmic origins and reality.

It is the state of one's being which is to be evolved over a period of time. All religions agree that God —the energy source is within you. To realize Him one must remove the veil of ignorance with the help of self knowledge. Similarly, peace is within and also all around. One does not have to create peace. One only needs to vacate noises, and distractions, listen to the sound of silence and enjoy peace and harmony.

Some people cannot face upto themselves. They are afraid of being alone and to them loneliness is a punishment. One must change such an attitude, look inward and contemplate. Solitude—is also a source of solace, peace and happiness—a bliss. One's intuitive mind or inner realm of oneself will start unfolding.

Though to the self-realized no crutches are required, yet for the new initiate or the beginner on the spiritual journey, in order to gain conscious control of one's different levels, it is recommended that, one has passion or anger under control (*yama*); one applies rule or principle to clear one's thoughts (*niyama*); one follows a body posture (*āsana*) to acquire control of intellect and allow free flow of inner-forces or energy of the body; one regulates inhaling and exhaling of breath—vital-force (*prāṇāyām*); and then focuses attention mentally on a select objective and then mentally moves on to the formless supreme.

It is a process of evolution not a matter of one' sudden decision and its implementation. In the best of circumstances one may be ill at ease mentally. One cannot say: I will be peaceful at a hill station or on a seaside but not in my office or home. Or one may think that one will be peaceful on a Sunday but not on any other day. If one's nature has evolved to be peaceful and has stabilised at that high level, one can be peaceful in all circumstances. As stated in verse 64 and 65 of chapter II of the Gītā, such a person has to have sense-control, equanimity or evenness of attitudes towards different aspects of life. It is not physical indulgence alone but mental indulgence also which needs to be controlled. Verse 6 of chap. III of the Gītā in the context of yoga of action says:

karmendriyāṇi saṃyamya ya āste manasā smaran
indriyārthān vimūḍhātmā mithyācāraḥ sa ucyate

Meaning: The deluded ones, who restrain their organs of action but mentally dwell upon the sense enjoyment, are called hypocrites.

The Gītā is not only against but harshly critical of persons who claim to renounce physical action but indulge in mental action involving physical objects. In fact, mental action by sense organs (*Jñānendriyas*) precedes physical action by the body (*Karmendriyas*) and not the other way round. Peace of mind cannot be switched on or off. Once attained, it stays with you all the time, in all situations. But it does not come easy. There are hurdles to overcome.

Mahatma Gandhi said:

"Any fool can find shanti (peace) in shanti. The greatness of man is to find shanti in ashanti (turbulence)".

The Great Indian poet Kalidasa said the following to the same effect:

"They whose minds are not disturbed when the sources of disturbances are present are the truly brave".

The import of the above two quotations is definitely more applicable to busy executives who work under great pulls and pressures from all sides. Persons whose decisions can make a real difference in business or their field of activity need to be peaceful at all costs. It is necessary for them as individuals as well as responsible executives or as leaders in the field of their activity. It is essential both as a principle and as a policy. He or she has to

---

कर्मेन्द्रियाणि संयम्य य आस्ते मनसा स्मरन्।
इन्द्रियार्थान् विमूढात्मा मिथ्याचारः स उच्यते॥ III (6)

interact with people at different levels or planes of activity. In a small stretch of time, he is dealing with people higher than himself; equal to himself or lower than himself. These different planes may be outside his own establishment or within his own establishment. He is in different modes at different times or he is in different gears at different points of time. But being in the driver's seat his dexterity in driving is important. Safety of himself, co-passengers, and the vehicle too, depends on it. He should be in control. He should be able to synchronise the various inputs. In the larger context of dealing with different people at different levels and possibly in different divisions of the organization and outside he has to create harmony among them, in addition to, himself being a peaceful mind or a peaceful person. Harmony implies more than one person or a source of sound or music and their producing harmonious sound or music to make the product a note pleasing to the ears. In business terms it means working in an orderly fashion without any friction, inter-se. They together make an orchestra and create a musical concert as against jarring or discordant notes having an unsettling effect on the mind, that is working at cross purposes. It is a cross traffic within the organization resulting in loss of energy.

That is why he out of necessity must be a peaceful person. A peaceful person thinks calmly, clearly and therefore rationally and logically. His communication with others is smooth, pleasant and effective. His own overall behavior is a pleasant experience. He comes across cheerfully and not with a tense face though he conveys, nonetheless that he means business. Neither a boss nor a subordinate avoids or resents meeting such a person. He himself is the biggest beneficiary. He achieves higher productivity with less fatigue or tension. Only a peaceful person can encourage others to be peaceful. Peace spreads peace, tension creates more tension and confusion creates more confusion.

In the modern world, particularly in business environment, speed has overtaken everything else. Corporates want speedier computers, speedier results, speedier deliveries etc. But it is necessary that we understand that there is a vast difference between speed and haste. Speedy decisions or actions are not the same as hasty decisions or actions. While the former come forth from a peaceful mind, the latter issue forth from an unpeaceful or an agitated mind. A good judgment is a natural expression of wisdom of a peaceful and harmonious mind.

> "It is only when we are not disturbed that we can always do the right thing, at the right time, in the right way".
>
> *(The Mother: Sri Aurobindo Ashram)*

Woodrow Wilson said:

> "One cool judgement is worth a thousand hasty councils (counsels). The thing to do is to supply the light and not heat."

The significance of a peaceful and harmonious mind can not be over emphasised in the life of an individual. Peace in the family, the business organization, society etc. is equally important. However it is the peaceful individuals who provide the right building blocs for peaceful families and other still bigger groups of individuals.

In practical terms in day-to-day life, we all experience the difference between the effort and achievement or between the capacity and the output of a person who is at peace with himself and the other person who is not at peace with himself. Even the same person achieves or gives a lower output when not peaceful as compared to when he is peaceful. An agitated person, disturbed person, having lost or at least reduced his power of reasoning and clear thinking, issues confusing, unclear and contradictory orders. Even after the fit of anger has subsided, it takes quite a while before one can resume one's normal work.

The person has not only lost out his self-control and peace of mind, he has also incurred a loss of time and energy. It all adds up to financial loss due to fall in terms of productivity and profitability.

His colleagues will not be able to work efficiently and give the optimum results. In both these states of mind viz. peaceful and unpeaceful a person consumes certain amount of energy. The peaceful mind is using the energy positively and optimally but an agitated mind is using energy negatively wasting a good amount of it. We all know that a wobbling machine is not an efficient machine. It moves with jerks and jolts and is counter—productive. Another comparison in mechanical terms may be made with an over-heated engine which is high on consumption (of oil i.e. resources) and low on performance (achievement or productivity).

After business life, let us come to the institution of marriage and family life. One does not get married merely because it is customary in society. It is often heard, particularly in India, that he or she is married and settled. Marriage is required and expected to remove or take away the feeling of being 'unsettled'. Man and woman both feel incomplete and less than full. Marriage is expected to bring about completeness and a fulsome feeling and lead the spouses toward happiness—the goal of everyone's life. Sex, no doubt, is an important part of married life in good measure. However, sexual pleasure can remain a physical pleasure only on a physical plane or can be sublimated into a bliss at a higher plane.

Cohabitation of the bodies should be accompanied by sharing of responsibilities and sharing of values to a certain degree. Marriage is more than sharing of bed and bodies. It is caring for each other. Home is a place one seeks to return after day's work in the world outside, to relax, to repair, to recoup in short, to enjoy oneself together with one's family, in peace without outside disturbance. What if one brings a part of disturbance from outside or disturbance inside the home itself is otherwise created. What if everybody in the family presents his or her list of complaints and charter of demands. The goal—of marriage and acquiring the family—of completeness, happiness and the hope to lead a fuller life disappears like a pipedream. The peace of mind of all concerned is disturbed or worse, shattered.

Marriage implies, *inter alia*, abridgement of one's freedom in return for love and support from the spouse. Same is the spirit behind sharing—to give something in the hope of receiving something. Both are givers and receivers and thus complement each other and are equal partners. There are those who consider wife and children bills of charges. On the opposite side, there are those who nearly think 'girdles and garters' to be 'bonds and shackles'. Neither kind should get into the bond of matrimony. Marriage also implies control or restraint. Control of mind and restraint of senses acquire a new meaning, so to say.

Senses may enjoy freedom, in moderation within certain fixed parameters but must observe restraint beyond those parameters. Home and family should become the focus of attraction for the wandering mind.

A family is not a group of people living together just as a home is not a structure where that group eats and sleeps. There is sharing of values, emotions and implied offer of support whenever needed. More importantly it is caring for one another, suffering for one another or suffering together which forges closer links. Those who stick together only in good circumstances are weak but those who close ranks further in suffering are the really strong. Such a family as sticks together, everyone doing his duty without complaints and demands or causing tension and disturbance of mind, promotes peace and prosperity. It has been said about nations that peace and prosperity are indivisible. The same applies to peace and prosperity at the family level. Togetherness, sharing responsibilities and privileges cheerfully makes achievement of goal easier and with less energy consumption because energy which would have been lost in friction and anger has been saved. Warring families have always ended up in disasters.

As brought out in the quotations from the famous poet Kalidasa and saint-politician Mahatma Gandhi, the brave are those who are not disturbed when sources of disturbance are very much present. Greatness or the peaceful nature of a person can be judged by the way he reacts to a particularly bad situation. A person with peaceful mind will respond in an entirely different manner to a bad situation as compared to the manner of the person devoid of peace of mind. Take an imaginary case of three persons traveling by a car and the car meeting with an accident somewhat away from a town. All three persons receive injuries but to different degrees. One has received a major injury but he is a calm person. He thanks God that accident took place just outside the town. He suggests going to a hospital in the town and getting the injury treated without much fuss. The second, passenger with a mild injury cries somewhat and shows discomfort but is willing to go to the town hospital as suggested by the first. The third, person has received only slight bruises i.e. has suffered the least, is most noisy and in distress without much reason.

He will be blaming the time he left his house as inauspicious etc. His suffering is in his imagination. There is hardly any relation between the degree of suffering and the response it has generated in different persons. The wise take suffering or adversity as an opportunity to learn the value of happiness.

Self-controlled and peaceful persons are bound to be harmonious people. They have a sense of altruism and are, therefore, competent to harmonise the interests of other members of the society so that friction or disharmony does not obstruct the path of progress in different spheres of life. Healthy building blocs have put in place a strong edifice of a healthy society. In the context of world it can become a 'global village', provided the interests of all the nations are harmonized. Society too can become a single big family provided there is harmonization of interests of all the members of society.

The Gītā looks at the world as one brotherhood, inter-connected and inter-dependent. Verse 20 of Chap. III, Gītā says:

karmaṇaiva hi saṃsiddhim āsthitā janakādayaḥ
lokasaṃgrahamevāpi saṃpaśyan kartum arhasi

Meaning: It was even by work (path of action) that Janak (king of Mithila and father of Sītā, the wife of Lord Rāma) and others attained to perfection. Thou should also do work (follow the path of action) with a view to the maintenance of the world.

Even kings such as Janak who had no need to work for themselves, had to perform action for the sake of the world. Therefore, even the self-realized, must act as the situation demands or occasion arises.

The message of the Gītā is very clear. The world is the responsibility of everyone, more so of those who are accomplished and self-realized, not for their own limited sake but for the larger interest of humanity. The Gītā has given this higher sense of purpose

---

कर्मणैव हि संसिद्धिम् आस्थिता जनकादयः।
लोकसंग्रहमेवापि संपश्यन् कर्तुम् अर्हसि॥ III (20)

through the concept of *'Lokasaṃgraha'*—world maintenance. Its purpose is to spiritualize society and to establish a brotherhood on earth through peace and harmony. If a section of society is neglected there can not be peace in other sections of the society. Adversity in any part of the world is danger to prosperity everywhere. Disturbance or turbulence anywhere threatens peace everywhere. That is how local, national or regional conflicts led to world wars in the past and, unless man becomes wiser, history may repeat itself.

A higher level of responsibility for the higher purpose of maintenance of social order (or even world order) rests with the more powerful and at higher levels of social and political hierarchy. Responsibility is directly (not inversely) proportional to power. The powerful, instead of being corrupted, partly or absolutely, must act responsibly for a higher purpose.

The Gītā, brings out the additional significance of the conduct of great men in the sense that the common men tend to follow them and their conduct.

Verse 21 of Chapter III, Gītā says:

yad yad ācarati śreṣṭhas tat tad evetaro janaḥ
sa yat pramāṇaṃ kurute lokas tad anuvartate

Meaning: Whatever a great man does, the same is done by others as well. Whatever standard he sets, the world follows.

The human tendency of following the leader or hero-worship is not anti-democracy. It is the truth of life. Masses follow the leader out of consideration of the latter's superiority. It is applicable to fields as different as politics, economics, education, sports, films etc. Real life can vouchsafe this principle being followed in all aspects by common men. Good leaders produced good following and good results even though over a period of time. Dishonest leaders because of their greed get surrounded by greedy followers. Minor functionaries cannot be honest when the top leaders are dishonest. Indifferent parents or indifferent teachers can not generate responsible or dedicated children or students. Decadence

---

यद् यद् आचरति श्रेष्ठस् तत् तद् एवेतरो जनः।
स यत् प्रमाणं कुरुते लोकस् तद् अनुवर्तते॥ III (21)

of the individual and the society sets in, leading to the destruction of the social and national moral fibre.

As the blame for decadence falls on those who are high up in different hierarchies of life, so does the responsibility to check the rot. They need to think coolly, reason out clearly and act rightly and righteously. In other words, they have to be selfless with a peaceful or tranquil mind, keeping emotions and senses under control with enough genuine regard for the concept of *Lokasaṃgraha*, more than an ordinary person.

Another important area of peace and harmony is man's living in harmony with, rather than in conflict, with nature in all its aspects. The Gītā's concept of *Lokasaṃgraha*—world maintenance by the man particularly when he is in a position to decide and command is receiving due awareness and recognition.

This concept is intended for those who are accomplished ones or those who occupy the position of power in society, governments, international organizations. Instead of sitting back as self-servers or silent spectators to the process of decadence and deprivation, they should use their position as trendsetters and opinion-makers, so that others may follow.

There are numerous movements in the world e.g. Greenpeace, Friends of the Earth etc. which are actively engaged in restraining mankind from violating nature any further because it is counter-productive. Man violates mother nature at his own peril. He is writing his own death warrant. Man must not be divorced from nature but be a part of nature.

Man is an insignificant part of creation. He is not competent to disturb or destroy the existing balance and harmony in creation and try to give it a new balance and harmony. Knowing his insignificance and incompetence in the scheme of creation, the intelligent approach would be to find his rightful place without falling foul of mother nature. Man, a microcosm, has to try so hard to find his own peace and harmony of mind—It is a tall order for him to find a new balance and harmony *inter-se* oceans, mountains, glaciers, rivers, forests, crest of the earth and the beautiful world of animal species. The human urge for search, discovery and exploration is search for truth. This is not what is being criticised. Scientists, on the other hand, are the ones who are warning mankind against global warming, damage to ozone layer due to emission from industry in the developed world. Population pressure in the developing world has led to deforestation which, in turn, changes the pattern of rain fall as well as flora and fauna. Other unintelligent uses of natural resources are sure to extract a hefty price in no distant future. It will be unfair to those engaged in the campaign of 'back to nature', if it is not mentioned that their good work is having some effect albeit not adequate. Certain animals have been declared as endangered specie and their killing is prohibited under the law. Laws against poaching are being enforced more strictly.

Hunting as a sport either by the brave or the rich is not allowed. Wearing of animal furs and animal skin is no more an insignia of high taste or station. Non-vegetarianism is on the decline. Use of animals even for medical research is being questioned. One comes across medicines with labels claiming that the product does not contain animal fat or it has not been tested on animals. Nature's mill is grinding though slowly.

In conclusion, one must say that peace and harmony in self and surroundings has a high place in Hindu scriptures. It will be interesting for some to discover that apart from the Gītā, the *Vedas* of India too have specific prayers for peace. In its invocation to God, the peace prayer asks for *Śānti* (peace): in the space/cosmos (*Antarikṣa*); on the earth (*Pṛthvī*); in the water-oceans (*Jala*) and the entire vegetation (*Vanaspati*) etc. The prayer seeks harmony among the spiritual needs (*Daivika*); body needs (*Daihika*) and supply by the elements (*Bhautika*). The most popular God of Hindus viz. Lord Śiva is also known as *Paśupati*—the lord of animals. Man needs animals, and therefore, must ensure their protection and preservation for his and world's peace and harmony.

Therefore, not only pray, but act also for peace.

CHAPTER 4

State of Mind and Action

"Since wars begin in the minds of men, it is in the minds of men that the defences of peace must be constructed".

UNESCO Constitution

What is true of wars between nations is also true of wars or battles or actions of individuals in the field of action viz. *Karma Bhūmi* or *Karma Kṣetra*. Thoughts precede physical actions. Thoughts pertain to mind and actions pertain to body. In other words, physical actions are thoughts translated into action. Therefore, one has to tackle the former first, the latter, then, gets tackled automatically, as a result. Thoughts arise in the mind. Therefore, the nature and quality of thoughts depend on how mind is impacted i.e. what is the state of mind when the body is performing an action. Generally speaking, action by itself is neutral in character. The state of mind behind the action determines whether an action is good, bad or indifferent.

According to the Gītā, depending on the right state of mind, while performing an act, the field of action viz. *Karma Kṣetra* becomes a field of duty viz. *Dharma Kṣetra*. In turn, the battle of life viz. *Karma Yuddha* becomes a righteous battle of life viz. *Dharma Yuddha*. The famous English Poet William Shakespeare also echoed the above truth in the play "Hamlet", as follows:

"Nothing is good or bad, only thinking makes it so."

Acts are neutral i.e. acts *perse* have no binding characteristics. Only the mind of the doer of acts, endows the acts with characteristics. Acts acquire a good, bad or neutral character, depending upon the state of mind of the doer. To begin with, an action is an effect not a cause. The seat of the cause is in the mind; hence the significance of control of mind and state of mind. Limbs will not itch for action if mind does not. Mind stuff is an internal problem. There are no external solutions to internal problems. It would be illogical to expect it to be any other way.

We talk about state of economy, state of finance, state of health of individuals, corporates and nations. It is time, we give due importance to the state of mind of individuals because they provide the building blocs for the state of health—economic, moral, secular and spiritual—of societies and nations. A sick mind can not generate a healthy action. The vital link between the state of mind and the action of an individual comes out clearly from the following examples from real life.

A painter artist would see a nude young female model as a beautiful creation of nature and focus on it to translate it into a work of art. An ordinary person may simply shy away. Still another person may suffer agitation of mind and even of body. All have different states of mind. That is why, female nude or semi-nude figures in sexy postures carved out of stone in caves e.g. Ajanta and Ellora invite appreciation of some and criticism of others. In temples such as those, at Khajuraho stone-depiction of men and women in all imaginable postures of sexual ecstasy, and even in act of copulation are considered work of great art by some but an example of decadent society of the time by others.

The very same physical act or situation could have different meanings to different people due to their different states of mind. Consider a family—husband, wife and a child, at a railway station. The train the family was to take, has been announced to be late. The husband gets upset, becomes angry, blames the railway authorities for upsetting his plans. The wife is not bothered much. The child completely ignores the delay and enjoys himself as if he were on an outing. Changing colors of signal lights, passengers embarking on or disembarking from trains, vendors hawking snacks etc. are interesting and absorbing attractions to him. The same situation causing anger to one person, is providing fun to the other and has virtually no effect on still another. Reaction of each to the same situation is different as per his or her respective state of mind. Depending upon one's state of mind, life can be a *panorama or a nightmare.*

This is virtually true of all events in life—happy or tragic. *What happens to a man is not as important as how he responds to what happens to him.* In festivity, some look for food and others for fun. In adversities, some lose nerve, start crying, blaming others while some remain composed, take charge and start organizing affairs in the new situation that has arisen.

Let us move from an individual to a larger scene in life. A commercial contractor and a team of free *Sewādāras* are busy constructing a road. A *Sewādāra* is a person who provides any service for a social or religious cause, free of cost. A passerby asks the contractor as to what he is doing? The contractor replies that he is linking such and such towns by a new road. When the same question is asked of the *Sewādāras,* the response is that they are working for the uplift of their own village and other villages nearby, as the link road would help the entire community. The state of mind of the contractor is different from that of the *Sewādāras*. The same physical work for the contractor is a selfish one whereas for the *Sewādāras,* it is selfless and is an act of sacrifice.

If a policeman kills a criminal in an encounter, it (act of killing) is an act of bravery, worthy of appreciation because the beneficiary is society. If a criminal kills a person to commit robbery, the act of killing is a murder, punishable with capital punishment because the beneficiary would have been the killer. Although, the act of killing is similar yet the act has been done with a different state of mind—in one case as part of duty while in the other, it is for a selfish end—a forbidden act, a wrong objective intended to be achieved through wrongful and forbidden means.

We watch the interplay of the states of mind within the family also. Around the time of marriage husband and wife look to each other as most important and loveable persons in their lives. When the relations, for whatever reason, become strained, they decide to get divorced. In that frame of mind, they see each other as worst enemies and as the biggest obstacle in achieving their respective goals of life. The state of mind has converted most-loved ones into most-hated ones.

"I love you" changes into *"I hate you."*

Another commonplace example is that of gifts given to family members, friends and others or care provided to elderly parents. Sometimes, giving of a gift or care of parents is a mere formality while at other times, it is just discharging a social obligation according to the social status of the giver and the receiver without one's heart in it or any love or emotions at the back of one's mind. *No emotions—only calculations.* The expensive gifts given to politicians and Government functionaries are not to felicitate them or to greet them on auspicious occasions but are in the nature of disguised bribery because the giver intends to establish a contact and use the contact for some favor later on. Rarely is there genuine love or even a sense of duty at the back of care of parents. Similarly gifts are very seldom tokens of emotion.

The mind has also been compared with a lamp connected to a two-way switch, as in the case of a light bulb in the staircase. The lamp is connected with one switch at the lower level of the staircase— near the first step—while the other switch is located at the higher level—near the last step of the staircase. Though, the example is a symbolic one its import is quite meaningful in the present context. Mind can be fed by the lower-self or lower values. Alternatively, mind can also be fed by higher-self or higher values. In one situation, mind becomes a *Devil's Workshop* and in the other situation it becomes *God's Kingdom.* The Gītā is, of course, for a higher and internal and not for a lower and external or superficial value-system. The example of a two-way switch given above must not be construed to imply that a state of mind can be altered at will, as if by pressing a switch. A right state of mind is achievable by following a right-value system over a period of time. Cheating in school examination, jumping traffic light etc. appear in themselves insignificant acts but acts such as these lead to bigger dishonesty and adoption of a wrong value-system in life, as against the right value-system.

The teachings of the Gītā were the need and a product of the circumstances prevailing when the Gītā was composed. Society in India passed at first through the age of rituals and later, the age of contemplation followed. Religious rituals had acquired the character and force of dogmas and even become an instrument of exploitation of the populace. As a result, reaction commenced and the select of the society started preferring contemplation over rituals. Social leaders realized, as is obvious, that mere contemplation or withdrawal from the activity of life was not conducive to a healthy society. *Actionless thoughts are as useless for society as thoughtless action. Both have a negative import for society though of different types. Thus, those who could think rightly would not act and those who could act would not think rightly.* This in brief is the paradox society then faced. The former would not act because they thought that worldly action would hamper their progress in the divine pursuit. They became passive peace-lovers. Arjuna was such a peace-lover. He was scared of war which would involve a lot of killings of cousins, kith and kin, *gurus* and other noble men. Arjuna was ready to give up more and more. He even said to Lord Kṛṣṇa that even if Kauravas have stooped low, they (i.e. Pāṇḍavas) should not stoop so low as to kill near and dear ones. On the other hand, Kauravas led by Duryodhana became devoid of right thinking and braced up as active war-mongers. They grabbed more and more and wanted still more, by force, deceit and other foul means. This analogy is quite apt in the present national and global politics. Thus, inaction by the right thinking and action by the wrong thinking types combined to set off a process of decadence in the society. Since wrong actions of Kauravas were meeting with initial success, their ranks were swelling. Even the wise *elders* remained mute in the face of the wrong doings of the Kauravas and even came to their support at the time of war because of dilemma at deeper levels.

Lord Kṛṣṇa, the great exemplar of supreme wisdom and righteousness, assumed the role of guide and philosopher of the Pāṇḍavas. For the benefit of Arjuna, the peace-lover and a just person and indeed for the benefit of the entire mankind, Lord Kṛṣṇa worked out a philosophy—value-based action viz. *Karma Yoga* as opposed to the- then prevailing tendency of inaction or withdrawal from activity, for the right-minded. Lord Kṛṣṇa brought out clearly that so long as one has a physical body, action is inescapable even for a moment. Action may be in any field of activity or even for mere physical survival i.e. for *Jīvan Yātrā* but it is necessary.

Verses (4) and (5) of Chapter III of the Gītā are relevant :

Verse (4), Chapter III, says:

> *na karmaṇām anārambhān naiṣkaramyaṁ puruṣo'śnute*
> *na ca saṃnyasanād eva siddhiṃ samadhigacchati*

> **Meaning:** One does not attain freedom from the bondage of Karma by merely abstaining from work. No one attains perfection by merely giving up work.

Verse (5), says:

> *na hi kaścit kṣaṇam api jātu tiṣṭhaty akarmakṛt*
> *kāryate hy avaśaḥ karma sarvaḥ prakṛtijair guṇaih'*

> **Meaning:** Because no one can remain actionless even for a moment. Everyone is driven to action, helplessly indeed, by the Guṇas of nature.

Inaction is neither viable nor desirable. Therefore, the Gītā is opposed to inaction. Action is choiceless. We cannot but act, choice is available only about the kind of action one may undertake. Naturally the choice of good people who are pursuing the goal of happiness in life or attaining *Brahma* or eternal bliss is for action which will not bind them to the cycle of cause and effect or birth and re-birth. Lord Kṛṣṇa through the teachings of the Gītā assures his devotee that if one engages in righteous action with right state of mind, such action will not only not bind him (doer) but even deliver him from the cyclical bondage of cause and effect. Thus, we come back to the question of the right state of mind because only a right state of mind is capable of generating right actions.

न कर्मणाम् अनारम्भान् नैष्कर्म्यं पुरुषोऽश्नुते।
न च संन्यसनाद् एव सिद्धिं समधिगच्छति॥ III (4)

न हि कश्चित् क्षणमपि जातु तिष्ठत्य् अकर्मकृत।
कार्यते ह्य अवशः कर्म सर्वः प्रकृतिजैर् गुणैः॥ III (5)

The life-long effort of a person is centred around acquiring the right state of mind. Through the analogy of two-way switch, we have seen that mind can be impacted in many ways. Various types of inputs impact the mind and play a part in determining its state. The resultant state of mind will be governed by a preponderance on the mind of stronger impacts over the weaker ones.

In this context of state of mind, it becomes rather important that we try to understand the functioning of the human body, mind and intellect and how these interact through nature's process of receiving inputs, subjecting these to analysis and arriving at a decision which is directed to body-organs as a directive or command for implementation. A human being is endowed with five senses of perception (*Jñānendriya*) namely—sight, sound, smell, taste and touch. These senses with the help of their respective sense-organs feed on the worldly objects or sense-objects, so to say. Stimuli in the form of desires are created and transmitted to the mind. Mind gets activated or even agitated and restless depending on how peaceful or under control it is and how strong the stimuli in intensity and speed are. At this point, the intellect is supposed to take over. Intellect has been endowed with the power to analyze, work out various options and arrive at a decision as to whether or not a desire should be fulfilled. Accordingly, after this sifting process, the intellect, conveys the decision, through the mind, to the body organs or limbs (*Karmendriya*) to perform corresponding physical-actions. This brings out that all actions are desire oriented. In the Gītā, desire has also been referred to as an enemy. It may be interpreted to mean that, if not controlled, it may act like an enemy. Therefore, body-mind-intellect system which acts in concert must remain in a state of balance. Since a mind unwatched by intellect is sure to go astray, mind has been compared to a child and intellect to an adult. As the parents keep an eye on the child even in the best circumstances e.g. in festivities at home or in holidays at sea or hill resorts, intellect has to stand guard on the mind, all the time. Even the best driver may cause an accident if he dozes off even for a brief moment. For ensuring a healthy, right or a righteous state of mind, intellect cannot afford to lower its guard even for a brief moment. Such is the nature of mind. The child in every person has to be watched and guided by the adult in the person.

If one attempts a brief summary of the inputs or ingredients, mentioned in various chapters of the Gītā, which help to create the right state of mind, the following are among the more significant ones. Call these the cleansing agents for or disciplines of mind, if you like. They are not exclusive of one another. Thus, there is a certain degree of overlapping also which only serves to emphasise the significance of teachings of the Gītā in our life.

(a) Act with an attitude of non-attachment to the result (or fruit) of action. One has a right to do one's duty but one has no claim to or control over the result. The famous much quoted verse 47 of Chapter-II of the Gītā says:

karmaṇy evādhikāraste mā phaleṣu kadācana
mā karma phala hetur bhūr mā te saṅgo'stv akarmaṇi

Meaning : You have Adhikāra (right) over your respective duty only but no control or claim over the results. The fruits of work should not be your motive. You should never be inactive.

This verse has two messages for living a life which is ideally correct and practically useful. Firstly, there is no escape from action even if one wishes for one. One may tend towards inaction but would never achieve it. Inaction is neither feasible, nor desirable. Worse, it may turn a person a hypocrite when he is engaged in action mentally all the time and physically also at times and still considers himself a renouncer of action.

Secondly, it concerns the result of action. Howsoever well we may plan and execute an action, there may be factors unknown to us, or not under our control which affect the result. Thus the result of an action may be different entirely or partly from what one would expect it to be. We are certainly aware of uncertainties, ambiguities or grey areas in universe and in all aspects of life, which refuse to be computed or calculated.The facts of life are too complex. The factors which go into making a result are indeterminate and are constantly changing. These hard realities make the result of any

---

कर्मण्येवाधिकारस्ते मा फलेषु कदाचन।
मा कर्मफलहेतुर् भूर् मा ते सङ्गोऽस्त्व् अकर्मणि॥ II (47)

action unpredictable with accuracy. Thus, knowing fully well that there must be a result of one's action, one must not desire, demand or expect a particular type of result. Desires and expectations cause fluctuations of mind and thus work against concentration of mind. Expectations may sometimes lead to excitement based on hopes of success and sometime to dejection due to fear of failure. The pendulum of mind oscillates between imaginary jubilation and frustration. There is not much point in asking for something which one is not sure to get. The best course in real practical life, is to put in the best efforts as per one's capability and capacity as an offering to God and to accept the result as it comes, as *Prasādam*—one's share of compensation or reward for the offering. There is always a next time when one may improve upon the effort, benefiting from the result of previous efforts. The biggest disadvantage of the tendency to think of the result while performing action is loss of concentration. A student cannot concentrate whole-heartedly on studies if he worries about the score in the examination. The same applies to a player in sports, a surgeon performing an operation in the hospital.

(b) Do not be caught in dualities due to ignorance of the reality. Rise above the pairs of opposites. Be even-minded and develop equanimity of approach to all situations affecting the physical being; emotional being and intellectual being. Similarly, one should be even-minded towards the entire creation—humanity and animal kingdom. Further, one's even-mindedness should extend to material objects (inanimate part of creation). This is achievable only when one understands, appreciates and adopts in life, the basic unity in the entire creation, behind the apparent difference in forms. The Gītā is replete with instances of pairs of opposites. Heat and cold pertain to physical being. Pleasure and pain relate to emotional being. Honor and dishonor belong to intellectual understanding.

One should be impartial i.e. even-minded towards friends and foes, lovers and haters; relatives and strangers; saints and sinners. One should also hold the rich and the poor; knowledgeable and ignorant; high and low; handsome and ugly in similar respect and affection.

Apart from human beings, one should also treat the animal world with due respect and affection, preserve and protect them as an essential part of creation, meant to maintain the balance in ecology —a need of humans, animals and plant life—the entire flora and fauna.

Lastly, even in the physical world or the world of inanimate objects, one should be able to rise above the worldly value-system. One's equanimity or even-mindedness should be so established as a result of self-realization, that a clod of mud, stone and gold have the same value for him.

(c) The Gītā says that one must undertake to perform action as duty. It is commonly said that there are no medals for doing one's duty. Therefore, one must not expect any reward for doing one's duty though reward may come in the same way as one gets *Prasādam* after an offering to God. Duty performed solely or partly with an expectation of compensation in mind ceases to be duty just as love ceases to be love if conditions are attached or a price is placed thereon.

Every member of human society—high or low, rich or poor, learned or ignorant, affluent, self-sufficient or deficient—has a duty to perform. He is an active, responsible entity in the inter-dependent and inter-connected world. His duty is someone's right and someone else's duty is his right. We are all engaged, in different ways, in preservation, protection and progress of the creation by doing our respective duties. Duty acquires different meanings in different contexts. There are different levels of duty. Like concentric circles, one's field of duty extends from the center to the bigger and still bigger circles.

One has a duty to oneself, to stay physically and mentally healthy in order that one may perform ones duty to others. One stays healthy by following disciplines e.g. regular cleansing of the body, regular exercising, and following a lifestyle of moderation *interalia* in the matter of eating and sleeping. In the next phase one's duty extends to one's family—parents, spouse and children. Duty further extends to friends, relatives, society, nation and indeed to the entire humanity and creation. As one progresses on the path of self-growth, the sphere or circle of duty keeps on widening. It is like extending the frontiers of one's own larger personality. One may start with self or family but must not stop there. The Gītā explicitly and implicitly lays down that man must give back to society at least a portion of one's resources as he has received a lot from society in terms of education, upbringing and capability to raise resources. There are various theatres of one's activity—home, workplace, society etc. Therefore, there are corresponding fields of one's duty also. Different considerations and criteria determine one's duty in a particular field of duty. Generally speaking, it is one's duty towards society which gets neglected. It is not the personal greed or need which should decide whether or not one should engage in a particular action.

One should see a higher purpose in life. That is why Lord Kṛṣṇa, through various approaches and insight into higher values goads Arjuna to do his duty in the context of a righteous war against evil and fight rather than give up or give in to inaction. It falls to the lot of the intelligent and the brave to protect and provide for the less intelligent and the weak. It is paradoxical but true that in the land viz. India, where the Gītā was preached in the first instance, society is most neglected by those who are able and duty-bound to help out. There is no voluntary or legally enforceable system of welfare run by the rich or the State. In the West, both exist and supplement each other. Education, scientific and other research, medical and social institutions are financed substantially through individual and corporate charity.

Alongside, the State runs a system of welfare for the elderly and unemployed, which is legally enforceable. Those in the West now increasingly acknowledge the value of the spiritual heritage of the East. TIME magazine of July 06, 2001, reported : "This ancient, Asian tradition (meditation) is booming worldwide—15 million Americans are doing it —in part because people believe it has real medical benefits." Belief, no doubt, is supported by medical observation and findings. It is time that those, in the East should accept that their brethren in the West are men of action with a sense of duty towards society and, therefore, better qualify for graduation to the level of *Karma Yogī*. In case of India, Indians swear by scriptures but hardly ever adopt the messages contained therein, in their lives. If one goes by the number of temples; saints and hermits, crowds at religious sermons, one would be led to believe that India is a heaven on earth. Unfortunately, it is not so. More funds go to temples (houses of God) than to the homeless and the hungry—more to godmen than towards God's cause. Scriptures are often quoted and preached to help perpetuate the status-quo, howsoever, unjust it may be.

(d) Exercise self-control. It is only a master not a slave who can quieten the mind and exercise self-control. The Gītā does not preach total abandonment of desires to attain peace of mind and self-control. The emphasis is only on being a master and not allowing one-self to degenerate to the level of a slave. One should be able to be selective between necessary and desirable on the one hand and unnecessary and undesirable on the other. Instead of being a consuming animal, one should try to rise to the level of a positive and creative being. The body-mind-intellect endowment of the human being provided by nature should, with practice, be evolved further into a regulatory system, one-self being the regulator.

Verse 64 of Chapter II of the Gītā says:

rāga dveṣa viyuktais tu viṣayān indriyaiṣ caran
ātmāvaśyair vidheyātmā prasādam adhigacchati

Meaning: A disciplined person (moves around in the world) enjoying sense-objects with senses that are under control and free from likes and dislikes, attains tranquility.

The art of living lies in developing the faculty of discrimination, and exercising the choices rightly. One practises this art in everyday life but on a mundane plane. When going out on shopping, one decides what one wants to buy as per one's requirement and for what price approximately. Normally, one would not buy the stuff not needed, or not suitable to fulfil one's need. Material wisdom would not allow him to empty his wallet or overshoot his budget in buying unnecessary or undesirable stuff. In the spiritual world of a person, it should mean not succumbing to senses —becoming a slave—to wrong desires and exposing one—self to undesirable

---

रागद्वेषवियुक्तैस्तु विषयान इन्द्रियैश्चरन्।
आत्मावश्यैर् विधेयात्मा प्रसादम् अधिगच्छिति॥ II (64)

influences which would only accelerate the downfall. There is a beautiful Urdu couplet which roughly translates to mean that : *"I do pass through the market but I am not a buyer."*

On a different plane it means that one physically lives in the phenomenal world but mentally one is free from or above indulgence. His senses, desires and mind remain under control despite temptations of a different nature. Such a state of mind is conducive to right actions of which both the doer and society are beneficiaries.

(e) Self is no doer. The Gītā aims at, among other objectives, to hone the ordinary human being into a superior being, diminishing gradually baser qualities in him. One such base quality is arrogance. The man arrogates to himself the claim that he is the doer, author or architect of what he does. He may be helping the wheel of creation to move. But he is neither the wheel nor the creator of the wheel. Far from that, at best he is a small cog in the wheel. The dictum that self is no doer has many more positive effects on a human being. Realising his insignificance in the scheme of things, he is sure to realize the existence of a higher power. He also comes to see a higher purpose in his own life. In the process, ego, arrogance etc. get dissolved and replaced by modesty and sublimity. One is enabled to seek guidance while doing one's actions and duty from that higher power and to leave the outcome of his actions to Him and even ask His forgiveness when things go wrong. Thus, it is not merely an idealistic but a very pragmatic approach in life.

Metaphysically also, the dictum of 'no-doership' is correct and tenable. One is not one's own creator in the biological or any other sense. Right at the point of time of conception certain endowments (called genetics) become part of one's person through the channel of transmission provided by the parents. Further attributes are added on during pregnancy, in the mother's womb The type of food mother eats indirectly becomes the food for the child in the womb. Her habits of drinking or smoking affect the child too. The kind of environment in which the mother lives or is forced to live, indirectly becomes the child's environment as well. After the child comes out of the womb and enters a much bigger world, to the role of nature (genetics) is added the role of nurture (including environment in various aspects) directly on a continuous basis and they together produce *Guṇas* that in turn make up one's nature or trait. According to the Gītā, the *Guṇas—Sāttvika, Rājasika* and *Tāmasika*—are present in a human being in different proportions and combinations. The preponderant *guṇa* or tendency is likely to dominate one's decision to undertake or avoid a particular action. Thus, *guṇas* in their unique proportions and combinations, in a person (not the Self) become the author of one's action. Of course, the proportion of different *guṇas* can be altered though gradually and moved to a higher category, with practice. Endowment, good, not so good or bad is not forever. *Guṇas* viz. strands (*Pravṛtti*) in an intelligent creature and definitely in a human being are alterable and thus improvable. This is what the movement to a higher plane or to a higher value system or self-improvement is all about. The Hindu law-giver *Manu* also said,:

> *"To improve upon the human race is everyone's duty."*
>
> (Everyone owes self-improvement to oneself, society and to humanity).

We have seen the significance of the state of mind of a person in its inter-action with events and situations and generation of action by body-mind-intellect apparatus; as also of essential disciplines needed to generate the right state of mind. A person with a positive, healthy, right-thinking mind is doubly blessed. He is blessed with his own positivity and righteousness. Society at large with whom such a person interacts, is also the beneficiary. Such persons must be encouraged and assisted to get associated with social activities rather than permitted to take leave of activity. Even if they themselves do not need to act for their own sake, they must act for others. The action by the self-realized is essential to maintain the balance of good and evil in the society. We say routinely that 'truth shall prevail' (*Satyameva Jayate*). However, we must assist the truth to prevail. Let good and capable members of the society be the building blocs for a better, healthier and a more positive society and, indeed, the world-free from unwarranted struggle but not free from activity. There is a difference between struggle and activity.

Free yourself from mindless struggle
and engage in mindful activity.

CHAPTER 5

Faith—A Positive Force

Broadly speaking, the Gītā describes three kinds of yogas. These are *Karma Yoga* (yoga of action or work); *Jñāna Yoga* (yoga of knowledge) and *Bhakti Yoga* (yoga of devotion). One or the other of these yogas should suit most people. Which one would suit whom depends on the endowment of the seeker. Physically active people are more comfortable with *Karma Yoga*. Since physical activity is a must even for mere survival, a large majority of people come in this category. The contemplative people are cut out for Jñāna Yoga. They are not satisfied with scratching the surface. They want to go deep and fly high mentally. They like to study, scrutinize scriptures and all else, to evolve, understand and reach culmination of self-realization. *Karma Yoga* has been rightly termed as a stage preparatory to *Jñāna Yoga*. *Jñāna Yoga* right in the beginning is, therefore, suited only to a small minority. The, third is *Bhakti Yoga*—devotion to and worship of a personal God. It does not mean that there is or there can be a separate or different God for different people. What it implies is that most people find it easier in actual life to perceive God in one of His many manifested forms. There are plenty of *Devtās, Devīs* (gods and goddesses) and saints of different hues (whose lives were not less holy than those of gods) adopted respectively from scriptures, and recent history, for worship as a personal God. Manifest God is easier to concentrate upon and thus meets the requirement of concentration with comparative ease. The important thing is that need for faith is common in all the yogas.

Verse 31 of chapter III of the Gītā, dealing with Karma Yoga Gītā says:

ye me matam idaṃ nityam anutiṣṭhanti mānavāḥ
śraddhāvanto'nasuyanto mucyante te'pi karmabhiḥ

Meaning: Those who always practise this teaching of mine (selfless action with detachment) with *faith* and free from cavil are released from (the bondage) of action.

Verse 39 of chapter IV, dealing with Jñāna Yoga, Gītā says:

śraddhāvāṁl labhate jñānaṃ tatparaḥ saṃyatendriyaḥ
jñānaṃ labdhvā parāṃ śāntim acireṇā'dhigacchati

Meaning: He who has *faith* and who is absorbed in wisdom (Jñāna or Knowledge) and has restrained his senses, gains wisdom and thus quickly attains to supreme peace.

Faith comes first followed by wisdom and later by experience. It is an important stage in self-growth and self-realization.

In Verse 2 of chapter XII, dealing with *Bhakti Yoga* Gītā, says:
śrī bhagavān uvāca

mayy āveśya mano ye maṃ nityayuktā upāsate
śraddhayā parayopetās te me yuktatamā matāḥ

Meaning: Those steadfast devotees who worship, with supreme *faith*, fixing their mind on ME as personal God, I consider them the best yogīs.

ये मे मतम् इदं नित्यम् अनुतिष्ठिन्ति मानवाः।
श्रद्धावन्तोऽनसुयन्तो मुच्यन्ते तेऽपि कर्मभिः॥ III (31)
श्रद्धावाँल् लभते ज्ञानं तत्परः संयतेन्द्रियः।
ज्ञानं लब्ध्वा परां शान्तिम् अचिरेणाधिगच्छति॥ IV (39)
श्रीभगवानुवाच
मय्य् आवेश्य मनो ये मां नित्ययुक्ता उपासते।
श्रद्धया परयोपेतास् ते मे युक्ततमा मताः॥ XII (2)

Sri Ramakrishna also said:

> "He who can resign himself to the will of the Lord with simple faith and guileless devotion, attains unto HIM without delay. He who has faith has all and he who lacks faith, lacks all."

The above words of Sri Ramakrishna are an echo of verse 40 of chapter IV of the Gītā.

ajñaścā'śraddadhānaś ca saṃśayātmā vinaśyati
nāyaṃ loko'sti na paro na sukhaṃ saṃśayātmanaḥ

Meaning: But the ignorant, who is without faith and is full of doubt, regarding Self, is bound to perish. There is neither this world nor the other world beyond nor happiness for the doubter.

As we have seen from the above verses and the quotation from Sri Ramakrishna, faith in God is a must for every one irrespective of the mode of life he may be following. It is a different matter in what manner one believes in God. It is faith not the faith i.e. not any particular faith, which is necessary. But without recognizing a higher plane of existence and only confining one's vision to a mere mechanistic or physical view of life one lives a life, less than complete, to say the least. Only after one has faith in God, can one have faith in himself or herself. Faith in God removes mental, psychological obstacles in the path of progress in different fields and planes of thought and action as if the faith in God has converted itself into a force of faith in himself or herself. One tackles the problems with redoubled speed and strength. Negative thoughts, uncertainty and fear of failure retreat yielding place to a feeling of reassurance. It may not be wrong to say that positivity of faith even changes the body chemistry. How else, otherwise, would frown change into smile or tension into relaxation. In the darkest hour of pessimism, one starts seeing light at the end of the tunnel. What is he or she himself

---

अज्ञश्चाश्रद्दधानश्च संशयात्मा विनश्यति।
नायं लोकोऽस्ति न परो न सुखं संशयात्मनः॥ IV (40)

or herself without that subtle, higher, superior force we call God. God is the nomenclature man's language has coined but the real implication is not a matter of language but of the spirit behind to be realized and experienced. We realize that we are much more than a sum total of bones, flesh, i.e. body, mind and intellect. *Our reality is that important extra bit, beyond, over and above, the physical sum total.*

Idol (*mūrti*) worship is very prevalent and popular. All the same there is a good deal of controversy about this practice and therefore it needs an elaborate discussion. Devotion to a personal God meets spiritual and emotional needs of a vast majority of people. That is why, there is such a large constituency of devotees or worshippers of personal gods in the form of idols. Idol worship of different gods has been touted by vested interests, on one hand, while its efficacy in helping the individual worshipper on the spiritual path has been doubted, on the other. To be fair to idol worshipper or the devotee with faith, it must be said that worship of a personal god as represented by an idol is not to be relegated to the level of a mere ritual much less to a superstition. To the one who does not support idol worship, the idol may not be anything more than a stone or a metal figure but to the worshipper, it represents all the qualities and power of his or her personal god. While worshipping, the worshipper is meeting—face-to-face—the representative of his or her god, who has full authority of god himself. The worshipper is not worshipping the medium of stone or metal but god and god's power, the physical medium represents to him/her. It is not uncommon that such a worshipper devotee closes his eyes while worshipping or praying. From the physical plane he is transporting the personal god into his inner being. Otherwise, closing the eyes does not make much sense. Much as a modern man keeps the picture of his wife or family on his desktop or in his wallet and looks at the picture occasionally as if to communicate with them, a devotee keeps the idol (*mūrti*) of his personal god in his house or office or visits a temple where it is installed and worships, to establish the channel of communication, with his favorite god. It is a user-friendly tool, to connect to the supreme to use a modern idiom.

It should also be recognized that for the majority of people it is far more difficult, if not impossible, to concentrate on the impersonal or unmanifest god than on the manifest god. The Gītā does recognize the difference in approach of different people. As a functional need of society and otherwise also, the Gītā does not denounce the devotion or *Bhakti* approach. On the contrary it declares that a devotee who fulfils certain conditions of good conduct is qualified and entitled to Supreme Bliss.

The closing of the eyes, even for a few minutes, suggests that the act of worship is neither a superficial formality nor an external act only. With eyes closed one should be looking inward and set one's mind's tune to the right wave length. Seated in front of the idol of one's favorite personal god, with eyes closed, one is totally engrossed within one-self. He is in communication with the Supreme through the medium of his personal god represented by the idol, he is sitting before with eyes closed. The object of concentration or prayer is not the stone figure. If that were the case, one would perhaps be praying with eyes, wide open. All forms of true devotion or worship is a matter of the mind, not of the external physical body. It is turning and tuning in to within.

Approaching God through devotion or Bhakti by some, while others do the same through *Karma Yoga* or *Jñāna Yoga* may also be compared with trying to get to the top of a mountain by a different route or arriving at the same destination by an alternative route. All the travellers, by whatever route they may travel are seekers. There is still another possible interpretation for the seekers to be content with yoga of devotion rather than pursuing other yogas. It could be explained through an example from the daily life of common men.

Finding it difficult or not within one's competence or means to establish contact and meet the top man in power—a politician, a bureaucrat or a senior executive of a company, one gets reconciled, to meet a functionary at a middle or still lower level. The middle level or the lower level functionary assures the seeker of the meeting that it is not necessary or feasible to meet the top man and that in any case, his request will be met. If necessary at all, the top man will also be consulted in the process. The benefit of comparative ease makes this yoga popular and the Gītā supports this form of yoga too.

Verse 21 of chapter VII of the Gītā says:

yo yo yaṃ yaṃ tanuṃ bhaktaḥ śraddhayā'rcitum icchati
tasya tasyā'calāṃ śraddhāṃ tām eva vidadhāmy aham

Meaning: Whosoever, desires to worship whatever deity (with whatever nomenclature, in whatever form and in whatever manner) with faith, I make his (devotee's) faith steady.

The Lord confirms that the faith of each seeker is rewarded. All worship (of course accompanied by right conduct, even after worship, i.e. as a part of daily life) is elevating. Similarly, all reverence, whatever we revere, is rewarding.

Verse 22 of Chapter VII, Gītā says:

sa tayā śraddhayā yuktas tasyā'rādhanam ihate
labhate ca tataḥ kāmān mayai'va vihitān hi tān

Meaning: Endowed with steady faith in the deity they worship, they obtain (the fulfilment of) their desires, the benefits (rewards) being decreed by ME alone.

The above verse implies that power of deities, in turn, is derived from the Supreme God only. The worshipper is also a seeker and with faith and good righteous conduct he is on the right path. Therefore, he too is to be encouraged in his path or journey by providing him with what he needs.

यो यो यां यां तनुं भक्तः श्रद्धयार्चितुम् इच्छति।
तस्य तस्याचलां श्रद्धां ताम् एव विदधाम्य् अहम्॥ VII (21)

स तया श्रद्धया युक्तस् तस्याराधनम् ईहते।
लभते च ततः कामान् मयैव विहितान् हि तान्॥ VII (22)

Verse 23 of Chapter VII, Gītā says:

antavat tu phalaṃ teṣām tad bhavaty alpamedhasām
devān devayajo yānti madbhaktā yānti mām api

Meaning: Verily the fruit that accrues to those men of little (comparatively less) intelligence, is finite (limited). The worshippers of the Devas go to the Devas but my devotees come to me.

Further, verse 23 of Chapter IX, the Gītā says:

ye'py anyadevatā bhaktā yajante śraddhayā'nvitāḥ
te'pi mām eva kaunteya yajanty avidhipūrvakam

Meaning: O, Arjuna, even those devotees who worship demigods with faith, they also worship ME, but not in a proper manner (not as enjoined).

The devotees' worship of demigods is "not in a proper manner" in comparison to or with reference to the worship of the absolute God. It is the devotee who has given the form to the formless as per his or her own mind-set. The deity is a conduit or a channel between the devotee and the God. The presence of a deity even though through the medium of stone, bronze or silver acts as a catalyst or a stimulant to start the process of spiritual cleansing or purification and concentration.

A careful study of chapter XII dealing with the path of devotion would clearly bring out a few important aspects of the Bhakti Yoga. Firstly, it is acknowledged in verse 5 of chapter XII that self-realization is rather difficult for those who fix their minds on the unmanifest Brahma, because comprehension of the

---

अन्तवत् तु फलं तेषां तद् भवत्य् अल्पमेधसाम्।
देवान् देवयजो यान्ति मद्भक्ता यान्ति माम् अपि॥ VII (23)

येऽप्य् अन्यदेवता भक्ता यजन्ते श्रद्धयान्विताः।
तेऽपि माम् एव कौन्तेय यजन्त्य् अविधिपूर्वकम्॥ IX (23)

unmanifest by an average human being is difficult. As is well-recognized and accepted as a practical methodology, the Gītā adopts a step-by-step approach for the followers. From the worship of form one may in course of time qualify to the worship of the formless.

According to Sri Ramakrishna, image or idol worship is helpful in the beginning, like a scaffolding in the construction of a building. Later on when the building is complete and can stand on its own, scaffolding can be removed. Further, *Bhakti Yoga* is not mere devotion. It is hollow without the inner strength of moral values or righteous conduct. It is not offerings nor their cost nor duration of the posture during prayer which matters. These are only external trappings and can be misleading. Importantly enough, different positive values which go into the making of right state of mind of *Karma Yogi* or *Jñāna Yogī* are as much necessary for the follower of *Bhakti Yoga*. An attitude of equanimity towards objects and beings having risen above the pair of opposites, non-attachment to the fruits of action; single-minded concentration; non-doership; selfless work for the higher purpose, with faith in higher power etc. are necessary values for the state of mind of the traveller on the path of devotion also.

While, faith is indeed necessary and desirable, there is no room for blind faith. There is a very thin dividing line between faith and blind faith. One must tread carefully. The latter viz. blind faith is based on ignorance and superstition. Therefore, it is recommended that reposing faith should follow a reverent inquiry by the seeker.

The Gītā advises the seeker to learn from the teacher or *guru* (wise man) approaching him with humble reverence and in a spirit of inquiry and service. The Gītā, further, advises us not to accept whatever is said in scriptures or taught by the teacher in unthinking trust. That is not enough. Reason must be satisfied. He who has no personal or direct knowledge but depends on what others have told him, does not have a right to pass his knowledge to others, as the truth. Scriptures are not against but rather recommend a combination of devotion to the teacher with unrestricted right of free examination and inquiry. *The demise of intellect is not a pre-condition to faith.* Reason is soul's left hand, Faith her right one. By these we reach divinity. A well-meaning Guru has his own qualities (rare now-a-days). He does not sell God. Sale of God is not allowed. Nor does he claim to offer ready-made, off-the-cuff, solutions to problems which need regular spiritual practices and right living i.e. right thinking and right actions. *Spiritualism is not fast food available a la carte or in suitable packages for a price.* Excess of money accompanied by perceived shortage of time and most of all, shortage of patience has made spiritualism cheap and the task of a real guru that much more difficult. It is said that the teacher has done his duty if he has inculcated in the taught the habit of self-study. Similarly a *guru's* job is to show the destination and the route, as if, on a guide map. Walking/ travelling has to be done by the seeker himself. The *Guru* can not walk on behalf of the seeker. If one wishes to enjoy dancing one must dance oneself not just watch from the periphery. In the modern parlance a guru has been called a spiritual doctor also. He is qualified to diagnose, prescribe medication and watch recovery. His knowledge and experience is far superior. That superiority must be acknowledged, respected and his advice—both preventive and curative—should be followed with faith.

However, there are ever so many teachers of different denominations now-a-days who take exception to the healthy spirit of inquiry even with reverence. They require of their followers unhindered, unthinking and unquestioning obedience. Such obedient followers are preferred and liked. To establish their external authority these teachers use such followers. They unwittingly become agents of the greedy and undeserving teachers for floating false stories about their miracles and super-natural powers. The rich and the powerful ensure all their teachers' worldly comforts though such teachers claim to have renounced the world. They claim to strike deals with

God or lesser gods for waiving sins of their followers, of course, for a handsome price. This route is quite popular with politicians also, in India. Large masses of the poor also spare something from their hard earned income to make an offering to them. Such is the influence of god's men over His (God's) common men. Thousands and thousands walk the streets of towns and villages playing on the faith of the common men. Some even play confidence tricks particularly on womenfolk. Such persons are not only parasites on society, they do disservice to the cause of spiritualism in a big way. The biggest disservice they are doing is to themselves. Far from self-growth or self-realization they degenerate by the day. Like other intelligent or educated persons they are doubly guilty—first for committing wrongs and secondly for passing the wrong acts as right acts. In fact, they perpetuate and propagate the antithesis of the Gītā. They preach escape from the penalty for wrong doing for a price. On the contrary, they all, with one voice should loudly proclaim from the rooftop that your sins must visit you. Water from all the rivers or ashes from Yajñas will not destroy your sins. This is the recipe for a healthy society. Even the sinners of yesterday would become the do-gooders of tomorrow. Hindus in India are aware of the practice wherein the priests on all auspicious occasions and *paṇḍās* on the occasion of death—ceremonies (at Haridwar, Allahbad etc.), ask the concerned relations to make a *Saṅkalpa* (vow or determination) as to how much money he would pay to the priest or paṇḍā, performing the ceremony. It is highly desirable that high priests of religion make it obligatory that the priests who perform worship of various types require the persons on whose behalf the worship is performed, to make a *Saṅkalpa* or make vows (preferably audible to others as is done by the boy and girl at the time of marriage ceremony) for leading an honest righteous life with righteous thoughts and actions in the future. They should also be told that there is no escape from the cycle of cause and effect. There is no point in repeating parrot-like, mantras unintelligible to them.

We are aware of the misuse of blind faith purposely

generated and spread among the simple gullible masses and used to exploit them by the rich and powerful. The kings of yesteryears and the powerful of the past and present have a vested interest in perpetuating the status-quo. They carried out metaphorically speaking, a division of the assets of the Indian nation. They kept the wealth for themselves and gave blind faith in the name of religon to the masses as their share. In India, Europe and elsewhere, the concept of divinity and divine powers of king was founded. Since king is in the image of God, he was above the law and he could do no wrong. In India, though, the kings were there (till 1955) by the hundreds, they were all above the law, and wielded unlimited powers. In short, they acted as superhumans supposedly blessed by God. In the East, apart from the King's super-human status in India, Nepal's king is considered as incarnation of Lord Viṣṇu. King of Japan is believed to be incarnation of Sun god. They lived in extreme luxury, most of them indulging in all sorts of vices in the privacy of palaces. As against these representatives of God, the poor-lesser images of God—were virtually living under the constant shadow of death. The poor masses suffered under the open skies against the backdrop of luxury of palaces.

All the wrongs of the powerful get righted. Such an unjust social order is justified on the basis of or due to blind faith in the inevitability of fate. Such a blind faith has been extended to absurd lengths. Even in the beginning of the twenty-first century, some spiritual leaders with large followings, explain earthquakes, famines, leave aside train and air accidents as punishment for collective sins. Such an approach might help soothe the aggrieved ones but is far from being logical even as per the Gītā. Belief in the cycle of cause and effect makes us more aware that for every effect there must be a cause. So, the state and society must look into the cause which led to the undesirable result in the form of accident etc. and must undertake to remove it for the future. That exactly is the purpose of enquiries into accidents. Sin committed to invite famine is maldistribution of food. Sin in case of deaths in accidents is the negligence of the pilot, or driver as the case many be. For physical effects—good or bad—there have to be physical causes only. It is hard to believe except with the help of blind faith that God has created or runs an agency for distributing rewards or punishments. Some actuated by their self-serving motives and others out of frustration contribute to the perpetuation of this blind faith.

Verse 15 of Chapter V of the Gītā says:

nādatte kasyacit pāpaṃ na caiva sukṛtaṃ vibhuḥ
ajñānenā'vṛtaṃ jñānaṃ tena muhyanti jantavaḥ

> **Meaning:** The Lord does not take responsibility either for good or bad deeds of anybody. The knowledge is covered by the veil of ignorance, thereby people are deluded.

Freely translated the first line of the above verse means that God does not take upon Himself anybody's meritorious or sinful deeds. He does not reward merit nor punishes sin. In other words, there is no remission of sin. God does not interfere in the cycle of cause and effect. Then how can saints or priests who claim to be endowed with some such powers can intercede where God Himself does not. They may, no doubt, help for the future by guiding their followers not to go astray, not to commit wrong action and stay on the right path. Even in the language of science, nature does not violate its own laws. The chance of the wrong-doer lies in abstaining from wrong doing in the future. While habitual offenders are dealt with harshly, first offenders are let off with lighter punishment. In the same way a regular indulgence in excesses punishes and damages his body far more than casual acts.

Faith in God, proximity and exposure to good influences will certainly help to bring about positivity of mind and righteousness in action and is, therefore, necessary and desirable. On the other hand, blind faith in the power of fate

---

नादत्ते कस्यचित् पापं न चैव सुकृतं विभुः।
अज्ञानेनावृतं ज्ञानं तेन मुह्यन्ति जन्तवः॥ V (15)

as an arbiter of one's good or bad existence is responsible for the suppression and exploitation of the man by the powerful with the help of social elite, and hence undesirable. The educated and those well-versed in scriptures particularly must not hold back knowledge and encourage superstitions or blind faith. More than any other institution of faith, religion must be humane. What good is it if religious people too have two faces—one for the rich and the other for the poor. *Help the faith, not the blind faith.*

An approach of enquiry, a thinking and reasoning mind or a scientific temper is necessary and desirable both in terms of scriptures as well as day-to-day common sense. Spirit of enquiry must, however, be backed with genuineness of purpose, concerted effort and devotion. These ingredients are there in all scientific research also. A scientist is as much devoted to his pursuit of knowledge as much as a seeker of faith. The one following or preaching scriptures only in part as per one's convenience and placing a narrow interpretation thereon, is a villain and enemy of faith. While an ever-doubting nature or resistance to faith is not helpful, doubt leading to genuine inquiry, and reasoning, has its own role and duty to perform. The state of mind behind the doubt or reasoning would decide. Reason may explode certain myths, expose falsehoods, or bring to light, traps of the greedy or the hypocrite. If doubt is a part of the seeker's search for truth, it has a positive role. In the scientific field, very basic concepts about the existence of the earth, solar system in particular, phenomenon of lightning, earthquakes have undergone immense changes because of the doubting and inquiring human nature. However, one must also not attribute dishonest motives to a discoverer whose discovery has become invalid in later years of research. In brief, reason and faith should be taken to be complementary. These should be synthesized and rationalized. In the seeker's search a stage comes when doubt must yield to faith. An ever-lingering or persisting doubt is certainly a factor against faith and peace of mind. Faith reposed after removal of doubt and completion of inquiry is not shaky and is long-lasting. The deeper one digs into the ground, the stronger is the foundation one can lay for the edifice of faith. Removal of doubts with right knowledge is like removal of weeds from the ground before planting flowers.

Verse 42 of Chapter IV of the Gītā says:

tasmād ajñānasaṃbhūtaṃ hṛtsthaṃ jñānāsinā'tmanaḥ
chittvainaṃ saṃśayaṃ yogam atiṣṭho'ttiṣṭha bhārata

Meaning: Therefore, resort to Karma Yoga and cut the ignorance-born doubt abiding in your heart by the sword of self-knowledge, and get up (to fight) O' Arjuna.

Although addressed to Arjuna in the battle field to help him remove doubts in his mind, the words convey a lot more, to all human beings. It is brought out that doubts arise out of ignorance. The words ignorance or ignorant should not be taken as contemptuous. These imply that further understanding or wisdom is required by the person to make up his own mind as to the correctness of his goal so that he may act with firmness and faith in pursuit of that goal. It is easy even for common people to appreciate that a doubting mind makes a wavering person whereas a person with faith in himself is a person with resolve and moves towards his chosen goal smoothly and successfully.

Reflecting on the nature of faith one finds that *both reason and faith are friends of the seeker and also that they are friends of each other and not each other's adversaries. Reason precedes and faith follows.* It is in our enlightened self-interest to have faith albeit after due satisfaction of the human faculty of discrimination. Faith serves as a well-grounded support for the human creeper to grow and reach higher and higher. Faith is also the foundation of all human relationships. There is no relationship which can be created, maintained, sustained or developed without faith in one another by the persons or the

---

तस्माद् अज्ञानसंभूतंहृत्स्थं ज्ञानासिनात्मनः
छित्त्वैनं संशयं योगम् अतिष्ठोत्तिष्ठ भारत॥ IV (42)

parties concerned. Faith is like Brahma the creator because no relationship can commence or can be created without faith. Faith is like Viṣṇu the sustainer, too, because no relationship can be sustained without continuing mutual faith. Disappearance or discontinuance or destruction of faith as a result of actual or sometimes even imaginary wrong doings, acts as Śiva the destroyer destroying the relationship. Like happiness it takes quite a while and a lot of interaction to develop faith, but one may lose it in a jiffy. Faith acts like an essential, efficient binding agent for all relationships. *Always keep faith in good repair*. The stronger the faith, the greater the binding force. The opposite is also true. The weaker the faith the weaker the binding force and this results in a fragile relationship. Strength gets replaced by fragility.

It has been said above that apart from the need for faith in one's spiritual journey, faith or trust is necessary in all other relationships also. Take, for example, the all important relationship between husband and wife. Faith is comparatively far more important in the case of young couples, particularly busy executives, who rightly or wrongly have to be physically away from each other due to pressure of work, business or social engagements. Mutual faithfulness to each other is the pivot of the relationship. Trust in each other's exclusive love and total sincerity is expected and even demanded. It is essential for physical love to generate emotional warmth and a lasting bond. Faith or trust needs to be kept not only intact but growing by fulfilling emotional needs of each other. To the young and immature it may seem that money would buy them happiness. A lot of wealth, a big house, a sleek car, a huge wardrobe are all that they would seem to need to secure faith and love of the spouse. Emotion would seem to have no importance in their lives. Only when they acquire wealth etc. and start missing emotional warmth and inviting eyes of each other, do emotions get the right recognition for a rightful place in life.

Mutual faith between husband and wife is at a greater risk in modern society, the more so if both husband and wife have their independent career pursuits. Even genuine reasons for staying late at the job in office seem mere excuses. Suspicion has started playing its role and doing the damage. Neither believes the reasons given by the other. On returning home, in the evening, each finds suspicion in the eyes of the other in place of the twinkle of invitation or welcome to the warmth of home. Kisses and hugs are either missing or at best have become a cold routine. The behavior of the spouses betrays mutual suspicion leading to arguments, quarrels, making life a virtual hell. In the absence of any efforts at damage-control and repair of trust, more serious consequences follow. Thanks to the Indian value-system, Indians come out comparatively lesser victims of the lack of faith in husband-wife relationship. They have not yet gone to the extent of hiring private detectives to spy on their spouses or to check through periodical telephone calls if the guy or the girl is there where he or she is supposed to be or is he or she faking up a business meeting to cover up an affair. Faith has walked out of the husband-wife relationships.

A simple inquiry with some M.N.Cs. (Multi-National Companies) in U.S.A. yielded a very important result, without having to go through the popular expensive method of surveys and opinion polls. They were asked about the reason for the popularity and comparative greater success of Indians in the corporate and business world of the U.S.A. The response pointed out that the ability of Indians to achieve greater productivity was due to peace at home as a result of understanding and faith *inter-se* the family members, particularly the husband and wife. The faith facilitated greater concentration without distractions caused by suspicions. The message : *Faith facilitates good results.*

Love begets love. Similarly, faith begets faith. When husband and wife have and evince faith in each other, children, an important part of the family, cannot remain positively uninfluenced, contributing to the feeling of togetherness and strength. On the other hand, if parents do not have faith in each other it is illogical to expect the children to have faith in parents, or the parents to have faith in children or the children *inter-se*. There is no emotional bond and therefore no trust. Each is for himself or herself. On the basis of survey and studies carried out, it is established that a major percentage of juvenile criminals are traceable to broken homes or homes where children grow in the shadow of suspicions and tension. As parents seek, though in vain, moments of peace and happiness outside the home, so do the children. It is not to suggest that the growing children should not be exposed to the challenges of a larger world but all the same home should continue to attract, and the growing children should have faith in home and parents both being a source of strength, love, peace and happiness. A lot of uncertainties get removed and replaced by trust in one another. Mutual trust, in turn, enhances one's confidence or faith is one-self and generates that important extra strength. That, perhaps, is the logic behind the concept of blessing by the elders or parents. They bestow blessing by touching the head of the young who pay their respects to the elders or parents. It is an exercise whereby a well-wisher transmits, at least symbolically his or her energy, to the young for success of his or her goal or objective. The same logic applies, may be to a bigger extent, to *Guru* and devotee relationship.

To have faith in a friend or to have a faithful friend is of utmost significance in real life terms. Let us take the case of an individual who is apprehensive of running into some financial difficulties or some other misfortune. He is caught between worries of the misfortune and the thought of finding a way out. In that state of mind, he thinks of a good friend of helpful nature in whom he has faith that he (friend) would respond helpfully. The very thought itself, far ahead of the actual request and response, fills him with hope, helps him to resume his calm and confidence and restores strength. He makes contact with the friend, shares his problem with him. The friend, helpful and faithful as he is gives a promise of help whenever asked, advises his needy friend not to worry. The need for help has not arisen, help has neither been requested nor provided but the faith has been re-established or reassured, so to say. A reliable channel of hope and help has opened up. It is in the interest of the needy friend to keep the channel open and unclogged. All of us are needy in some way or the other; sometime or the other. Therefore, have good friends and have faith in them. If faith in a friend can be so comforting and rewarding, it is not difficult to gauge how much more comforting and rewarding faith in a higher power can be. What a wonderful thing it would be if the channel is established with the Supreme self. Knowing His nature as an inexhaustible reservoir of cosmic energy and our own basic cosmic nature, it should be possible, to establish the channel with the Supreme and draw benefit from it to one's heart's content.

Young students at a school were asked to write an essay on 'A friend'. One student wrote that everybody needed company and therefore a friend, except a hermit who preferred to be alone. The other wrote that everybody, needed company without exception. He added that a hermit also was not without company or a friend. He was in the constant company of God and God was his friend. Friendship creates, in a person, the psychology or feeling of not being alone. The feeling of not being alone or togetherness grows rather slowly and needs regular nurture to be able to withstand kicks of adversity from all sides and of all types like a strong football and unlike a fragile glass jar.

Another category of people, one necessarily comes in contact with for one's physical health is doctor. Faith in the ability of a doctor is necessary in his diagnosis and prescription for the ailment of the patient to be efficacious. If the patient has no faith in the ability of a doctor, particularly a surgeon, the latter will have a hard time treating the patient. To develop faith and entrust his health to a doctor, the patient does want to know the doctor's academic qualifications, practical experience and skill. To that end, the patient makes some enquiries directly as well as indirectly about the doctor's reputation. For example, he wants to know whether the doctor has a sense of duty, or ethics in addition to professional skills. The patient having satisfied himself, in all respects, after due relevant enquiries, puts faith in the doctor. At times, one prefers even to wait for the doctor one can trust rather than consult anyone else readily available.

Similarly, in the legal field, wherein the interaction of an ordinary person is comparatively much less, one does need to have faith in the impartiality of the concerned judge (if not in the whole of judiciary). The law does provide for the transfer of legal cases from one court/judge to another, in case a party to the legal case has reasonable doubt or does not have faith about the impartial trial by the concerned court. Faith in one's own lawyer is also essential both as to the lawyer's ability as well as his integrity in the sense that the rival party will not be able to influence him.

Even, while choosing an airline for air travel, one goes by the reputation of the airline as to the trustworthiness of its aircraft, pilots, punctuality etc. That is how relative greater faith in a particular airline over others is built. Even in this matter of travel, faith implies peace of mind for the traveller and better revenues for the airline.

The world of business, which gives financial means to sustain and survive to everyone and opportunity to rise and prosper to some, is no different. All business relationships hinge on basic faith although one takes practical, feasible precautions against breach of faith, fraud, dishonesty with the help of written contracts and agreements. At the back of all agreements, there is that element of faith. Whenever faith is breached, agreements and contracts become mere pieces of paper. Management has to have faith in the employees and vice-versa. A trusted employee is definitely more productive. While blind trust is risky, the employer needs to understand that trust is a two-way traffic. The employees' trust needs to be respected and rewarded occasionally. Partners in business have to have faith in one another. All partnerships in life hinge on the integrity of partners. One partner's instinct to play smart and go dishonest with the other partner in the expectation that it will not be discovered wrecks the partnership even to the disadvantage of the dishonest partner. A manufacturer has to have faith in the suppliers of raw material to ensure timely supplies and the suppliers need to have faith in the manufacturer for timely payments.

The next and the most important in the business chain is the consumer. A company engaged in production of consumer goods or in providing services needs to have faith of the consumer in their goods or services. It is common knowledge that some companies with healthy business and manufacturing practices really give importance to the image of the company and its brand names. Their products are asked for by the consumer by name. They stay in the market over longer periods and earn better profits than those who adopt unhealthy practices with an eye on quick buck. One can develop faith in some one or something, with good credentials. Faith can not be forced on the consumer. On a bigger scale, shareholders need to have faith in the directors of a company for its success and progress and the directors have to deserve it by watching the interests of the shareholders. Two-way loyalty between the concerned parties generates and sustains the faith. The same basic criteria of faith which apply to business and commerce among companies and parties within a country also apply to commerce between or among countries, also. From the world of business, let us move to the world of politics and see the role of faith there. A political leader is one who has the faith of the followers in him. When the leader ceases to enjoy the faith of his ranks he has to yield the pedestal of the leadership to someone who enjoys such faith. In democratic system of politics and governance the phrase 'no-confidence motion' is quite familiar. When a 'no-confidence motion is passed' it is established that the ruling party and its leader have lost the confidence of the legislature and thus of the people to rule. Thus faith or trust or confidence and its expression as such are so crucial in political arena also. Loss of faith leads to loss of face and loss of power. Elected leaders should earn the faith of the public as a result of their deeds and not by mere words and promises. Only then will the public have faith in the government and in the established systems.

Similarly, in the field of international relations, the phrase 'confidence building measures' is well-known. The logic is to develop verifiable faith and trust in the concerned countries before any settlements are arrived at and substantive agreements signed. Each country or group of countries wants to be sure that the other country or group of countries has a genuine desire for settlement of disputes and establishment of peaceful relations. A relationship of good neighbourliness and peace has to be built on faith or trust. When the erstwhile U.S. President Ronald Reagan was asked by his Soviet counterpart to trust U.S.S.R. the latter responded with his political motto: 'Trust but verify.' Both—*prior verification and trust*—are necessary in the same way as enquiry followed by faith. Whenever doubts crop up, these should be removed like weeds so that the seeds of faith and trust take root and produce desirable fruit. As between men so between nations.

In conclusion, one may say that faith is a friendly escort, and an anchor of life. Without faith one is likely to drift in life. Faith is a healer. Faith is an inspiration, a source of hope–a positive force. But it should not be used as a trademark or put on display. Let it remain in its own sanctuary of the mind. However it can not be forced upon anybody. It is wrong and unethical to make people change their faith through, exploitation of their circumstances or their simplicity. On the contrary, everyone is entitled to his or her own faith. Even an atheist is entitled to his views. As a matter of fact, he too has faith which is something different from or the opposite of someone else's object of faith. It is also said that communism did not destroy religion or faith. It only replaced one faith (religion) by the other (communism). No one should be expected to throw stale water, until fresh supply is assured, i.e. till one of one's own search and volition, finds for oneself a more convincing and satisfying faith.

A faith, by whatever name, makes for peace for the individual and for the world. However, the faith of a particular denomination asserting its superiority over others or its claim as the only route to the supreme God generates avoidable tension and conflicts in the world. It is contradictory and incongruous to find men of faith (on the extreme fringes) promoting and supporting conflict rather than making a common cause for peace. Let such a negative situation throw up a positive opportunity such as in the form of Millennium World Peace Summit held in August 2000 in New York under the auspices of United Nations. Let essence of faith, not its form, be the core. Let universality of essence of different faiths, not the supposed uniqueness of a faith be the message to the world. Faith in the universal and universality of God is sure to fill the human being with positive force, enhancing his potential for improvement in all aspects of Life.

Faith should spread like glue in order to be a positive binding and abiding force behind all relationships.

CHAPTER 6

Self-control

We have noted that the philosophy of the Gītā is mainly action-oriented. The Gītā concerns itself with the self-growth of the individual but is not oblivious to the social cause. Its author realized that actions of the individual did not impact on him alone. His actions affected the society too. Thus, his actions ought to be such as would not benefit him alone but the society at large also. At least his actions must not run counter to the good of the society and hence the significance of the nature and quality of actions. It has been said that one does not become a good individual simply by performing actions which are only externally good. Men must first acquire or adopt righteous principles and such men would not fail to perform virtuous or righteous actions. This is where the role of self-control comes in. Self-control, mind-control, sense-control and self-restraint are almost synonymous. Self-control is neither suppression nor repression of one's physical, mental or intellectual energies or being. It is a self-imposed regulatory system, put in place to ward off merely selfish actions (even if they be good for the individual but harmful to others) with the help of self-knowledge and self-control. Seeing self-control as a self-regulatory mechanism, it is easy to comprehend the positive effects of self-control in all spheres of human life. In one's demeanor, smile replaces physical stress and strain; clarity of vision replaces mental confusion. Happiness being the goal the journey of life becomes smooth and struggle-free. There are neither waves nor troughs nor booms nor depressions in life (It is a different matter if some compulsively dislike a smooth life). Sudden or sharp rise and fall, as in the case of blood pressure, sugar level or heart beat in the human body are disastrous for the body. All forms of energy—from water, wind or any other form—in order to be beneficial must flow smoothly. Water which benefits crops and helps to feed millions, when in the form of flood destroys the villages and their crops. Similarly, wind can be a soothing breeze or a damaging storm. There is no aspect of life which cannot benefit from self-control and there is none which will not suffer from the absence of self-control.

In the simple matter of eating also, one has to exercise self-control in choosing what to and what not to eat and in what quantities. Neither too much nor too little is recommended. In Chapter XVII, the Gītā goes into great detail as to the nature of food. The same applies to sleep—neither too much nor too little. The golden principle is MODERATION AS AGAINST INDULGENCE. The Gītā does not preach self-denial. Avoid both self-indulgence and self-denial and one becomes self-regulated and moderate in habits with a healthy lifestyle.

Chapter VI (Verses 16 & 17) of the Gītā recommends moderation in eating, recreating, working, sleeping and waking.

Verse 16 of Chapter VI, Gītā says:

> *nā'tyaśnatas tu yogo'sti na cai'kāntam anaśnataḥ*
> *na cāti svapnaśīlasya jāgrato nai'va cā'rjuna*

> **Meaning:** Yoga is not possible, O Arjuna for one who eats too much, or who abstains too much from eating; who sleeps too much or who keeps awake too much.

Do not be a victim of cravings. Thus one would not need to resort to excessive indulgence to satisfy craving.

नात्यश्नतस् तु योगोऽस्ति न चैकान्तम् अनश्नतः।
न चाति स्वप्नशीलस्य जाग्रतो नैव चार्जुन॥ VI (16)

Verse 17 of Chapter VI, the Gītā says:

> *yuktāhāra vihārasya yuktaceṣṭasya karmasu*
> *yukta svapnāvabodhasya yogo bhavati*
> *duḥkhahā*

Meaning: But for one who is moderate (or temperate) in eating food and recreation and who is restrained in action (working), Whose sleep and waking are regulated (moderate), all sorrows are destroyed by the yogic disciplines thus generated.

It is important to note that it is not total abstinence but restraint in action which is advised. Escape from action is neither feasible nor desirable.

The above words of counsel of the Gītā may well be compared with the Buddha's middle path and Aristotle's doctrine of the Golden Mean.

No enjoyment should spring from or cause misery to others. Derive no pleasure from others' pain as you would not like to warm your body by burning your own house. No society or state can afford to give unfettered freedom to its members. Similarly, no individual must give uncontrolled freedom to his senses. Identify the difference between enjoyment and indulgence. Stop before enjoyment becomes destructive indulgence. One must know one's limit or **Lakṣmaṇā Rekhā*. It will not be wrong to say that indulgence is at one's own peril.

All pleasures are followed by pain. Contact-based pleasures are particularly short-lived; they have a beginning and an end. The law of diminishing returns starts working. No sensible

---

युक्ताहारविहारस्य युक्तचेष्टस्य कर्मसु।
युक्तस्वप्नावबोधस्य योगो भवति दुःखहा॥ VI (17)

**"Lakṣmaṇā Rekhā is the line marked on the ground by Lakṣmaṇā of the epic Rāmāyaṇa, which he instructed Sītā (wife of Rāma) not to cross for reasons of her safety. She did cross it and was abducted by the demon king, Rāvaṇa".*

person would bargain for short-term gain and long-term loss in business or otherwise. Indulgence whets appetite for more and more pleasure with less and less satisfaction. Instead of providing satisfaction it only enhances the craving. Indulgence to such a degree can be called sinful—a source of consuming pain. Sin visits the indulgent without mercy. From the level of a human being, one falls and becomes first a consumptive animal seeking more and more indulgence, and later a living corpse.

The Gītā's instructions recommend a practical and a feasible course of life. Enjoy life in moderation, avoiding extremes, maintaining self-restraint or self-control. Restraint or control must be seen both in terms of right degree and right time. In other words, whatever activity e.g. sex, is permissible on attaining adulthood may be harmful at a tender age. Premature sex burns out the budding youth before reaching the threshold of youth. What could have been a healthy, legitimate, acceptable, enjoyment of life—even a bliss— has been turned into a curse and a cause of regret due to wrong timing. Similarly, one should observe one's own limits without competing with anybody else.

In the absence of self-control, all actions or courses of action would appear to be right as all colours seem to agree in darkness. It may not be out of place to mention that the proverb: *'all is fair in love and war'* is the rule of the blind or the blind-folded. It amounts to taking leave of discretion, judgment of good and bad, right and wrong. In other words, it is abandonment of self-control. Such a wild approach has a serious damaging dimension both for the individual as well as for the society. True love can not flourish on unfair or deceitful means and methods. A righteous war or *Dharma Yuddha*, as fought between Pāṇḍavas and Kauravas, representing respectively, the good and the evil in society is in a different category. Unfortunately, self-control has been replaced by selfish control. The cliche, *'all is fair in love and war'* is being extended to all fields of life. After all, it is argued, that the entire life is a war— a continuing struggle. The obvious areas which suffer are politics, business and other money-making pursuits where in the name of competition, scruples are thrown overboard. The game is more foul than fair. This virus is infecting other areas too, to different degrees.

Contrary to the impression, that self-control or mind-control is a form of suppression or repression, self-control is an expression of one's will to be doing what is unselfish, desirable and eschewing what is selfish and undesirable. It takes a strong man to develop that sort of will or self-control. Though, difficult and slow, it is within the realm of the possible. In verse 34 of Chapter-VI of the Gītā, Arjuna express his diffidence about self-control i.e. control of mind.

The Verse 34 of Chapter VI, the Gītā says:

> *cañcalaṃ hi manaḥ kṛṣṇa pramāthi balavaddṛḍham*
> *tasyā 'haṃ nigrahaṃ manye vāyor iva suduṣkaram*

> **Meaning:** Because the mind, indeed is very unsteady, turbulent, powerful and obstinate, O Kṛṣṇa. I think restraining the mind is as difficult as restraining the wind.

Lord Kṛṣṇa, in response to Arjuna's despair in Verse 34, comes out with an important assurance.

The Verse 35 of Chapter VI, the Gītā says:

> *asaṃśayaṃ mahābāho mano durnigrahaṃ calaṃ*
> *abhyāsena tu kaunteya vairāgyeṇa ca gṛhyate*

> **Meaning:** Undoubtedly, O Mighty armed (Arjuna), the mind is restless and difficult to restrain, but it is subdued by *Abhyāsa* (regular practice) and detachment, O Arjuna (son of Kuntī).

चञ्चलं हि मनः कृष्ण प्रमाथि बलवद् दृढम्।
तस्याहं निग्रहं मन्ये वायोर् इव सुदुष्करम्॥ VI (34)

असंशयं महाबाहो मनो दुर्निग्रहं चलम्।
अभ्यासेन तु कौन्तेय वैराग्येण च गृह्यते॥ VI (35)

No doubt, the key to learn and acquire any discipline is *Abhyāsa* (practice)—the higher the goal, the harder and longer is the practice required. All good things in life need practice before they become part of one's character e.g. compassion, composure, equanimity, peace of mind. Self-control or control of mind is no exception.

In the context of self-restraint or self-control, it is also worthwhile to deliberate on the relevant verses in the Gītā, on the influence of nature (*Svabhāva*) on one's mind and therefore on one's action.

Verse 33 of Chapter III, the Gītā says:

> *sadṛśaṃ ceṣṭate svasyāḥ prakṛter jñānavān api*
> *prakṛtiṃ yānti bhūtāni nigrahaḥ kiṃ kariṣyati*

> **Meaning:** All living creations follow their tendencies; even the wise man acts according to the tendencies of his own nature. Of what use is external restraint?

The relevance of this verse must be seen in the context of Arjuna's hesitancy to fight even though he being a warrior, it should be in his nature to fight. Indirectly, Lord Kṛṣṇa is advising Arjuna not to try to misuse (so to say) self-restraint against fighting because under the circumstance fighting was selfless or righteous action and his duty. Self-restraint is advisable against selfish action, wrong or undesirable action or forbidden action but not against doing one's duty particularly for a higher purpose. Therefore, Lord Kṛṣṇa's arguments in favor of Arjuna taking up arms and fighting can not be extended in life, by anyone to fight for selfish gains. Man cannot afford to indulge in impulses or be slave to one's nature. If that were so, the very concept of self-restraint, mind-control and sense-control would lose all meaning.

सदृशं चेष्टते स्वस्याः प्रकृतेर् ज्ञानवान् अपि।
प्रकृतिं यान्ति भूतानि निग्रहः किं करिष्यति॥ III (33)

Another possible interpretation could perhaps be that Lord Kṛṣṇa is alluding to force of one's nature as a challenge to be faced with resolve. The next verse 34 of Chapter III seems to support this interpretation as it warns of attachment and aversion–(which are part of nature of most men) being two stumbling blocs in one's journey to the goal of supreme bliss and happiness.

In Verse 34, Chapter III, the Gītā says:

indriyasye'ndriyasyārthe rāgadveṣau vyavasthitau
tayor na vaśam āgacchet tau hy āsya paripanthinau

Meaning: *Rāga* (attachment) and *Dveṣa* (aversion) remain rooted in all sense-objects. One must not come under their sway as they are the two principal enemies standing in the way of his redemption.

The import of the two verses (33 & 34) of Chapter III, taken together would imply that man should act according to his understanding not on impulse. In this way, we would not be mere victims of the play of Prakṛti. We would succeed in warding off the above-mentioned stumbling blocs in the pursuit of self-realization. One's nature need not be looked upon neither as a master nor an invincible monster but a dominant tendency or a trait giving birth to certain impulses likely to generate impulsive actions. A controlled mind being guided by intellect endowed with reasoning power can neutralize such impulses and render them ineffective. Their speed and intensity is reduced gradually till these are completely quietened and pacified. (It may be noted that there is no underlying conflict or contradiction between nature and

---

इन्द्रियस्येन्द्रियस्यार्थे रागद्वेषौ व्यवस्थितौ।
तयोर् न वशम् आगच्छेत् तौ ह्यास्य परिपन्थिनौ॥ III (34)

self-control. The self-controlled too has followed rules of nature— cause and effect— but of a higher order and for higher purposes having an understanding of eternal-unity, universality and happiness.

However, it may not be correct to overlook the influence of nature entirely. Extent or degree of influence, of course, varies from person to person depending upon one's level of self-control. It is neither desirable to go against one's nature unnecessarily nor to fall victim to it. What it essentially means is that going against nature is far more difficult, an uphill task, than going along. But the ease in going along (rather than going against) is not a good enough reason. On the contrary, if nature tends to take one the wrong way it is best to resist, put in greater effort to go the right way. All upward journeys— from lower to higher altitudes are arduous. The same applies to upward movement from a lower value to a higher value-system.

One needs both *Will* (determination) and *Skill* (discipline). In the physical sense, it means going against the pull of gravity as in the case of a lift going up to higher floors in a building. In the spiritual sense, it means not being attracted, tempted or pulled by baser, negative instincts e.g. greed, lust, anger, vengefulness etc. even if these frailties be inherent part of one's in-born nature.

As in the case of a lift, the control or regulatory system provided in the lift would effectively check its slipping back downwards. Both kinds of upward movements are difficult but not impossible. Skilful use of mechanical or electrical energy in the case of physical movement and human energy gathered as a result of self-discipline in the case of spiritual movement are the requisite means. Self-discipline or self-restraint will take care of the counter-forces like desires, greed, lust, anger etc., which cause a setback or sliding downwards.

If one had only to be a slave to one's nature, emphasis, on

acquiring and practicing self-control as a pre-requisite to self-realization, would be a complete contradiction. Emphasis on self-control, restraint of senses, is the very basis of any yoga. It must also be understood that self-control does not imply a state of inaction nor forcible repression of senses. It is tantamount to evolving a regulatory system whereby the baser instincts in one's nature e.g. greed, lust, anger etc. would be reined in (till they die their own death) and the finer ones e.g. detachment, equanimity, peace would be nourished and developed further to their full bloom. No doubt, this is a long and slow journey, but one must strive and remain hopeful of success. Even rough stones change into shapely ones when impacted by flow of water over a long period. There is a beautiful Hindi couplet which is very relevant in the above context.

> *Karata karata abhyās ke, jaḍmati hota sujāna,*
> *Rassī āwat jāt se, sila per paḍata niśān.*

It translates as follows:

> Through practice (regular), an ignorant person becomes intelligent. A stone acquires a dent due to rope rubbing against it (on its upward and downward movements).

The simile is based on the old practice in villages, where a bucket tied to a rope is used to draw water from a well, and the rope rubs against the stone structure on top of the well and cuts into the stone. Canyons are examples of the same process in nature on a grand scale, where rivers have cut into mountains as deep as over a mile.

In spite of one's predisposition or nature (*Svabhāva*) or predominance of certain traits due to presence of three guṇas (*Sāttvika, Rājasika* and *Tāmasika*) in a certain proportion, it should be possible to modify, rectify and improve. Actions as per one's nature, no doubt, will be comparatively easy to perform, but acting against one's nature, for sure, is going to be as difficult as swimming against the current or climbing uphill. However, if pursuit of righteous life through performance of right actions, requires going against or acting at variance with one's nature, all religions and philosophies require that one must choose the difficult path and strive for success with the help of regular practice (*Abhyāsa*) to the extent necessary depending on one's nature and endowments. For different travellers, the amount of preparation, effort and control required would be different.

In principle, however, one must accept that both nature and nurture operate in life. One cannot remain slave to nature—from birth to death a long journey indeed. If modern science is to be believed, innate nature or endowment as transmitted through parental genes plays a minor role whereas influences of various kinds, one is exposed to play a major role in shaping one's life. Indeed, if there is no scope for improvement or movement from lower to higher realms by practice then education, scriptures and sermons would be a waste. The key, of course, is practice.

A slave to nature must transform himself into a master of nature, through regular effort and self-control. A small story makes the message of the Gītā, quite clear. A dervish met a king. The king said: *"Ask a boon of me."* The dervish replied: *"I will not ask a boon from one of my slaves. I have two slaves who are thy masters: Covetousness and expectation (jealousy and desire)."*

The Gītā acknowledges that the journey from the slave stage to the master stage is long, arduous, and full of pitfalls with all the risk of setbacks. The goal of self-control is, indeed, very high and more so for an ordinary person who is engaged in active life (which the Gītā also recommends) and for whom meditation is not the sole or even the main occupation or activity.

Seemingly, out of the realm of possibility, the goal of sense-control and self-control is intended by the Gītā, to be made a part of one's character, through a practical step-by-step approach. Verses 25 & 26 of Chapter VI, of the Gītā are relevant.

Verse 25, Chapter VI, the Gītā says:

śanaiḥ śanair uparamed buddhyā dhṛtigṛhītayā
ātmasaṃsthaṃ manaḥ kṛtvā na kiṃcid api
cintayet

Meaning: Little by little (gradually and in small steps) let him attain tranquility of mind, with intellect in firm control and concentrating on self to the exclusion of all else.

Verse 26, Chapter VI, the Gītā says:

yato yato niścarati manaścañcalam asthiram
tatas tato niyamyai'tad ātmany eva vaśam
nayet

Meaning: Wheresoever (and for whatever reasons) this restless and unsteady mind wanders away, one should (gently) bring it back to the control of the Supreme.

The significance of the above verses can also be understood and appreciated by reflecting on the childhood of Lord Kṛṣṇa Himself. The child Kṛṣṇa plays pranks, runs here and there in different directions, alone or with other friends. Mother Yaśodā chases the child Kṛṣṇa , makes use of love, guidance, reprimand and even punishment to control and bring Him back on course. The process continues till the child matures into a responsible well-behaved adult. Restless nature of mind

---

शनैः शनैरू उपरमेद् बुद्ध्या धृतिगृहीतया।
आत्मसंस्थं मनः कृत्वा न किंचिद् अपि चिन्तयेत्॥ VI (25)

यतो यतो निश्चरति मनश्चञ्चलम् अस्थिरम्।
ततस् ततो नियम्यैतद् आत्मन्येव वशं नयेत्॥ VI (26)

and its tendency to follow wrong leads in the absence of proper control can also be understood with the help of the example of a cowherd or a shepherd. No sooner do the watchful eyes of the cowherd or the shepherd look elsewhere than one or two members of the herd are likely to go astray breaking away from the main herd. If the shepherd or cowherd is not alert enough to immediately respond to the situation and act to bring back the member who has wandered away, more and more members escape from his control, follow those gone astray before, with the resultant problems and even loss. On the contrary, if control (gentle or harsh if need be) is exercised, even unobtrusively, the herd as well as the herdsman get to the destination, after they have fed themselves and reasonably satisfied their hunger, grazing in the fields during the day.

The Gītā's advice of gently bringing back the mind to the control of the Supreme has a rather practical application. In different contexts, the Supreme may mean different objects of concentration. For a student it is study; for a painter it is painting, for a poet it is poetry, and so on. Advice is applicable in all fields of activity where concentration is required. The beauty of the verse is the implied recognition of the fact that mind does wander here and there and needs to be brought back. The wandering nature of mind is not a reason to give up the goal.

The comparison of mind with a child is very appropriate. One tries to keep harmful things beyond the child's reach but in case the child does get hold of a dangerous object it should be possible to take it away from him through creating awareness of the harmful nature of the object, reasoning, persuasion and even reprimand. Love might make him lovable, adorable; reason may make him reasonable and reprimand may make him responsible. Such an approach will help his (child's) own intellect grow. The Gītā tells us and we acknowledge that intellect is superior to mind. Adult-nature of the intellect in man will take care of the child-nature in man till such time that the desired stable state of mind has been attained, restraint has to be actively and consciously practised on a regular basis.

Unfortunately, regular practice is like a treatment with slow-acting medicine which people find difficult to accept and use. Like medicine, practice also need not be a life-long affair. Through practice desired characteristics become part of one's temperament and character. Eventually, one reaches a stage when no further conscious practice may be necessary. There is a saying that *"that Government is the best which governs the least."* Behind this saying about an ideal Government is the faith that in course of time citizens of the country have grown mentally and acquired a state of mind where external control by the Government becomes unnecessary and unwarranted. A mature mind takes care of the fact that such a citizen has been, of his own volition, rendered incapable of reposing a belief in anything wrong or harmful. His/her actions cannot result in harm to society, country, humanity and, therefore, to self. One of the couplets of Saint Kabir says that water (or whatever else) having once changed into a pearl, may not be reconverted into water again. An individual having given up slowly and steadily, through practice of his own, the baser instincts of body and mind is unlikely to reacquire such traits, in the normal circumstances. The same logic applies to an individual who, by practice, has reached the stage when self-control, as opposed to external control, has become part of his being. Such a person has his senses under control and his intelligence is firmly set. Having imbibed the habit of self-control, no external controls are needed any more.

Let us try to understand the interrelationship of thoughts and actions. Nature has endowed man with five sense—organs (*Jñānendriyas*) and five abstract working senses or capacities to undertake actions or action-organs (*Karmendriyas*). The *Jñānendriyas* are: Power to hear (*Śrotra*), Power to See (*Chakṣu*), Power to Smell (*Ghrāṇa*), Power to Taste (*Rasana*) and Power to Feel (*Tvak*). In simple words, the following functions are performed by the respective sense-organs:

1.	Hearing	through	Ears
2.	Seeing	through	Eyes
3.	Smelling	through	Nose
4.	Tasting	through	Tongue
5.	Touch	through	Skin

There is a definite purpose in nature providing two eyes and two ears. This endowment facilitates us in comprehending the physical world from both right and left sides—the two views complementing each other to provide a fuller picture. All the same, nature has not given the ordinary creature the mythological third eye to look behind. Therefore, let us remember in humility that man has evolved a lot, but not to perfection. The *Karmendriyas* are the Power to Express (*Vāk*), the Power to Grasp (*Pāṇi*), the Power to Move (*Pāda*), the Power to Procreate (*Upastha*) and the Power to Excrete (*Pāyu*). Five sense-organs (parts of the body) perceive the external world and transmit the stimuli in the form of feelings, emotions or desires into the mind. Then, there is intellect which has been endowed with the power of discrimination using logic to differentiate between good and bad.

Stimuli in various forms act like a crowd trying to gate-crash into the mind. The crowd, as is normal, is a mixed·lot consisting of good and not so good people, or in the words of the Gītā unselfish and selfish desires. Inspite of the nature and preventive mechanism of intellect providing the filter or an instrument for sifting and selection, certain undesirable inputs do sneak into the mind as Satan entered the Garden of Eden. Intellect is not driven by selfish desires but still it cares for positive desires like reputation, name and fame. In simple words, intellect has a role and a duty to control the mind. One who controls the mind can control the matter—meaning the material world. There is an interesting story relating to Alexander the Great which brings out the right message about the mind and its control or self-control. Diogenes was the great philosopher-saint who lived a rather simple life. He himself hardly travelled but his followers and others who learnt about his greatness would come to see him. As his reputation and popularity grew, Alexander the Great decided to pay him a visit.

No wonder that the Saint did not show any respect or pay much heed to Alexander the Great, but Alexander asked—*"What can I do for you, Master?"* Master-Diogenes responded by saying—*"Nothing. Pray stand a little aside, so that the sun can keep shining on me."* Further, the Saint inquired as to where Alexander was going next. Alexander replied—*"Master, I have to conquer the entire world. I have conquered half of it, but there is more to conquer."* The Saint responded—*"You will never be able to conquer everything. For a part is always left, Yourself."* The Saint Philosopher wanted to convey the message which the Gītā has been giving as part of its perennial philosophy. Alexander's story also has it that having been forced to abandon his mission of world conquest, he sought to discover the deeper meaning in the words of the philosopher-saint. It is said that he (Alexander) ordered that after his death his right hand should be left outside the shroud to signify that even the greatest of the Kings—Alexander left the world as empty-handed as he had come into it.

Swami Vivekanand said succinctly: *"Conquer the mind and you will have conquered the world."*

We have noted that mind and intellect serve the body system as a control-room. It decides about actions to be undertaken by the body that is by *Karmendriyas*. The *Karmendriyas* singly or in combination, come into play for carrying out the commands received from the control-room by performing or producing actions in the external physical world. This is the short journey from the point of time of sense perceptions by sense-organs and performance of actions by action-organs. The journey commences from the external world and terminates in the external world. Thus, it also becomes clear that output in terms of actions is not independent of inputs in terms of thoughts. In the computer language also it is said : "Garbage in Garbage out." Input of thoughts is translated into output of actions. In other words, actions are physical expressions of thoughts.

The Gītā takes cognizance of the fact that there cannot be any life without activity of some sort. The nature, extent and type of activity will differ from person to person but otherwise is a sine qua non for everybody. Sense perceptions, thoughts, precede actions and are like a seed for the fruit to be produced.

The importance of thought is thus obvious.

> "Thought without Action makes one a recluse, Action without thought makes one a machine."

Nature has given man an enormous exclusive and unique capacity to be able to see things from the point of view of another person only if he is noble and sensible enough to use it with the help of self-control. Absence of self-control spells doom for the individual and society in which he lives. Individually, without self-control, he finds himself incapable of any concentration in whatever work he undertakes. His mental and physical capacities are not operating at the optimum level of efficiency and productivity. He is not an asset to himself or to others in the family or in society. There are many stories, old and not so old, about the benefits of concentration which led to the success of great persons. There is a recorded fact about the great scientist Newton. He would keep busy at his desk and hardly leave his room and certainly not for trivial things.

The story goes that he was called several times to dinner by his servants but he failed to show up at the dining table. In fact, his concentration or what we call single-mindedness shut out the call for dinner which never registered in his mind. Newton continued with his work in his room and the servants of the house decided out of frustration to retire for the day without waiting for Newton to eat. Eventually, Newton's spell ended and he went to the dining table. Finding no food on the table, he remarked that he had forgotten having already eaten his dinner. Such is the sublime level of concentration of the great people for lofty achievement. *A scientist can be as much in Samādhi as a saint.*

The impact of self-control or lack of it or total absence of it, is not less important from the angle of the community and society. Looking at self-control in a different way, it implies abridgement or partial surrender of one's freedom so that others may enjoy their freedom.

The whole purpose of civilization in a community and society is to restrict the individual freedom to some extent, so that it does not interfere or unreasonably diminish others' freedom. British law expounds that everybody is free to move around his stick but not in a way that interferes with the other person's freedom to move his stick. Like the constitution (National Charter of Rights and Duties,) of some other countries, Indian Constitution too has its own philosophy of fundamental rights for Indian citizens.

However, no right is so fundamental that it cannot be reasonably abridged in the larger interest of other citizens. The basic philosophy behind such legislative measures is the same as has been proclaimed in the Gītā, i.e. living in peace and harmony with others, controlling one's own thoughts and activities through self-control. One may call it the Gītā's Jurisprudence. Lack of self-control generates stress and strife in the individual mind leading to harmful actions. Similarly, in a society led by or composed of people who are devoid of self-control, struggle and strife are commonplace and a part of everyday life.

Rights and duties are not opposite to each other. These are the two sides of a coin. Individuals and societies have rights as well as duties. Each flows from the other or each exists because of the other. The same is true of freedom and control. Art lies in the balance between the two and avoidance of excesses and extremes. The Gītā, with the help of different arguments, encourages Arjuna to act and fight (for a righteous cause against evil and wrong). On the other hand, the Gītā discourages unrighteous action and advises exercise of Self-control over body and mind (against a tendency for wrong action).

Even in terms of simple worldly wisdom or practical prudence, self-control is a useful ally in life. A busy executive who has a lot of demands made on his energy, time and other resources needs self-control more, not less, than others do. The higher or the more powerful a person, the more composed and controlled he must be. He has to ration his resources of various kinds among various demands.

Only with a peaceful and composed mind which follows self-control; can he achieve that goal. Productivity and profitability can be optimized only with a cool mind which can grasp and take stock of his business in its entirety without getting confused, without a splitting headache or pulling at one's hair. Make your own mind a friend, not a foe. As brought out beautifully in verses 5 and 6 of chapter VI, mind can be one's friend or one's foe.

Verse 5 of chapter VI, the Gītā says:

uddhared ātmanā'tmānaṃ nā'tmānam avasādayet
ātmaiva hyātmano bandhur ātmaiva ripur ātmānaḥ

Meaning: Let a man elevate (or raise) himself by himself. Let him not degrade himself. Because the Self (higher) alone is the friend of self (lower) and Self (higher) alone is the enemy of the self (lower).

उद्धरेद् आत्मनात्मानं नात्मानम अवसादयेत्।
आत्मैव ह्यात्मनो बन्धुर् आत्मैव रिपुर आत्मानः॥ VI (5)

Verses 6 of the chapter VI, the Gītā says:

bandhur ātmā'tmanas tasya yenā'tmai'vā'tmanā jitaḥ
anātmanas tu satrutve vartetā'tmai'va satruvat

Meaning: For him who has conquered his (lower) self by (higher) Self his Self is a friend but for him who has not conquered the (lower) self, (higher) Self will act in enmity like an enemy.

Self with capital 'S' denotes universal self and self with small 's' denotes personal self. The two are not antagonistic to each other. Everyone has the discretion and scope to rise or fall, to connect with the universal self or not. If one can subdue lower desires and cravings, the channel of higher energy becomes available i.e. the (higher) Self becomes a friend. On the contrary if one is subdued by lower desires, the channel of higher energy is shut against him.

The Higher Self is the friend of those who have control over the lower self (those whose higher self has conquered their lower self). But it *acts like an enemy* (implying that one can make it act like an enemy though it is not an enemy) for those who have no control over it (those men whose higher Self is unable to conquer the lower self).

No resource is available in unlimited quantity. A controlled mind is a saver of energy and other resources available to the executive and thus the supplier channel viz. higher channel or Higher Self becomes a friend. An uncontrolled mind is a waster of resources and, therefore, the higher channel seems to act like an enemy.

The statement in verse 5 and 6 of chapter VI quoted above is to be noted. An uncontrolled mind acts like an enemy implying that its basic nature is not inimical. Universal Self is full of energy. It depends on the man as to how much he

---

बन्धुर् आत्मात्मनस् तस्य येनात्मैवात्मना जितः।
अनात्मनस् तु शत्रुत्वे वर्तेतात्मैव शत्रुवत्॥ VI (6)

is able to benefit from this flow of energy to his advantage by providing a smooth flow or let it be used to his disadvantage by putting up impediments, resistance blocking the channel against smooth flow due to lack of self-control. Presence or absence of a regulatory technique by way of checks and balances, in the mind, (as we have for the external activities) will make all the difference, *not only in BUSINESS LIFE in a limited sense but in the entire BUSINESS Of LIFE itself.*

Conflicts and contradictions in the mind are self-destructive. They raise walls of resistance against peaceful and clear thinking. Energy is all around us. To let it in, we have to remove all forms of resistance and obstruction to let the light and energy come in to remove darkness and energise the body mind apparatus provided by nature. The lower self has to be readied for ascendancy. Effect-friendly or inimical—will depend upon the use energy is put to. Man, the user of energy has to decide its use for the lower destructive; or for ordinary worldly purpose or for higher constructive purpose. Basically, one must be aware of the complex but flexible nature of body and mind. For we all know the difference between a tense body and a relaxed one, an angry face and a smiling one—one helps the free flow of blood and Prāṇa (breath) while the other hampers both. We also know as to how fear raises hair on the human body. Thus knowing the link between mind and body, it is common sense that we devote ourselves more and more to self-control. Further, it is not one time exercise. One has to protect the conquered territories with constant vigilance. Similarly, the command system for control of mind has to be kept in place forever for ever-lasting benefits. Balance sheet of life is much larger and more important than the balancesheet of business.

One must include in one's balancesheet of life not only the monetary outgoings but also emotional and spiritual wastefulness. Pause a little and think what emotional price one is paying for material benefits, which, one knows for sure, are not going to serve one beyond a point— in terms of quantity and in terms of time. If too little is bad, too much may be worse. A child's smile, or wife's hug or a mother's fondling is worth more than the extra buck one may make by over-working, stressing and straining oneself and keeping away from happiness within one-self and within the family. Worldly activities, be it money-making business or something else need not and must not diminish or take away happiness. No activity is worthwhile if, instead of giving happiness, it takes it away or even diminishes it.

Executives are aware that teachings of the Gītā are receiving more and more attention, appreciation and are being adopted by the corporate world. E.Q. (Emotional Quotient) has been added to I.Q. (Intelligence Quotient) in the functioning of executives. They are advised and trained to take care of the emotional needs of their team members to make them—the executives—more effective team leaders. No one can perform at one's optimum level with emotions bottled up. Thus, the executives must deal with their juniors not just mechanically but with a human touch. Executives have to be more humane. Warmth of emotions should be added to cold calculations of the job to make the man a fuller man rather than reduce him to a machine. Such an attitude follows a fuller, wider and deeper view of life.

If the executive cares for his team in office, chances are that he would care for his own family also. It is interesting and satisfying to learn that corporations have started involving their executives and others in community services. This is a small but significant step in the right direction of working for a social cause or higher purpose espoused in the Gītā. Make the Higher Self your friend and goal. The chief external foes e.g. anger, greed, lust etc. viz. the lower self will then be controlled and conquered.

Control and conquer the lower self.
Make the higher self the goal of life.

CHAPTER 7

Desires, Anger and Fear

Verse 28 of Chapter V of the Gītā says:

yatendriya manobuddhir munir mokṣa parāyaṇaḥ
vigatecchā bhaya krodho yaḥ sadā mukta eva saḥ

Meaning: With senses, mind and intellect (ever) controlled having liberation as his supreme goal, free from desire, fear and anger the sage is verily liberated for ever.

Lord Kṛṣṇa asks the seeker to renounce desire, fear and anger. The link between desire, fear and anger is clear. Firstly, there is a desire to acquire certain objects. This desire itself gives rise to a struggle for success in fulfilling the desire. All along this struggle for success, the fear of failure is accompanying the struggle and haunts a person. Perhaps, failure itself is not so much bad as the fear of failure. The pendulum of the mind is oscillating between hope and fear; success and failure. Anger is generated due to unfulfilled desires.

It has been said that there is no greater sin than too many desires. One must know the difference between what is necessary,

---

यतेन्द्रियमनोबुद्धिर् मुनिर् मोक्षपरायणः।
विगतेच्छाभयक्रोधो यः सदा मुक्त एव सः॥ V (28)

sufficient and superfluous. Further, one should know the difference between what is desirable and undesirable. For fulfilling any desire, some struggle is necessary. In this struggle, there are bound to be some good actions and others not so good. Desires which can be fulfilled with the help of good actions without consciously or unconsciously resorting to bad actions or *adharma* are part of the life of even a righteous person and these need to be fulfilled. Desires cannot be wiped out or eliminated altogether. What is recommended in the Gītā is a control over these desires. There is a difference between reduction and removal. Regulation is different from suppression or repression. One does not even have to try removal or repression as it is neither possible nor desirable. One's aim should be to control them, be their master, not letting them control you instead. One has to try to control or reduce the multiplicity of desires as also their intensity. Sometimes, a simple desire with too much intensity does the same damage as do many desires.

Therefore, one must first endeavor to reduce (a) the intensity (*vega*) of the desire so that its impact on one's mind is less forceful and (b) reduce the number. We are all aware that one desire fulfilled means another one arising in the mind. The process goes on endlessly and the man is ever engaged in the struggle to fulfil them, so much so that one loses interest in the ones fulfilled but those unfulfilled fresh ones only bother him. Such a man is struggling by choice not out of necessity. Such a man can never be content or peaceful.

Verse 70 of Chapter II of the Gītā says:

āpuryamāṇam acalapratiṣṭhaṃ
samudram āpaḥ praviśanti yadvat
tadvat kāmā yaṃ praviśanti sarve
sa śāntim āpanoti na kāmakāmī

आपूर्यमाणम् अचलप्रतिष्ठं
समुद्रम आपः प्रविशन्ति यद्वत्।
तद्वत् कामा यं प्रविशन्ति सर्वे
स शान्तिम् आप्नोति न कामकामी॥ II (70)

> **Meaning:** He attains peace in whose mind all desires enter without creating any disturbance, as river waters enter the full ocean without creating a disturbance. Not the one who loves (hugs) desires.

Satisfying desires is like feeding fuel into the fire or trying to fill a bottomless pit. The state of mind is such that one does not even know what he has got. He only knows what he does not have.

There are desires of lower level, higher level and still higher level. These can also be called *Tāmasika*, *Rājasịka*, and *Sāttvika* desires of a person with predominantly these *guṇas* or strands of nature, respectively. (The highest level of desire is of course, desirelessness. This is not the objective of a *Karma Yogī*).

Verses 34 of Chapter III of the Gītā says:

> *indriyasye'ndriyasyārthe rāgadveṣau vyavasthitau*
> *tayor na vaśam āgacchet tau hyāsya paripanthinau*

> **Meaning:** *Rāga* and *Dveṣa* (likes and dislikes or longing and loathing) for the sense-objects remain in the senses. One must not come under their sway. These two are his enemies.

Verse 37 of Chapter III, the Gītā says:

> *śrī bhagavān uvāca*
> *kāma eṣa krodha eṣa rajoguṇa samudbhavaḥ*
> *mahāśano mahāpāpmā vidhyenam iha vairiṇam*

> **Meaning:** This is craving (strong desire or *Kāma*), this is anger born out of passion mode or strand of nature (*Rajoguṇa*). These are all consuming and sinful. Know them to be enemies here.

इन्द्रियस्येन्द्रियस्यार्थे रागद्वेषौ व्यवस्थितौ।
तयोर् न वशम आगच्छेत् तौ ह्यास्य परिपन्थिनौ॥ III (34)

श्रीभगवानुवाच
काम एष क्रोध एष रजोगुणसमुद्भवः।
महाशनो महापाप्मा विद्धयेनम इह वैरिणम्॥ III (37)

Spinoza, mentions three types of desires or cravings which men hanker after. These are Riches, Fame and Sensual pleasures. The last one is followed by satiety and repentance. The other two are never satisfied; the more we have, the more we want to have. We work hard—honestly and dishonestly to acquire these; worry to protect these and grieve over their loss. Dishonesty in acquisition means social crime in appropriation in any form whatever, class privilege, racial or national superiority as it involves pain to others.

Wordsworth, advises,

> "Never to blend our pleasure or our pride with sorrow of the meanest thing that feels."

Likes and dislikes act against the equanimity of mind and distort one's correct view or judgement. All material or sensual pleasures (i.e. *Kāma*) are insatiable. The more one tries to satisfy these, the more demanding they become. A person may not be able to exhaust them but they can exhaust him or her. There is an interesting anecdote which is relevant here. There was a king in India, to whom the British rulers had given the title "H.E.H."—'His Exalted Highness'. Because of his rather poor physique, he came to be known as 'His Exhausted Highness'. If one lets the roles be reversed against oneself i.e. instead of controlling desires as a master one becomes a slave to them, one falls down an exhausted and defeated one, eventually.

The Gītā repeatedly tells us to be watchful against these waylayers, stumbling blocs or enemies by whatever other names one may call them. The Gītā also warns against the potential danger inherent in a desire for pleasure viz. it producing an anger when not fulfilled.

The answer lies not in trying to fulfil each and every desire as it is not possible. One fulfilled desire leads to atleast one more new desire. One should try to acquire the right mental attitude. We all suffer from *Vāsanās* or desires directly or from its side effects indirectly. It has been said that world has enough resources to meet the needs of all human beings but not enough to satisfy the greed of even one person.

Man would not have needed education or erudition if he were to fulfil desires mechanically without application of mind. In some aspects of life, man behaves worse than an animal. Unlike most animals, man is accumulative and possessive by nature. He accumulates things he does not need. Possessing is not appreciating things of beauty or pieces of art but man does just the same. A person with a higher level of desires appreciates a painting or another piece of art in a museum. His desire would be to buy it out and place it in his house. His gaze of appreciation would fall on it a few times till he spots another, perhaps better or a more expensive one, somewhere. It is not an appreciative mind but a desire to possess or acquire which is at work. Acquire, guard against loss and suffer from fear of possible loss in the bargain—one struggle leading to another kind of struggle. It is struggle or lack of peace all the way. Therefore, train the mind to be satisfied with fewer necessary desires and even these should be regulated in terms of intensity.

Even having avoided failure and succeeding in fulfilment of desire of acquiring an object, the fear of losing the object achieved, sets in or as it were takes over from the fear of failure. Thus, the fear has two aspects—one before success and the other after success. First whether he would succeed or would not in his objective keeps haunting the mind of an ordinary person. Secondly, after making success of one's mission of fulfilling the desire(s), an ordinary person, has to guard the success zealously lest it should be lost. In both situations it is one's mental attitude, the attachment to, not the appreciation of, objects of desire, which is doing the harm.

Where does anger enter into the interplay of desire, fear, success and failure? Anger is a reaction to an obstacle, in any form—human or otherwise, between a person and success. It is over someone or something which has taken away success from him and pushed him towards failure. In other words, anger results from unfulfilled desires.

Verses (62) & (63) of Chapter II of the Gītā respectively bring out clearly the sequence which anger follows and causes harm to the man.

Verse 62 of Chapter II of the Gītā says:

dhyāyato viṣayān puṃsaḥ saṅgas teṣu' pajāyate
saṅgāt samjayate kāmaḥ kāmāt krodhā' bhijāyate

Meaning: One develops attachment to sense objects by thinking about these sense-objects. Desire for sense-objects comes from attachment to sense- objects and anger comes from the unfulfilled desires.

Verse 63 of Chapter II of the Gītā says:

krodhād bhavati saṃmohaḥ saṃmohāt smṛti vibhramaḥ
smṛti bhraṃśād buddhināśo buddhināśāt praṇaśyati

Meaning: From anger arises bewilderment; from bewilderment loss of memory; and from loss of memory; the destruction of intelligence and from the destruction of intelligence he perishes.

Anger has been called a temporary madness. In that state of mind, one can not think clearly, because as explained in the above verse II(63) of the Gītā, the intelligence and reasoning are destroyed by anger.

Francis Bacon who lived as back as late 16th and early 17th century, in his essay "OF ANGER", advises that to calm the habit or natural tendency to be angry one must meditate upon the effects of anger. First, anger is like a ruin which breaks itself upon that it falls. In other words, alongwith causing harm to the target of anger one harms, oneself, perhaps to a much greater degree. He or she is the first victim before anybody else gets affected. Anger works to one's own disadvantage and to the advantage of the enemy. Men must not behave like bees in the sense that a slight disturbance to the beehive provokes them into an attack on the

---

ध्यायतो विषयान् पुंसः सङ्गस् तेषुपजायते।
सङ्गात् सञ्जायते कामः कामात् क्रोधाऽभिजायते॥ II (62)

क्रोधाद् भवति संमोहः संमोहात् स्मृतिविभ्रमः।
स्मृतिभ्रंशाद् बुद्धिनाशो बुद्धिनाशात् प्रणश्यति॥ II (63)

unwary. Secondly, in refraining from anger, it is best to buy time giving oneself any reason or even an excuse. The chances are that in the meantime it will calm down. One must be careful about two things while in a fit of anger. One must not break off a relationship irrevocably. Be it business or matrimony. Words are like arrows shot, which cannot be made to return without piercing the victim. Words are worse than physical wounds and wounds of words are more difficult to heal. When one's soul is possessed by anger, one should not become so weak as to reveal secrets one would otherwise not.

Whosoever knows how to practise restraint, does not get into anger and thus lasts forever. This message is conveyed in an interesting story of a saint. A saint lived in the vicinity of a small town. He would go to the nearby river every morning, for a bath. He became very well-known for his piety, patience and peaceful nature. But some villagers vowed to exhaust the saint's patience and thus damage his reputation. They engaged a prostitute for this purpose who would take a suitable position on the route of the saint from his hut to the river and back. When the saint returned after bath by that route, she would spit on him. But the saint, instead of losing patience and getting angry, would go back for a fresh bath to the river. On his return from the river, the prostitute would spit again and the saint would restart towards the river for a fresh bath, another time. The process went on till the prostitute but not the saint, got fed up. She kneeled before the saint, begged his forgiveness and told him that she had been hired for a price to make him lose patience and get angry. The saint, interestingly, said, that had she told him the purpose, he would have displayed his anger for her sake the very first time she had spat on him.

Fear is a state of mind. It is the opposite of courage or fearlessness. It is induced by ignorance—sometimes on a lower plane and at other times on a higher plane—of a person. In the beginning of the Gītā, Arjuna (Chapter II of the Gītā) is not willing to fight out of fear that fighting would involve killing etc. Lord Kṛṣṇa explains to Arjuna the inevitability and true nature of death, concept of soul etc. and thus removes ignorance of Arjuna. Fear of death is mainly due to uncertainty attached to what happens after death. Once one knows that death is not the end of life but a continuance of journey in a different form, performing a different assignment or a different role, half the fear is gone.

Further, more significantly, when one learns that man himself can decide (depending upon actions done during his lifetime and state of mind at the time of one's death) his future birth, the remaining half of the fear also disappears. Uncertainty due to ignorance has been removed. Everything—small as cells of bodies and big as planets and stars in the cosmos, must keep on dying and be reborn.

It may not be wrong to say that the bulk of the Gītā, Chapter after Chapter, is devoted to the discovery of the true nature of man, nay, the true nature of the entire creation by removal of uncertainty due to ignorance and eventually prepares Arjuna to fight (Chapter XVIII of the Gītā). The context is the war of Kurukṣetra which Arjuna shuns to fight because of cowardice and fear born out of ignorance and Lord Kṛṣṇa wants him to fight fearlessly this righteous war but the logic can be extended to everybody's daily struggle in life.

Wise men both of the East and the West agree that fear comes in the way of right reasoning and right acting.

Yajur Veda says:

> "Be brave and overcome evils with daring courage. Realise thy own inner strength. Fear no one. Be steady and strong."

Edmund Burke. (1729-1779) the Irish Philosopher and Statesman said:

> "No passion so effectively robs the mind of all its powers of acting and reasoning as fear."

One may not escape noticing the closeness of contents of the respective statements made in the Yajur Veda and that of Edmund Burke quoted above. The Gītā speaks of fear as destroying the reasoning and Edmund Burke reaffirms that fear effectively robs the mind of its power to reason and act.

Verse 56 of Chapter II of the Gītā also says:

> *duḥkheṣv anudvignamanāḥ sukheṣu vigataspṛhaḥ*
> *vīta rāga bhaya krodhaḥ sthitadhīr munir ucyate*

> **Meaning:** He whose mind is not perturbed in the midst of sorrow, and who is free from desires for pleasures and from whom passion, fear, and rage have departed, he is called a sage of stable (settled) intelligence.

Fear is also an animal instinct. Need of food, sleep and sex along with fear of their deprivation are common to man and animal. An animal is afraid of a stronger animal, of its own species or of another species. The animal retreats when faced with a stronger enemy which it knows by nature or discovers in the process of fight. Generally speaking, the fight is for food (or sex) i.e. for survival. But man is not merely an animal. He does not live to eat alone. Other faculties make him different from and higher than animals. Man can differentiate, discriminate and decide. He can overcome his nature (of fear of the strong) because he can see a higher purpose in life, which he can reckon and work to achieve. Lord Kṛṣṇa tells Arjuna to overcome this nature of weakness showing itself as fear, by making Arjuna bear in mind not the fear born out of ignorance but the fearlessness brought about by removal of ignorance. The example of a rope being perceived as a snake in the darkness is very common. To know its true nature one needs to replace darkness with light. As soon as light is there, rope shows itself as a rope and ceases to suggest that it could be a snake.

Darkness is physical absence of light. Ignorance is absence of mental awareness. Even in the modern world a majority of crimes such as robbery, theft, murder etc. are committed in the darkness of night. Ignorance is like a veil or a cover which hides the reality from the watcher or the viewer.

दुःखेष्व् अनुद्विग्नमनाः सुखेषु विगतस्पृहः।
वीतरागभयक्रोधः स्थितधीर् मुनिर् उच्यते॥ II (56)

Verse 38 of Chap. III of the Gītā says:

dhūmenā' vriyate vahnir yathā' darśo malena ca
yatho' lbenā' vṛto garbhas tathā tenedam āvṛtam

Meaning: As fire is obscured by smoke, as a mirror by dust and as an embryo is enveloped by amnion, the same way this (wisdom or Brahma Vidyā) is also obscured by that (vāsanā or desire).

The three examples are not selected by the author of the Gītā, at random. These are qualitatively different and perhaps relate to three types of persons namely *Sāttvika*; *Rājasika* and *Tāmasika*, respectively. Removal of the physical veiling takes different amount of effort. Removing of the smoke seems the easiest, by letting some more air come in and the bright light from the fire would show. Next, cleansing the dust from the mirror may take greater effort— use of cloth, water, soap etc. Next and last, the embryo, has in addition to the veil of amnion, the thick walls of mother's stomach and one can not see it at will. Only after a fixed period, the full grown child wrapped in the amnion comes out of mother's womb and then by piercing the amnion, child is taken out and becomes visible. The three similis bring out that different amount of time and effort is needed to remove ignorance and attain wisdom by people with different mental traits or tendencies.

Ignorance has also been compared to a mirage— a physical deceptive phenomenon wherein a surface looks like water under the light. It is common in desert lands when the seeming water keeps on receding as one tries to approach it. There is a narration of a similar false imagery in Mahābhārata also. Kauravas have been invited by Pāṇḍavas to the latter's palace. Duryodhana the eldest of the Kauravas is misled into believing, due to the reflection of light, that a shining floor was water. He cautioned himself lest he should step on to water. Draupadī (the sole wife of the five Pāṇḍavas) at this point of time, remarked that, no wonder, son of a blind person

---

धूमेनाव्रियते वह्निर् यथादर्शो मलेन च।
यथोल्बेनावृतो गर्भस् तथा तेनेदम् आवृतम्॥ III (38)

(Dhṛtarāṣṭra—The blind king) had to be blind. This unprovoked insulting remark took a deep root in the mind of Duryodhana and is believed to have actually caused the Mahābhārata—the epic war. The episode, apart from explaining the effect of ignorance about reality also brings out the fact as to how poisonous the sting of human tongue can be in destroying the entire body. The body can be an individual, a family, a society, a race or a nation. We all know how the insults are avenged by ordinary people—even with bloodshed.

Drunkenness is also self-imposed ignorance. It lets you say and do things which you would not when in your senses.

Now, let us examine the fear or worry about the result of one's actions.

The Gītā's answer to the fear about the result is, that one must not expect the result to be of one's own choice. Result will be there as cause and effect process, whether one wants it or not. With the best of scientific and other tools it remains unpredictable. It may be or may not be as one wishes. Therefore, it is futile to pin hopes or fears in the result. Take the result as it comes. Next time one may try for the better. Previous effort has already produced or will produce result and thus it is a waste of time, to worry about the result even from the practical view-point. Having put in the effort, it is the best not to be attached to the fruit of action or to be concerned about the result of action. Further, with an attitude of unconcern, pendulum of the mind, oscillating between one extreme of success and the other extreme of failure would yield to 'Samāndrṣṭi' or equanimity between success and failure. Like another pair of opposites, failure and success should not disturb you. Success will not intoxicate you, call for celebration or in the language of the Gītā, it will not prompt you to revel in it. Similarly, failure will not deject you. There is always a next time. Thus, the practical philosophy of the Gītā will make you fearless and courageous to fight your own righteous battle of life, as an ongoing process.

There is a rather interesting story relevant to the phenomenon of fear. Unfounded fear or suspicions of one another did lead to a bloody murder of ten persons, as the story explains. This story, has ten human characters. Each of the ten characters has in the past committed some crime or the other. They are all invited by a wealthy friend for an enjoyable holiday in his luxurious house on top of a hill. The only access to the house on the hilltop is by a ropeway. All the guests reached the house of the host with the hope of having a good time, but the host was missing. A good deal of talk among the invitees and surmises as to the reason for the absence of the host is going on, some suggesting that enough was enough and they should all leave the house, having been humiliated for no reason. The ropeway snaps as planned by the host. The only link with the world outside and the house is destroyed. Naturally, there was an uproar and concern among the guests. Suddenly, a tape recorder, switches on. The recordings reveal the past evil actions of the invitees against someone in the lot of ten which included a judge, a doctor, lawyer, and so on. A fear psychosis sets in. Each of the invitees fears at least one of the remaining ones. Each one is afraid lest he be murdered by way of revenge. One by one, each invitee gets killed by one of the remaining invitees who in turn are also afraid of being killed. In this process, all the invitees get killed by one another.

Such tragedies do happen in real life also. There are scenarios when a person believing that offence is the best form of defence does kill his rival in anticipation. Such is the grip of fear on the human mind.

Sometimes, one feels that life itself is governed by fear and fear only. It does not loosen the grip over one's mind. In daily life, we often hear someone remarking, "I am afraid that I may miss this or that—bus, train or flight. I may not wake up in time. Having woken up and left the house in time I am afraid that I may not be caught in traffic and get delayed. If so, all my plans would fail." The solution is simple. Plan and organize yourself better. It is not good to be always running late. One can be an early bird also. How much early or timely one should leave for journey by train or air would depend on one's mind as the seat of fear is in the mind. You may compensate yourself by simply relaxing or reading a book, if you have arrived early.

A little fear or worry may act as a caution and spur one into activity or preparation. Parents may worry about their children and as a result help them to stay on course and study properly. Students may worry and as a result, start putting in hard work right from the beginning. They can be better planned and prepared about their studies. Others may be better devoted and determined to achieve their respective goals of life. Such fear as may lead one to plan and prepare is not a negative fear. Once having put the plan in action or having executed the plan or having done your duty to the best of your ability, do not worry about the result. The result will be produced as a part of a cause and effect chain. In simple words, do not just worry only. Replace worry at the earliest by work. A little worry which acts as a caution or a reminder of the ugly consequences and whips up suitable action or decision is not bad. Only worry or fear which does not lead to good work or action or does not keep one away from bad action, is negative.

One has to worry about symptoms of a disease and take suitable medicine. Further, one has to avoid certain types of food and drinks. Fear of disease followed by suitable action is a positive one.

In today's world one cannot presume that if one does not have any bad intention towards anybody, nobody will have bad intention towards him or her. One has to be watchful about the activities of others with whom one interacts as an individual or as a businessman etc. One's goodness alone without proper defence of one's territory can invite trouble and can be exploited. Therefore, it is also said in the Gītā that to avoid exploitation one must not play up even one's good emotions.

Fear of attack from a neighboring country leads a nation to prepare its defence. Similarly, for the statesman the fear of misuse of nuclear weapons is a cause for concern and has to be addressed properly.

Fear of engaging in any activity which is *adharma* is good. Fear that if one commits a sin, the sin will visit the doer and exact its price, is good. As against it, the belief or fearlessness that one can get away with committing a sin by paying a price in the form of an offering to the priest, on behalf of God, is bad. That is why in international relations, it is said that the cost of aggression should be made so high as would deter the aggressor from committing the aggression. The Gītā has a similar message both for the individual and the society. Social angle or social welfare requires that fearl-essness should not be allowed to be an attribute of the wrong-doer or an unrighteous person. Whenever the good of the society clashes with that of the individual, the former must prevail. 'Might is right' is the rule of the jungle and cannot apply to any civilized society of human beings. The Gītā is about emboldening or making fearless the righteous who like Arjuna act as a weakling or a coward in the face of his unrighteous cousins.

Fear of censure or sanction is a great enforcer of rectitude of good conduct. The fact of life, one may like it or not, is that while a small minority would follow the good value-system *per se*, the large majority would follow this system if an element of fear, for retribution here and now, in this world or in the world beyond is added to it. History of jurisprudence tells us that broadly there are three types or three levels of sanctions available to society against wrong-doers. These are: religious sanctions; social sanctions and state sanctions.

Every major religion of the world prescribes a code of conduct. For example, Hinduism has *Dharma Ke Dasa Lakṣaṇa* or ten indicators of *Dharma*.* These include speaking the truth, non-stealing etc.

The Old Testament too records the ten commandments given by God to Moses. These include injunctions against lying; stealing, coveting other's wife etc.

The above indicators or commandments were considered inviolate and thus the followers were expected to adopt and follow these in their lives. Promises of God's love and favour for the adherents have been made in the respective religious scriptures. Conversely, going or working against religious instructions were believed to invite the wrath of God in this or the next world. Unfortunately for society, religion and its sanctions have lost their effectiveness. At best, only illiterate masses may follow but not sufficiently.

Just imagine the social scenario wherein all members of society, without exception, would speak the truth. Everyone would readily believe the other without question. No record of dealings,

---

* According to Manu, they are (i) Steadfastness (2) Forgiveness (3) Application (4) Non-Stealing (5) Cleanliness (6) Restraint of Sense- organs (7) Wisdom (8) Learning (9) Truth and (10) Freedom from anger.

commitments, in any field would be necessary. Litigation and courts of law would be rendered unnecessary. Similarly, lie-detectors would not be needed. Computers have led to paperless offices, men can help the process further.

Society had its own code of conduct to be followed by its members. Such a conduct had a more matter-of-fact approach. The area of authority of the society included marriage outside one's caste, depriving family members particularly the poor ones of their share of property or not paying off one's debt etc. In fact, society derived its authority from the *Pañcāyata*-system wherein the *Pañca* had the powers of a court. Pañcāyata, however followed tradition and custom but had no written and codified rules or laws.

Lastly, there are state sanctions. A modern state has codified laws relating to most fields of human activity. Customary laws based on religion and tradition have also been adopted by the state and are enforced in the manner of codified laws. State laws have essentially evolved from the religious tenets and social tradition, considered good and essential for a civilized society. For example, the laws relating to forgery, perjury are rooted in the injunction against lying; patent laws are based on non-stealing and laws on adultery are based on the injunction against coveting other's wife. These laws have the good of society in preference to the good of the individuals, in mind.

Unfortunately, with the passage of time the hold of the religion over society has weakened. Therefore, religious sanctions have practically no effect. When people do not worry about religion, how can they be worried about religious sanctions? Religious sanctions basically had moral appeal and no system of temporal punishment. It was a matter of belief and one's volition.

With the power of money and muscle ever on the rise, social censure and sanctions have also lost their efficacy. Society's biggest weapon against wrong doers was social boycott as a result of which a large majority of society would cease to deal with the erring member in such matters as marriage, other social functions or even in business. Society's double standards are too infamous. Money and muscle power of the rich, creates fear in the minds of people, This is how fear degrades individuals and society. Instead of the wrong-doers being afraid, they instil fear in others.

Sanctions of the state through the operation of its codified laws, however, survive. This is not to suggest that these are followed in letter and spirit. On the contrary, the state laws are manipulated right and left, the motivating force being provided by the influence and power of money or other forms of influence. As in physics, one form of energy can be converted into another form of energy, one form of wrong influence can be converted into another form of wrong influence. All the same, the only surviving friend of the civilized society, howsoever feeble, is the institution of state laws. There are well-defined and codified laws, rules and regulations and there are courts to enforce them. However, the mill of law like the mill of God grinds slowly.

Seeing in the context of the positive role of fear against wrong-doing it is important that fear of the state sanctions, remains to help society to keep its members on the righteous path. Even as the fear of religious and social sanctions has been eroded a great deal, the fear of state laws should be enhanced. The Gītā expects the social leaders as well as the men of religious learning to set an example as masses are prone to follow a hero.

Verse 21 of Chapter III of the Gītā says:

> *yad yad ācarati śreṣṭhas tat tad evetaro janaḥ*
> *sa yat pramāṇaṃ kurute lokas tad anuvartate*

> **Meaning:** Whatsoever, a great man does, the same is done by others as well. Whatever standard he sets, the world follows.

The great men are path makers who blaze the trail that other men follow.

The religious leaders in particular, must stop trading in sins i.e. take on themselves others' sins. They may advise the sinner to take a vow to neutralise the past sins by future good actions and not to commit any fresh sins or wrongs. For the ordinary, it may be worldly-wise and good for the larger good of society if the fear of

---

यद् यद् आचरति श्रेष्ठस् तत् तद् एवेतरो जनः।
स यत् प्रमाणं कुरुते लोकस् तद् अनुवर्तते॥ 3 (21)

the wrongdoings of others or wrong results of one's your own actions keep one vigilant and on the right track.

A little fear for the ordinary people for the larger good of society is not bad. Better a little fire to warn than a big one to burn.

In conclusion, fearlessness should replace the cowardice born of ignorance about the real nature of death, of soul, of actions etc. in the righteous person, in his pursuit of righteous action. Instead, we find in real life, in the modern world, that we need something to fear or to worry about all the time. We have not graduated to a level where we can enjoy a problem-free life. When someone asked a person as to what his problem was, the latter replied that his problem was that he did not have any problem. And that made him worry. We have to learn to be fearless and to enjoy fearlessness, doing our duty. It takes us back to the nature of desires—cause of fear before fulfilment; cause of fear after fulfilment, and cause of anger when an objective is not achieved. Desires one can do without are not at all worth chasing. Channelise the saved-up energy elsewhere.

Therefore, rein in the horses of desires and be happy.

CHAPTER 8

Self is No Doer

The concept 'Self is No Doer', like many other concepts in the Gītā operates on more than one level. It operates on a lower level or what may be called a popular level at which we attribute all actions to a superior or higher power. In other words, there is no freewill, available to man absolutely. We often hear people saying that a particular happening was in God's hands. Man has to accept it as His will. Man must reconcile himself to and accept whatever comes his way without a thought that this could have been different in any way. God is seen by such believers as ordaining every activity of life, howsoever big or small, significant or insignificant. Events as important as death, accidents, illnesses and events as unimportant as the stirring of a leaf in a breeze are decided upon by God. He is portrayed as and believed to be intervening in every matter big and small. He is seen as directing, deciding and awarding rewards and punishments. Fate or destiny is also held responsible for one's faculties and fortune. Further, the destiny is not alterable to any degree whatever the amount of effort put in.

Saints and poets have contributed to the spread of this popular belief. Probably it was not considered necessary or practical to explain this concept logically in terms of the Gītā or otherwise. To encourage man to be non-egoistic, to shed 'I' and 'Me' approach and to be acting righteously, saints and poets stressed the inevitability and unalterable nature of destiny.

The Indian Sufi poet Kabir says :

> "Karam Karīma likhi rahā, Aba Kachhu likha na Jai
> Māsā[1] ghate na tilā[1] baḍhe, Jo kotin[2] kare upāi"

The above concept means that God has (already) written down the destiny (of man) and now nothing can be written (afresh); neither can it be reduced nor increased by the smallest measure of weight, even with innumerable efforts.

The same thought is behind the Rubai of famous Persian poet Omar Khayyam. It says:

> "The moving finger writes, and having writ, moves on: nor all thy piety, nor wit shall lure it back to cancel half-a-line, nor all thy tears wash out a word of it."

In another Rubai, he says:

> "Yea, the first morning of creation (He) wrote what the last dawn of reckoning shall read."

It implies that the book of fate for the entire life is complete, final and shut. Omar Khayyam is very sure and emphatic about the force of destiny. According to him, neither man's wisdom, piety, nor his appeal for mercy will change the destiny. Everything in life is pre-determined with no scope for change.

William Shakespeare, the famous English poet, compares men with actors on the stage of the world. They come on to the stage, enact their respective roles and leave the stage, implying that they had no say whatsoever in selecting their roles. The big Director or God did that in advance, wrote the script not leaving any opportunity for the actor to question or alter it even a bit. This simile is closer to the philosophy of the Gītā. With the help of make-up and costume that go with the role, one assumes a suitable form and creates relationships with other actors for the duration of the play on the life-stage. Thereafter the curtain falls, different actors disappear behind the curtain. They go to the green room and remove the make-up and change. Green room is the melting pot where separate manifest identities dissolve,

---

1. Māsā and Tilā were the smallest units or measures of weight in olden times in India.
2. Kotin meant a number equivalent to ten million.

disappear and merge into the unmanifest, before emerging afresh in a different make up and costume. This concept of one being a mere actor dovetails into the concept of life after death. End of one play and one role does not necessarily mean the end of an actor's career. The actor has to exhaust all his roles before the big Director (God) deems him or her deserving enough to be released. Omar Khayyam also compares men with pieces on the chess-board, where destiny plays its games.

Before going into the rationale or otherwise of the popular concept 'Self is No Doer' supported apparently by poets and saints vis-a-vis, the concept that man makes his own destiny (or man does have power of free-will or the power of determinism), it may be worth while to go into its advantages and disadvantages. One has also to examine whether the God is willing to accept this onerous responsibility for all of man's actions, or is it only that man in his frustration uses God only as a scapegoat.

On the side of advantages, one may say that the concept: "Self is no Doer" makes a person modest. His ego, expressed as 'I' and "ME' is replaced with 'He' and 'HIM'. He does not claim any credit or merit for his worldly success and attributes it to God's grace. Chances are that such an attitude, at some point of time would change his outlook in favor of sharing the fruit of action with others. He would draw more satisfaction or he would be more inclined to atleast share the fruit of action with God's creation (poor men of God rather than rich God's men). Gradually, he will go on decreasing his own share and increasing, instead, God's share. In this process of decreasing his own share, in fact, he is increasing himself.

Self-importance assumed by an egoistic person is like the psychology of a bat. The bat while clinging to the ceiling, upside down, foolishly believes that he is holding the ceiling, In fact nothing as such is being done. Awareness of the reality only makes him comprehend his own insignificance in nature's scheme of things. He realizes that, *Action is not being done by him but through him.* He is a mere agent not the doer nor the author of action. Actions are like anonymous books of life. Man may act on behalf of the king or on king's order but he is not the king. He must not assume that he is a king. Believing in this truth and behaving accordingly he has saved himself from going through the experiences of a passing glory following a boom and a gloom following a bust. He comes out as a clever winner in all situations.

Then, there are hypocrites who remember and forget God according to their convenience. God becomes a convenient scapegoat or a whipping boy for them to pass on discredit for failure. Such hypocrites heap the blame on poor God who is not physically there to defend Himself.

In the legal world and in the law books there is a whole lot of discussion on the doctrine of Principal and Agent and their respective responsibilities or rights and duties. An agent always acts on behalf of his principals as per the latter's directions in general or specifically for a situation. As recompense, he gets his salary and commission. Having acted within the domain of duties as per the agreement, the agent has no responsibility for profit and loss. Another interesting example is the institution of Ambassadors appointed as pleni potentiary of one's own country to act in another country. The country concerned whose Ambassador he is takes full responsibility for his actions. Good and bad results accrue to the country or the Government he represents, not to him personally or individually, provided of course, he does not overstep his authority. The temptation or weakness for over-stepping one's jurisdiction or not acting as expected has an inherent danger.

Verse 27 of Chapter III of the Gītā says:

> *prakṛteḥ kriyamāṇāni guṇaiḥ karmāṇi sarvaśaḥ*
> *ahaṃkāra vimūḍhātmā kartāham iti manyate*

> **Meaning:** While all kinds of actions are performed by the modes of nature (material *guṇas*) though he whose soul is bewildered (or deluded) by the self-sense (I - faculty), thinks, I am the doer.

The deluded soul wrongly assumes authorship of actions forgetting the role of nature. The nature restricts the freedom of ego soul.

The moment the agent starts assuming and acting as a principal or the ambassador starts behaving as being the king or

---

प्रकृतेः क्रियमाणानि गुणैः कर्माणि सर्वशः।
अहंकारविमूढात्मा कर्ताहम् इति मन्यते॥ III (27)

the Government, the problem starts. It is over-stepping one's jurisdiction of duty or activities. It attracts the wrath of the principal wherefrom the authority of the agent has sprung with unpleasant consequences. Having reconciled oneself to the insignificant role of an agent, one has also to watch one's own conduct. One cannot afford to assert like a principal and still be free from blame. An error of judgement is execusable but selfish conduct or misconduct due to ego is not.

The Chinese philosopher La Tzu says: *"He who does not assert himself, thereby remains free of blame."*

One can, in the present context modify the above statement to say that he who does not assume himself to be what he is not, will remain free of blame.

On the side of disadvantages, one may say that the concept that "self is no doer" can make one a pessimist or a fatalist. He would think that his own effort either by way of thought or action is not going to make any difference. Atleast some would settle into a convenient belief that since everything is predestined, not changeable at all, there is no point in doing any action with a view to bringing about a change. It may lead to sluggishness or inertia in society at large.

This cannot be a message of Lord Kṛṣṇa emanating from the Gītā. On the contrary, the Gītā is a mandate for action. The Gītā is to encourage and mobilise the indecisive, the good but weak by removing fears of various kinds due to ignorance which comes in his way. The Gītā is tackling the problems arising out of weaknesses born out of misconception in the society wherein the good is abdicating its role, by bringing out the physical and metaphysical truths. Since man's personality operates on different planes, so do the messages of the Gītā. By interpreting the different messages of the Gītā in the right context, one may not only not find any contradictions but discover a unified message based on eternal truth.

That the 'self is no doer', means that there is a higher power which is the actual doer or the architect of all actions. Behind the visible 'self' there is an invisible "SELF", on a higher plane. As a result we tend to presume that higher 'SELF' is responsible for all the actions. But verses 8 & 14 of chap. V of the Gītā, together make the truth clear.

Verse 8 of Chapter V, the Gītā says:

naiva kiñcit karomīti yukto manyeta tattvavit
paśyañśṛṇvan spṛśañjighrann aśnan gacchan
svapañ śvasan

Meaning: The man who is united with the divine and knows the truth thinks 'I do nothing at all' in seeing, hearing, touching, smelling, testing, walking, sleeping, breathing.

We are asked to understand that 'SELF' is different, higher and unchangeable. It is not involved in the actions of body and mind which are the handiwork of ego which is impermanent and changeable.

Verse 14 of Chapter V, the Gītā says:

na karttṛtvaṃ na karmāṇi lokasya sṛjati prabhuḥ
na karmaphala saṃyogaṃ svabhāvas tu pravartate

Meaning: The sovereign self does not cause, create nor prompt men to act. Nor does He act. Nor does He link up actions with their fruit. It is nature that works out (these).

Even God has a non-intervening role as a mere witness. So should the man of realization have.

Who, then, is responsible or is the doer of actions? The answer, lies in verse 27 of the chapter III of the Gītā referred to earlier. The verse 14 of Chapter V reinforces the verse 27 of Chapter III.

Analysing the verse 27 of Chapter III, further one finds three key phrases therein : first is 'performance of all actions'; second is 'material tendencies or material guṇas' as different from self or SELF and the third is 'deluded by self-sense or ego'.

'All actions' imply that there is no exception. The important message which comes out is that if one wants to change the character of one's action, one must change one's material *guṇas*.

नैव किञ्चित् करोमीति युक्तो मन्येत तत्त्ववित्।
पश्यञ्शृण्वन् स्पृशञ्जिघ्रन् अश्नन् गच्छन् स्वपञ् श्वसन्॥ V (8)

न कर्तृत्वं न कर्माणि लोकस्य सृजति प्रभुः।
न कर्मफलसंयोगं स्वभावस् तु प्रवर्तते॥ V (14)

In the first place one must understand that material tendencies of a person is not the same as his/her 'self'. This 'self' is a microcosm of the 'SELF' the macrocosm and the macrocosm is not Prakṛti nor material tendency nor trait. *Guṇas* or material tendencies is a part of the body whereas 'self' is not. *Guṇas* are a variable admixture of three *Guṇas—Sāttvika; Rājasika* and *Tāmasika*—in different proportions. This admixture is peculiar and unique to each person. One is born with it. The Gītā calls it *Prārabdha* (the scientific equivalent, perhaps, is genes in the body). When the *Guṇas* interact with physical objects, desires, thoughts are born and actions are perforce performed, whether one likes to act or not. Further, all actions must be exhausted by living them out. No action can remain unaccounted or unexhausted. Every action must produce a result, sooner or later. It is a different matter that in the process of exhausting past actions, one acquires and adds fresh actions. One may cancel out the previous ones (from this life or previous lives) by the new ones. Both have acted and neuterialized each other leading to zero sum like a disease disappearing after use of medicine. Disease is the result of one type of action and recovery is the result of another type of action viz. use of medicine . The process of each action producing results is purely individual. No one else can do it for someone else. I must suffer or benefit from my actions, and nobody else.

One of the messages of verse 27 of chapter III and 14 of chapter V is that a self-realized yogī, or even God HIMSELF does not take upon himself the suffering or punishment for someone else's actions. There is no recognition or sanction in the Gītā for the system of giving power of attorney to the priestly class or *sādhus* and *saints* to take over the punishment for wrong actions by someone else. Both the sinner and the undertaker are deluded and egoistic. Neither the performer who engages the other on the basis of devotion and donation nor the undertaker understands the significance of prayer which is a pacifier, a tranquilizer and has to be preceded by ego-destruction. No one can and therefore, no one should claim to act as an intermediary between God and the sinner. As against this practice in India, passport to Heaven is issued by holy men in the West, for a price.

The most effective way of entry into Heaven of one's own perception is through righteous actions by oneself not only to neutralise the past wrong actions or sins but save some good actions to one's credit. There is an interesting story told about the famous Indian king Akbar and his prominent minister Birbal—considered as one of the nine jewels of the king. The king drew a line and asked his ministers and courtiers if it was possible to make that line small without in any way erasing it. All, except, Birbal as usual, were non-plussed. Birbal drew another line, somewhat longer, alongside the one drawn by the king. The king was greatly impressed.

In the same way, a line or a heap of accumulated sins can be shortened or reduced by a longer line or a bigger heap of accumulated good or righteous actions. In the context of performer of actions and the promiser of release from the result of actions, the way out is to impress upon, the performer of actions, the inevitability of past sins visiting him as also the desirability of good actions or righteous action in the present. Logic is simple. Past is like arrows already shot from the bow which cannot be recalled. One can make a turn-around in one's life by acting rightly or righteously in the present. Hopefully, acting righteously in the present will mould him enough to continue acting righteously in the future too. In fact, what is future now will be present, then.

The big important question is as to how can a person's actions, by *guṇas*—natural tendencies be changed from one type to another i.e. from wrong to righteous. It is a wrong and misleading notion prevailing in the society that nature or tendency is a fixed one and not subject to change, over a length of time extending from birth to death. A tendency does have a force but a counter-force can definitely be generated to change a given tendency or trait or strand inherent at birth or acquired later albeit slowly, gradually, and surely.

Lord Kṛṣṇa's imploring to Arjuna to engage in the battle, without faltering (in verse 31 of Chapter II of the Gītā) because he was a *Kṣatriya,* should be seen in the context of a fair fight and circumstances—action against inaction—not merely just Arjuna's role as a *Kṣatriya* the warrior defender.

Right from birth, one is exposed to a variety of influences which may not necessarily augment the material nature or tendency. Sources of influences may include, mother, father, brothers, sisters and relatives living as part of the family or outside the family. Thereafter the influence of friends, school mates, playmates plays its role. Teachers, the education, books, T.V., Computer sites, scriptures are other sources of influence. There is hardly a moment when one is not subjected to some sort of influence in one's interaction with the outside world—both animate and inanimate. After all what is the role of the *gurus* and education if it were not to mould a person's outlook towards oneself and to the world. Everybody's *guṇas* are undergoing a change for the better or worse and manifesting the change through one's actions. The admixture of three *guṇas* like body-chemistry is impacting the nature of actions. If the mixture of contents or ratio-proportion of its ingredients changes, it is logical to expect that its influence on the person concerned would also change. It is like a medicine affecting different disorders of a person differently. If that were not so, the Gītā would not take cognisance of such simple matters of life like food and sleep. Food and sleep, *inter alia*, not only provide vital energy but also impact directly the *guṇas* and therefore actions. There is the famous story of Vālmīki, who later authored the beautiful epic Rāmāyaṇa, but was earlier a dacoit. There must by many more examples of changes of *guṇas* and, therefore, of actions, all around us, only if we cared to discover and benefit form such examples.

In conclusion, one may say that (1) self is no doer. SELF does nothing i.e. He does not interfere with the laws of nature; (2) one's own *guṇas*, tendencies, traits or strands manifest themselves in the form of actions by producing first desires through interaction with physical objects, then developing these into thoughts and finally implementing these thoughts into commands for action; and most importantly (3) guṇas can be altered. An improvement of *guṇas* is not at will but slow as a result of following discipline. What the *guṇas* were at the time of birth is the destiny. Since it belongs to the past, it is indeterminable. What changes one may bring about through various influences belong to the realm of free-will. However, one must concede that all changes are as per laws of nature or laws of change. Therefore, changes must follow these laws and the resultant changes will be achieved accordingly. Man has the competence to change himself and his *guṇas* but not for changing the laws of 'change'. Everything changes except the laws of change. The free-will, therefore, has a parameter beyond which one may not tread.

If *guṇas* were not impermanent and changeable the whole discourse of the Gītā, which *inter-alia*, tells us to control ego, anger, greed, lust, desires etc., and to acquire peace of mind, an attitude of equanimity towards the entire creation etc. would have been an exercise in futility.

There is hope for betterment. Rise, improve and act.

CHAPTER 9

Work Without Concern for the Results

The famous verse 47 of Chapter II of the Gītā says:

> *karmaṇy evādhikāraste mā phaleśu kadācana*
> *mā karma phala hetur bhūr mā te saṅgo' stv*
> *akarmaṇi*

> **Meaning:** To action alone hast Thou a right and never at all to its fruits; Let not the fruits of action be Thy motive; neither let there be in Thee any attachment to inaction.

In the above verse, there is a very intelligent fusion between the Gītā's command for action without desire or motive of fruit on the one hand and the injunction against inaction or passivity, on the other hand. The practice of renunciation was being encouraged by Buddhism and Jainism. This was naturally not good for society at large. Society is a mixed bag of a lot of people—good, not so good and bad. If good people renounce the world of action, it is not difficult to imagine what sort of society it will become eventually. The Gītā harmonized or fused the two old doctrines, one of Karma and the other of renunciation. The Gītā advocates that *Karma* or action, *per se,* does not necessarily

---

कर्मण्येवाधिकारस्ते मा फलेषु कदाचन ।
मा कर्मफलहेतुर् भूर्मा ते सङ्गोऽस्त्व् अकर्मणि ॥ II (47)

produce attachment for the fruit of *Karma* or action. It is the attitude behind the action which generates attachment to the result and thus concern for fruit. Therefore, it came up with a solution that one must do actions or worldly duties but without being attached to or concerned about the result. In other words, *renounce not the actions but the concern or anxiety for the result,* by changing one's attitude, by being a *Karma Yogī* i.e. by joining or fusing the two—action and renunciation.

There is logic too in this essential principle of disinterestedness contained in the verse 47. It is not the same thing as lack of objective. It is an active policy of a *Karma Yogī*—man of action, not the passivity of a laid back man.

The phrase 'Work alone is your privilege, never its results' might sound quite contradictory, an exercise in double speak, unnatural, unreasonable and even ridiculous to a modern man whose only motive behind an action may be result flowing from his action. It is all the more so in the world of today when we are increasingly talking of result-oriented policies and action-plans. However, the real meaning becomes clear when one looks deeper in the matter. It is true that every action must produce a result. The cycle of cause and effect is always at work. There is no escape for any action from this cycle. This cycle of cause and effect applies both to animate and inanimate world. The effect of a cause becomes the cause of something else and thus the cycle continues. Every action must exhaust itself by producing a result. Problem arises when one desires the result—result of a particular kind—not just any result. Such an attitude gives rise to hopes and desires, leading to either excitement or frustration.

As a practical compromise, the advice of Lord Kṛṣṇa is to engage in action but not to be concerned about the fruits of action. The very word 'concern' implies anxiety for the fruits of action. In other words, the performer of action is trying to prejudge the outcome of actions. He has set his mind on a particular type of outcome or result to meet his desires. The advice of Lord Kṛṣṇa is against this type of attitude for the result or concern for the result because it is counter-productive. Desire-motivated actions lack concentration and are incapable of producing the best results. One crosses many bridges in life without fear even without being conscious of the fact of crossing the bridge. But when afraid due to concern for the consequence viz. falling off the bridge, the same person would waver and falter.

As soon as the desire enters the mind, the thought of possible success or the fear of possible failure starts bothering the performer. Both the hope for success and the fear of failure are sure to interfere with the performance itself. Hence, the advice to *delink the action from the fruits* or the results thereof. It does not by any stretch of imagination mean that the performance may become below standard or the efforts put in may become slack or half-hearted. On the contrary, the performer is free from one major distraction viz. attachment to the fruits of action.

The later part of the above verse (47) of chapter II, Lord Kṛṣṇa again warns against the tendency towards lethargy or inaction. His advocacy in favor of action as against inaction, dynamism as against passivity becomes more reinforced. It guards against any possibility of misinterpretation of His message of disinterestedness in the fruits of action, leading to aversion to action or providing an escape route to those who are not able to decide between action and inaction.

In practical terms, if one thinks of success, failure, profit, loss, fame or obscurity, while performing action, it means that his mind is wavering instead of concentrating on the action. He is worried about the outcome of action. Such an attitude or state of mind is not the attribute of an equipoised or a balanced or a peaceful mind and does not essentially lead to the best performance of action. This verse of the Gītā meaning that 'Work alone is your privilege, never its results' brings out that the work (action) and result are in two separate realms. The one (work) is in your control and the other (result) is out of your control. Even referring to work as under one's control may not be a fair interpretation of the verse. The word used is right or privilege which has the same connotation as honor. Performance of action has been elevated to the level of privilege. We, sometimes, hear noble people saying that to serve humanity is their duty as well as their right. There is a change of emphasis according to the persons involved in an act. Of late, we note that good institutions, while honouring distinguished persons with prestigious awards, say that the institution is privileged that the awardee has consented to receive the award.

To sum up, this verse of the Gītā implies:

a) Mandate for action,
b) Mandate against inaction,
c) Right to action does not extend to result of action and that the thought of result should neither impel you to nor repel you from action, and
d) 'Right' really means 'duty'.

Concern for result of action or for anything else for that matter is an anti-thesis of concentration. One can't be concerned about the result and still concentrate on the action to produce that result. Mind can not do both simultaneously. In trying to do this, mind is oscillating between the two possibilities like the pendulum of a clock continuously moving from left to right and from right to left. The two possibilities in the context are success and failure (in attaining the desired results). The former creates hope and happiness and the latter creates fear and unhappiness. Both ways, concentration is disturbed, Neither hope nor fear is justified at the time, when concentration is needed to perform action. The lesser the concentration becomes, the farther from the goal one is pushed. Is it not a net loss?

We are all too familiar with the homely advice which generation after generation has been given to posterity. We often hear parents telling their young ones: 'Put your mind in the work.' We do not hear parents telling them—'put your mind in the result of work.' The advice on the Western pattern 'work while you work and play while you play' is an even-handed advice between different activities. The advice significantly implies that at a given time, engage in one activity and must perform that activity alone to the exclusion of other activities. It is also said that it is not important what you do, what is important is how you do it. Therefore, in whatever activity one may be engaged in as part of one's business, occupation or profession, the art lies in doing it whole-heartedly with a steadfastness, as opposed, to a wavering mind.

To understand the logic behind the advice of Lord Kṛṣṇa given in the verse under discussion, one must try to understand the relationship or linkage between action and result. We have noted that all actions produce results. The problem arises when we think and try to focus on the type of results. No doubt there is a linkage between action and result, as there is between cause and effect. In our obsession with desires we try to pre-judge the result and this is where we go wrong. We wrongly presume that we know all the laws of nature which govern our actions and produce results. While assessing the outcome of our actions we believe, we have taken all the laws of nature into account. In other words, we arrogate to ourselves the knowledge of the process as to how our actions, being the cause, will produce certain effects. We assume a convenient linkage between our actions and results. Based on our assumption and calculations, we create hopes and start building castles in the air, so to say. A slight jolt of failure, or a rude shock of reality, brings down the imaginary castle to the ground like a house of cards.

Unfortunately, we are wrong on two scores. Firstly, we do not know entirely the laws of nature. We are also wrong in over-estimating our capacity to rightly calculate the impact of working of the laws of nature. We must accept that there is a lot more unknown than what is known, about the working of the laws of nature. This immense gap between what is known and what is unknown, is an important factor in our lives which makes our calculation inaccurate and unreliable. That is why, Lord Kṛṣṇa's advice to delink the action from its result becomes more convincing. To recapitulate, the attempt to pre-judge the result makes the mind unsteady and thus incapable of producing the best results. Right determination of result or fruit is not within the human capacity of knowledge or understanding of the laws of nature. Further, concern or worry about the outcome of actions is not only not logical or useful, but explicitly harmful. It dilutes concentration on action or effort being put in.

Examples of human calculation going wrong are commonplace in life—individual, social and economic. We often learn that individuals, corporations and governments, making certain important decisions after consultation with experts in the specific fields; discussions and deliberations in committee meetings to produce desired results *in toto*. When the results do not conform to the expectations, inquiry commissions are set up to go into the reasons for mismatch between the desired and the actual results. Similarly, politicians, when they lose elections, make efforts to discover the reasons therefor. Often, incalculable or unpredictable human psychological factor or shifting public mind and opinion are held responsible. Predictions about weather go wrong even with the use of supercomputers. Too little or too much rain, destroys agriculture and causes misery. Unpredictable weather is also known to have altered the outcome of great wars. Hitler is said to have commented during the Second World War, after suffering defeat at the hands of the U.S.S.R., that it is not Russia (U.S.S.R.) but the winter of Russia which has defeated Germany. Hitler must have miscalculated the impact of winter on his troops and the war effort. Thus, we have ample evidence of the existence of forces or of the laws of nature which human mind is not equipped to discover or contend with and take into account fully. Those who keep the existence of these invisible and incalculable factors in mind are more mature and prepared mentally to accept the results of their actions, as they come. Others, not so mentally advanced, meet frustration.

While taking cognizance of the invisible forces of nature at work, one must sincerely believe that nature is not partial against you. The result of your actions, even though not as per your desires or liking is the net outcome as per the laws of nature. Nature does not violate its own laws. Such a belief would make you more inclined to accept the result of your action as it comes to you and will not allow frustration or inactivity to creep into your mind.

It has not been said in vain that man's best-conceived and best-laid plans and schemes often go awry and the grief and pain follow, instead of the desired, expected and sometimes promised joy. It is the experience of individuals, institutions and governments that instead of achieving the desired goals; they land up with a mixed bag of desired and undesired results or worse with the result completely opposite to the desired one. The planner's scheme for helping the poor, at international or national level, for example, only produced more poor people. The planner might have forgotten to take into account factors opposed to the success of the plans, namely corruption by the intermediaries involved in the distribution of aid to the poor. Or the poor themselves might have diverted the aid money to the purchase of drugs, tobacco or alcohol, instead of food. There may be other invisible or unforeseeable factors in the pro-poor schemes or other schemes in general, which come in the way of desired result of an action.

An American academician, Steve M. Gillon of Oklahoma University, has come up with an explanation. He calls his formulation "The law of unintended consequences". He says, one cannot predict the results of any action, howsoever purposeful it may be.

There is an element of randomness in nature. Laws of nature are so numerous that all may not even be known to man, leave aside, being calculable by him. Human psychology is the biggest grey area. A good product may not take off the ground whereas a bad product may do very well. The buyer may wish to have benefit in the short-term and sometimes in the long term. This is true of the spiritual field also, wherein modern spiritualists are coming up with easy and quick solutions for all-problems, like fast food.

Some call invisible factors (to the man with a limitation of five faculties only) the invisible hand. A person with a scientific temper may like to rope in Newton's Third Law, which says, "To every action, there is an equal and opposite reaction." One would think and logically so, that as soon as an action is undertaken, with a normal projected result, the process of an equal and opposite reaction sets in, with a countervailing result, somewhere, sometime if not in the same field and at the same time. Communism intended to wipe out capitalism, did the job in part only and now communism itself seems to be on the way out, because of the opposition generated by the process of communism. A commonplace example is in the field of business. As soon as you bring out your product, the rival company becomes more active to dampen your efforts. On the positive side in the process of promoting your own business, you, unintendedly promote others' business also, for example, of suppliers and buyers—a good example of 'unintended consequences'.

The Gītā puts this phenomenon in a succinct manner through its unique concept of 'pairs of opposites'. For example pleasure has pain in its womb and prosperity has adversity in its womb. Newton's Third Law seems to be embedded in the philosophy of the Gītā. The above discussion shows the fallibility of prejudgments of the result of action because of unknown, incalculable factors, unintended advantages and disadvantages. Mr. Gillion, however, is at pains to explain that his formulation of 'Unintended consequences' is not a recipe for inaction. The Gītā too is a mandate for action through *Karma Yoga*. A *Karma Yogī* is doubly blessed. Since he is not attached to and not concerned with the results or fruit of action, he is better able to concentrate and he will not be upset with the type or kind of fruit of action produced because he did not prejudge the result.

Following the spirit of the Gītā's verse 47 of chapter II, one can only try to do one's job efficiently according to one's physical and mental faculties, operating in conjunction or harmony, at the optimum level. It will generate a positive feeling. Performing one's action to the best of one's ability is a satisfying reward in itself. Having driven anxiety and fear out of the mind, about the result, one saves a lot of energy which would have been consumed wastefully by these negative tendencies.

There is a famous story about the British Prime Minister Sir Winston Churchill. Someone asked him as to how he managed to get sleep when Britain was caught up in the crucial World War, he is said to have replied to the effect that after a day's honest work and before retiring to bed he would say: "Let everything including Britain go to hell". Sir Churchill worked hard to the best of his capability but at the end of the day, he was not concerned about the outcome of the war. He got the message of the Gītā in the right earnest. After honest hard work he would get his well-deserved sleep in addition to the final victory in the world war and a place in the world history. This is the right attitude conveyed in the verse 47 of Chapter 2 of the Gītā. Sir Churchill was not great for nothing. One may contrast it with the presumptuous over-confidence of Hitler.

On the practical side we have to agree that the formulation of an action-plan needs to be result-oriented. But while executing the plan i.e. in the stage of implementation you must be action-orientated i.e. full concentration on the act rather than on the result. In military terms, having decided the target, action-plan follows full steam, without concern for the outcome. The entire focus has become the performance itself. A worker or a soldier does not have to worry about the correctness or otherwise of the decision and similarly about the nature of the outcome. He must only focus on the performance of action.

There are numerous examples of concentration in daily life. A student preparing for examination does not pre-judge the result of the examination. His whole attention is focussed to prepare himself for the task with concentration and steadfastness of mind without fear or hope. Senior Executives give instructions to their staff not to disturb, to the extent, that incoming phone calls are also not to be passed on to him. It is not that he has become rude or arrogant or is not bothered about what goes on in the office. The singular purpose is to screen off himself in order to be able to concentrate fully on the task before him without any external disturbance. Having blocked other energy-absorbing channels the energy force gravitates into a single channel. Another familiar example is hitting the bulls eye while practising shooting. The whole idea is to concentrate on the bulls eye to such an extent that the shooter does not see anything else except the bulls eye. Such a level of concentration is expected of a good shooter in life who wants to fix his mind on things and goals higher than average. We are also familiar with the famous story of Arjuna about an incident which took place in Mahābhārata earlier than the dialogue between Lord Kṛṣṇa and Arjuna. As the story goes, Arjuna with his four other brothers, landed up in a **Swayambar* ceremony. The princess Draupadī, daughter of king Drupada was to be married only to the prince who will successfully carry out a rare deed of archery. There was a wheel on top of a pole rotating in a circular horizontal motion. Attached to the wheel underneath was a fish. The reflection of the moving fish could be seen in the cauldron of oil placed below. The prince trying his luck to win the hand of the princess, was required to shoot an arrow in the eye of the fish while looking at the reflection of the fish on the surface of oil. The story has it that prince Arjuna alone was able to perform this feat and thus got married to the

---

* Swayambar was a ceremony among royalties in ancient India wherein a princess would accept a prince as her husband, from amongst the princes gathered, after he fulfills the conditions laid by the princess or by her parents.

princess. This may not be indicative of a real life situation but illustrates the need for a very high degree of concentration to achieve positive results.

We have seen that concern for the fruits of action really means attachment to fruits which attitude acts as a counter to a balanced mind. There are numerous illustrative examples of this unique fact and its application in real life. Judges are debarred from trying cases involving their kith and kin. They are required to declare before hand if they have any personal interest in the case and if so request for transfer of such a case to another judge or court. The reason behind this principle is amply explained in the Gītā. Having an interest in the case, the trial judge, would be supposed to be attached to or concerned about the result of litigation, one way or the other. He can not be balanced in his thought process. His mind will waver. As against this danger the judge is required to apply his mind in a just, fair, impartial and a balanced manner without concern for the result i.e. as to how the result would impact the parties to the litigation. Another area of application of this principle relates to the medical field. A Surgeon is not expected to carry out a surgical operation on his near and dear ones. The logic is simple and contained in the same principle of detachment from the results of one's actions. A surgeon's judgement may not be fair or balanced as the result of surgery is going to impact his own near and dear one. His hands and instruments might shake while performing the operation because of the fear about the success or failure of the operation. The above two examples-of the Judge and the Surgeon-amply prove that the Gītā's golden principle of detachment from the result of one's action or action without concern or anxiety for the result has been appreciated in real life and accepted by human society, the world over. The above two prohibitions are observed and applied the world over. As stated earlier behind these two prohibitions is the need for detachment from result while performing action. It will be nice and sensible if the concept of detachment from result while performing action is followed in daily life by all.

There is still another way of looking at the concept of 'Action without concern for results' in a purely scientific manner. Time is an accepted fourth dimension, in addition to three dimensions of space viz. length, breadth and height (or depth). The present is the center point of time between the two lateral points viz. past and future. Thinking of past or future implies movement of mind backward or forward respectively i.e. in the opposite directions with reference to the centre point. Though we act only in the present thinking of result while performing actions, the mind is moving between the present and the future. If past memories of the actions performed are also bothering, it means mind is travelling in the opposite direction as well i.e. between the centre point of present and the past. The mind is in a state of constant flux. It is moving between present and past or present and future. It is not exclusively in the present. This is against the requirement for a mind to be under control and steady, for the best results.

If concern for or attachment to the result were advisable and capable of altering the result to one's liking in actual practice, in the real physical world, there would not be any failure in life. Everybody will be an achiever and a success story, which is not the case. Hence the inadvisability of the approach of concern for the result of one's action.

In brief, the Gītā's advice to perform actions most efficiently according to one's capability without concern for results is the most practical advice. It is a panacea for concentration and therefore, for the best practical results. It applies to all men of action, particularly the modern young man.

However, it is the concern for the result of action, the Gītā is advising against, not the concern about what goes on around you. An attitude of supreme or holy unconcern in the face of evil is not preached by the Gītā and can not be peddled as a virtue. Even, in law, silence is tantamount to agreement with a statement or an act which needs to be contradicted or opposed because the statement or the act is wrong. Unfortunately, this is the type of society, we are heading to, where opposition to the wrong will become more and more muted.

Concern for result while performing action is anti-thesis of concentration.

CHAPTER 10

Work Without Selfish Desire

Verse 43 of Chapter III of the Gītā says:

evaṃ buddheh paraṃ buddhvā saṃstabhyātmānam
ātmanājahi śatruṃ mahābāho kāmarupaṃ durāsadam

Meaning: Thus, knowing the *Ātmā* to be superior to the intellect, controlling the mind by the intellect, one must smite (hit hard), this mighty enemy, Kāma, which is difficult to get at.

The word *Kāma* is not to be interpreted in the narrow sense of sexual pleasure only but in a much wider sense to include all kinds of desires, *Vāsnās or Kāmanās*. It has been explained in the earlier verses of the Chapter III that senses are superior to desires; mind is superior to the senses and intellect is superior to the mind and above the intellect is the *Ātmā*. This *inter-se* superiority among desires, senses, mind, intellect and Ātmā has been kept in mind in the verse 43 for the control and subjugation of *Kāma* or desire which is described as mighty; very powerful and difficult to get at.

The control mechanism of desires has been popularly illustrated with the help of the analogy of a chariot. Horses

---

एवं बुद्धेः परं बुद्धवा संस्तभ्यात्मानम् आत्मना।
जहि शत्रुं महाबाहो कामरूपं दुरासदम्॥ III (43)

pulling the chariot are senses; reins represent the mind and the charioteer is the intellect, intelligently guiding all decisions. Intellect must control the mind and through mind the senses and desires. Or else the desires will end up controlling the mind. Use of the discriminatory power of intellect will determine whether one is a master of or a slave to desires.

Desires have been called a mighty enemy and difficult to get at because these destroy or atleast impair the knowledge and discrimination of a *Jñānī* by veiling his *Jñāna*. Desires when acted upon become pleasures of different types. Spiritual pleasures are of course, in the top category, followed by three types, on the pattern of dominant guṇas: *Sāttvika*; *Rājasika* and *Tāmasika*. *Sāttvika* pleasure may mean pain and restraint, like poison, in the beginning but is nector in the end. (verse 37 of chap. XVIII). *Rājasika* pleasures include sense pleasures which appear like nectar in the beginning but become like poison in the end. (verse 38 of chap. XVIII). *Tāmasika* pleasures are those which delude a person both in the beginning and in the end (verse 39 of Chapter XVIII).

Verse 37 of Chapter XVIII, the Gītā says:

> *yat tad agre viṣam iva pariṇāme'mṛtopamam*
> *tat sukhaṃ sāttvikaṃ proktam ātmabuddhi prasādajam*

Meaning: That happiness (pleasure) which is like poison at first and like nectar in the end, is *Sāttvika* in the nature of goodness born out of clear understanding of the self (due to self-realization).

Verse 38 of Chapter XVIII, the Gītā says,:

> *viṣayendriyasaṃyogād yat tad agre'mṛtopamam*
> *pariṇāme viṣam iva tat sukhaṃ rājasaṃ smṛtam*

Meaning: That happiness (pleasure) which arises from the

यत् तद् अग्रे विषम् इव परिणामेऽमृतोपमम्।
तत् सुखं सात्त्विकं प्रोक्तम् आत्मबुद्धिप्रसादजम्॥ XVIII (37)

विषयेन्द्रियसंयोगाद् यत् तद् अग्रेऽमृतोपमम्।
परिणामे विषम् इव तत् सुखं राजसं स्मृतम्॥ XVIII (38)

contact of the sense-organs with objects, and which is like nectar at first (in the beginning) but like poison at the end (later), that is declared to be 'passionate' (*Rājasika*).

Verse 39 of Chapter XVIII, the Gītā says:

yad agre ca'nubandhe ca sukhaṃ mohanam atmanah
nidralasya pramadotthaṃ tat tamasam udahrtam

Meaning: That happiness (pleasure) which deludes the soul in the beginning as well as in the end and which arises from sleep, sloth and negligence is declared to be in the nature of dullness (*Tāmasika*).

All of us feel always, in all circumstances incomplete and inadequate and search for that missing piece or ingredient that will make life complete or adequate. It is happiness that one misses. Happiness is the universal aim of every one in life. We search for it, even without knowing as to what we are searching for. But we seek it in the form of various pleasures. For sure, we can not succeed in our pursuit of Happiness in this way.

The Gītā is not for elimination or suppression of all desires. The Gītā is also not for destruction, renunciation, or rejection of life. It is for reconstruction or readjustment of life in general with the help of control of desires. Ṛight approach may lie in the compromise or arriving at a balance between abstinence and indulgence. Manu goes to the extent of saying that it is easier to control the senses after senses have enjoyed pleasures and one has discovered the meaninglessness and even the harmfulness of sense pleasures.

It has been said that man minus desires is equal to God or in the reverse, God plus desires is as good as a man. The state of desirelessness may be the highest aim or goal but that is not for a common man. Just as, some action has to be performed for mere survival, some desires need to be satisfied for the journey of life. These should be the means of life, not the goal of life. In fact,

---

यद् अग्रे चानुबन्धे च सुखं मोहनम् आत्मनः।
निद्रालस्यप्रमादोत्थं तत् तामसम् उदाहृतम्॥ XVIII (39)

minimum or inescapable action follows minimum desires. Even one may move somewhat further from the level of unavoidable or inescapable desires and enjoy pleasures in moderation so that one may know the essential nature of pleasure and be able to control the desire for pleasure, as advised by Manu. All pleasures have side-effects. They are habit forming and make one an addict. Having known the nature of pleasure, one should be able to say, '*deja vu*' or like Socrates, say on looking at the shop windows, "How many things I can do without!"

In the material world of a worldly man, money, property or other possessions are never enough. His goal of getting to a certain level, in terms of finance, goes on moving higher and higher. In fact, he is moving further and further from himself. From the level of necessity or adequacy he passes on to the level of sufficiency and superfluousness. He is not even able to keep track of his wealth or worth as they call it. The difference, all his mad efforts have made are the changes in the name of bank account holders. Various names have been replaced by his name. Probably he will never have the need or opportunity to use that money in his bank accounts. He is worried though, that it may not slip out of his hands and therefore he is protecting it. Amassing, protecting what is not needed by him. How different is his lot from a security man or at best a custodian or a trustee?

In the Indian mythology, the goddess Lakṣmī represents wealth, the goddess *Śakti* power and goddess Saraswatī, knowledge (*Jñāna*). While wealth can be stolen (or suffer a loss); power can be reduced or destroyed, knowledge or *Jñāna* has no such risk. Even sharing knowledge enhances rather than reducing it. Therefore increasing wealth beyond a point and make it overflow is not worthwhile. It is a doubly losing game in which one is caught. First, one struggles to acquire it and secondly one works to protect it. If the struggle includes wrongful or sinful activities or means to acquire wealth, it is a worse scenario. It is everyone's right to seek and realize happiness as his goal and, therefore, everybody's happiness is sacrosanct. Even a sinner has happiness as his goal. What sets him apart from others is that he causes misery to others. A person using wrongful means to acquire wealth falls in this category. Apart from religious philosophy that such a person can not achieve his goal of happiness, no social system should permit it. One cannot be allowed to build palaces over the debris of huts of the poor.

On the other hand, those who do not snatch others' happiness or still better, work for others' happiness are working for a higher desire, or without selfish desires (*Niṣkāma*) for the welfare of society.

Verse 12 of Chapter III of the Gītā says:

iṣṭān bhogān hi vo devā dāsyante yajñabhāvitāḥ
tair dattān apradāyaibhyo yo bhuṅkte stena eva saḥ

Meaning: The Devas, worshipped by Yajña will provide the desired objects. One who enjoys the gift of Devas, without offering (to others) is indeed a thief.

Verse 13 of Chapter III of the Gītā says:

yajñaśiṣṭāśinah santo mucyante sarva kilbiṣaih
bhuñjate te tv aghaṃ pāpā ye pacanty ātmakāraṇāt

Meaning: The righteous who eat the remnants of Yajña are freed from all sins but the wicked who cook food only for themselves, virtually eat sin.

The words of the above verses need not be taken literally but symbolically. Life itself has been compared with a long drawn out *Yajña*. Verse 12 implies that one makes offerings and obtains token *Prasādam* immediately after the Yajña and the desired objects in the course life, as a result of one's actions. The message is that the resultant objects must not be usurped by the performer of action alone but must be shared with others. It is not the visible effort of a certain person which produces a result but is the result

---

इष्टान् भोगान् हि वो देवा दास्यन्ते यज्ञभाविताः।
तैर् दत्तान् अप्रदायैभ्यो यो भुङ्क्ते स्तेन एव सः॥ III (12)

यज्ञशिष्टाशिनः सन्तो मुच्यन्ते सर्वकिल्बिषैः।
भुञ्जते ते त्व् अघं पापा ये पचन्त्यात्मकारणात्॥ III (13)

of collective invisible efforts of many. Many causes have combined to produce a particular effect or fruit of action. Therefore, the Gītā requires of members of society to offer and share the fruits with others. Those who do not follow this dictum have been termed as thieves—a strong word but well-deserved all the same. In the production of a commodity or product—agricultural or industrial—there are the silent poor behind the man in the forefront. Sharing in the terms of the Gītā could have meant, in the past, only commodities but in the modern world it would mean fair wages to other contributors. The second verse (13) would mean that ideally one should put oneself as a beneficiary of the fruit of action (Yajña) at the end. He would eat whatever is left after meeting the needs of others. Such a righteous person, no doubt, is modest and highly responsible towards society. He himself would eat last after feeding others like honoured guests. Naturally, he is freed from all sins.

The Chinese sage, Lao Tzu says this about such a man,

> "He disregards himself, and his self is increased. Because he desires nothing as his own His own is completed."

It is creating and contributing not acquiring and retaining, that makes a person great.

On the other hand, wicked or cunning people who are concerned about fulfilling their own selfish desires only eat sin. The word "sin" can have more than one implication. Actions of such people are sinful. Their achievements and resultant pleasures are in the nature of wages of sin. Since these wages of sin are entering the body of such people, so to say, their body system is bound to be afflicted.

Verse 16 of Chapter III of the Gītā says:

evam pravartitaṃ cakraṃ nānuvartayatīha yaḥ
aghāyur indriyārāmo moghaṃ pārtha sa jīvati

Meaning: The one who does not help to turn the wheel

एवं प्रवर्तितं चक्रं नानुवर्तयतीह यः।
अघायुर् इन्द्रियारामो मोघं पार्थ स जीवति॥ III (16)

(of creation) set in motion is evil in his nature, sensual in his delight and he, O Arjuna, lives in vain."

Inter-dependence or constant inter-change in the creation is a fact of life. One can not be a taker only. It has to be a two-way traffic. One must give back in some form or the other , to society and indeed to the entire creation, so that the wheel of creation remains in motion i.e. the creation remains sustainable. The emphasis is on exchange—give and take as against the parasital or exploitative tendency. Those who do not follow this principle, live in vain i.e. their lives are not useful for themselves or for the society.

It is correct thinking and correct acting, not the abundance of things, which bring about the right attitude. One ought to know what is enough and should be able to feel that it is enough. There is a beautiful story which may drive the point home. A rich person asked his accountant as to how much wealth he had. The accountant, having checked different account books told the rich master the amount of wealth he had and added that it would suffice for seven generations of the rich master. The rich master queried what would happen to the generations, thereafter. The accountant applied his mind and came up with a plan. He told the master that there is a poor religious person living on the outskirts of the town. If the master could give him food for a day, he can pray to God and get a guarantee that even the eighth generation will be taken care of. The master agreed, went to the home of the poor man with some quantity of food. When the poor man was requested to accept the food, he wished to check with his wife if there was already food in the house for the day. The wife confirmed that it was there. The rich man pleaded with the poor man that he might keep the food for the next day. The wife intervened and rejected the offer and said that there is a night between today and tomorrow. Why keep the food overnight, protect it for an uncertain tomorrow. The plan worked, the rich man got the message.

Therefore, it becomes evident that plenty does not give peace or happiness. It is not the sufficiency of material things or money but the mental attitude of sufficiency and security which is important in life.

> *"There is no greater sin than many desires;*
> *There is no greater evil than not to know sufficiency;*
> *There is no greater defect than wanting to possess."*

No education, discipline of mind or use of intellect is required to follow desires indiscriminately. But to resist desires, one must listen to the voice of intellect. Since only the intellect is capable of generating a red signal, or raising guard, one must develop and strengthen the intellect. Strong or intense desires need strong bulwark of resistance. A simple or a moderate desire needs to be fulfilled. However, if it is allowed to become intense, it is like adding speed (*vega*) to it and increasing the potential for damage on impact. It is another area where Laws of mechanical physics apply to human behavior. The impact of energy released when a moving body strikes a stationary object is directly proportional to the mass of the moving body multiplied by its velocity. Speed, Velocity or *vega* of the desire makes it more and more intense and difficult to resist.

Therefore, it should be the endeavor of a person, not to respond to a desire (or a situation) dis-proportionately. A steady or even a low key response as a result of a steady intellect is likely to reduce the intensity of desire for pleasure.

One may try to categorize pleasures as sense pleasures, emotional pleasures and intellectual pleasures. The commonality is that all the three types manifest human weakness and have their opposites. Most dangerous are, no doubt, the sense pleasures.

Verse 22 of Chapter V of the Gītā says:

> *ye hi saṃsparśajā bhogā duḥkhayonaya eva te*
> *ādy anta vantaḥ kaunteya na teṣu ramate budhaḥ*

Meaning: Pleasures derived (or springing) from the

ये हि संस्पर्शजा भोगा दुःखयोनय एव ते।
आद्यन्तवन्तः कौन्तेय न तेषु रमते बुधः॥ V (22)

> (outside) contact (of senses with objects) are sources of misery, and have a beginning and an end. The wise, O Arjuna, do not rejoice in them.

Four aspects of pleasures stand out in the above verse. Firstly, the verse relates to sense pleasures i.e. to the pleasures which spring from the contact of one or more of the five sense-organs with sense objects or objects which are perceivable by the senses. The five sense-organs are : Eye (sight); Hearing (sound); Smelling (smell); Tongue (Taste) and Skin (Touch). When one or more than one organ, singly or in combination, with other sense-organs, produce on the recipient mind (as different from intellect) a pleasing effect, it is called a sense or sensuous pleasure. The same or similar contact or interaction of the senses and objects may produce a different effect on different recipient minds depending upon one's own *guṇas.* The same physical sight, landscape or creation in general, animate or inanimate, may be perceived differently by persons with different dominant *guṇas.* The same sound, may appear low pitched, pleasing to some and high-pitched, noisy and displeasing to others. Smell can be attractive or repulsive depending upon the recipient mind. Similarly, the same food may taste hot and spicy to some and cold and bland to others. Touch pleasure may be as a result of physical contact with an inanimate object such as water in the process of bathing, massage by a machine or as a result of physical contact with an animate object e.g. cuddling a pet, holding a baby to one's breast, hugging, embracing or kissing a loved one. The most dominant touch pleasure, of course, is through cohabitation and act of sexual intercourse. Whatever is pleasing to whosoever, is a pleasure with all the concomitants, to him or her.

Secondly, the verse brings out the fact that all these pleasures are a source of misery. Thirdly, that they have a beginning and an end. In other words, they are fixed or limited in space (because of objects) and time (because of having a beginning and an end). They cannot be eternal or timeless. One cannot enjoy them at will because one has to struggle to procure them before one can enjoy them.

Such pleasures have to be supported and sustained with the company of not only objects to be enjoyed but also of friends and companions who would encourage more and more indulgence. Fourthly, the verse emphasizes that the wise do not rejoice in them. The attitude of the wise is to look at them as necessities of life to fulfil physical needs of body during the journey of life. These are good as a means to an end but certainly not as an end in themselves. The Gītā does not advocate or ordain a life wherein pleasures are out of bounds. Enjoy the creation, by enjoying pleasures as a means, to the necessary extent, but not for the sake of pleasures themselves. As the saying goes "eat to live, not live to eat." Thus, the Gītā provides a pragmatic philosophy to modify, and reconstruct life, suitably. A repressed desire is likely to bounce back in the face and damage one disproportionately more. All the same a reasonable enjoyment of pleasures is no cause for show and celebration. These are not achievements for celebration and rejoicing. If through delusion, one gets caught in rejoicing in these, it will halt the progress towards the higher purpose of eternal Happiness and Bliss.

Happiness is the missing piece of the puzzle which in man, gives rise to a feeling of unhappiness; incompleteness or inadequacy or emptiness. Happiness is not something which can be created or generated with or without the help of physical objects. It has only to be discovered with the help of self-knowledge leading to self-growth. If one can continue life's journey towards the goal of happiness, caring periodically for the needs of body—hunger with food; thirst with drink and sexual desire with cohabitation, enjoying beauty and music of nature on the way, the Gītā approves of it. However if periodical satisfaction of these needs converts into often and oftener attempts at satisfaction of desires, the resultant pleasures are sure to become a pain. Generally speaking, quenching thirst should not further whet the thirst or desire. Or else the feeling of emptiness would keep on returning with more and more intensity. And a deluded person would seek to remove the feeling with more and more objects. Unfortunately for the enjoyer of pleasures, the same amount of physical-objects, gives less and less pleasures as the time passes. The Law of diminishing returns starts functioning.

Verse 38 of Chapter of XVIII of the Çītā, quoted earlier, inter-alia, brings out the deceptive nature of certain pleasures. The pleasures called *Rājasika* appear as nectar in the beginning but prove poison in the end.

Persons with dominant *Rājasika guṇas* are active mentally and physically, are passionate and pleasure-loving. In brief, a mix of activity and pleasures-seeking pursuits make a *Rājasika* person. Naturally, because of their *guṇas* they are attracted to pleasures which have a veil of goodness about them. In the beginning, these seem to satisfy a genuine need of the body but have a tendency for converting the need into addiction till such time that the very human body these were intended to nourish and develop, becomes diseased and falls a hapless victim to these pleasures. One is caught up in the trap and the pleasures become the weakness and the goal of life instead of the means to a goal.

For example, a weakness for hot, spicy or otherwise tasty food for one's tongue or palate becomes a weakness. One starts consuming more and more of it, tries out different and new recipes to satisfy the palate, not the hunger or the body need.

Excessive intake, particularly of wrong type of food, cause diseases of the body. More people die at least in the western world of over-consumption than of starvation, though we may call, the death due to over- consumption, by different names given, to disease caused by over-consumption and wrong consumption.

Eye is another organ which perceives objects and thus can be a source of pleasure, for the perceiver. One gets attracted by and develops a weakness for a beautiful creation—woman, man or something else and may even fall in love with it. Wise men do not suffer such a weakness. That is why is has been said *"that it is impossible to love and to be wise."* It is the sensual, pleasure seeking physical love, that is the subject of discussion here not the love for God wherein the physical eyes have no role. That love is a weakness, is confirmed by the phrase, 'falling in love' itself. It is the fall or descent, not the rise or ascent of man. Wise, practical and successful men do keep out this weak passion out of serious affairs and business of life. Bacon said, "*Men ought to beware of this passion, which loseth not only other things, but itself.*" All pleasures involve perils and hence the need for caution. Sight-based pleasures are no less perilous. These produce attraction to a fleeting object of beauty even though it is known and declared by Bacon too that "*Beauty is as summer fruits, which is easy to corrupt and cannot last.*"

Even so, beautiful faces of women in history have been responsible for starting wars. None, particularly the powerful, can appreciate a thing of beauty in someone else's possession, much less a beautiful woman. It is also true that in a large majority of cases men who intensely love someone or a few, lack the capacity to love many. The inclination to love, in the really great people, spreads to love many. The Gītā goes a step further and asks us to love the entire creation even-mindedly.

Love, for someone else in a way originates in the feeling of incompleteness. One seeks in the loved object, man or woman what one lacks in oneself—completeness, happiness. But the spell of love breaks, when love ends, forcing one to think beyond the temporary magic of physical love. Marital love is designed by the society to help responsible procreation in addition to satisfying the body-need. Friendly love perfects it and hence the need to combine, (a) responsible procreation, (b) satisfaction of the body-need and (c) togetherness, as friends, confiding, sharing, helping through thick and thin. A healthy institution of marriage must provide for all the three plus more to help reduce the feeling of incompleteness.

Bertand Russel, said:

> "Many people when they fall in love look for a little heaven of refuge from the world, where they can be sure of being admired when they are not admirable, and praised when they are not praiseworthy."

Fed by the eyes, agitated by the mind and propelled by the desire to satisfy the physical body-need, sexual pleasure or sexual activity for the ordinary is normal. It calms the mind and the body albeit temporarily. As already discussed in this Chapter healthy sex is a necessity both for the individual and society.

In Hindu mythology, sex is not regarded as dirty. Hindu gods do have their spouses and progeny. *Ṛṣis* (holy learned men) also had their families. But one has to be wary of the perilous nature of pleasures and thus of sexual pleasure also. One needs to regulate the sexual activity and also confine it to one single partner. Intriguingly, man is worse than animals in the matter of sex. As we know, in the animal kingdom, the sexual activity is more or less seasonal. An animal practically seeks consent of the member of the opposite sex. If he or she is not in heat or does not give out or respond to a call for mating, the mating does not commence and the seeker turns away. But for man, the season of mating extends all the year round. Consent can be induced or even forced. Probably man and the animal are programmed differently in this matter, Man has other strengths but also has this weakness. To increase one's sexual prowess, for sexual pleasures, man resorts to many methods, including use of aphrodisiacs. Man wants to maximize this pleasure and make it perpetual enjoyment. There are treatises, including the famous Indian '*Kāmasūtra*', describing and depicting sexual activity as a form of art. There can be arguments for and against making sexual activity an object of human imagination and its depiction in different forms of art and in real life. On the one side there is an argument that God intended this activity between man and woman (or more generally between male and female) to be used as a means of procreation in order to provide a continuum in the creation to offset destruction due to death etc. It was not meant to be a source of pleasure and thus should not be resorted to for pleasure. The argument on the other side is equally plausible. Human body was not designed for playing golf, other games and sports. Fingers also could not have been meant for painting, sculpting or playing a piano or a sitar. While the male is busy discovering different methods for enhancing his male prowess, the female is busy discovering new methods of attraction by means of dresses, and beauty aids. Incidentally, the modern dress, revealing the tentalizing parts more than concealing them have given a ready excuse for fundamentalists in all religions to spread their wings.

The act of Sex, as long as it lasts, can give to the participants in the act an experience of elevation, esctasy, even an experience of bliss. But it is a pleasure all the same and cannot last forever. It takes away all concerns and worries from one's mind as if the outside world, for the duration of the act, has ceased to exist. Procreation might have been the object of nature, but man mainly resorts to it as a source of pleasure. Therefore, man has to be cautious against becoming a victim of it. Wanton love is harmful and dangerous both for the individual and for society. It develops into a craving and one seeks it more and more often with different partners. He contracts different venerable diseases. To the list of old sexual diseases, the deadly disease viz. AIDS (acquired immuno-deficiency syndrome) has been added. The victim walks like a dressed up corpse and finally the body drops dead. AIDS, as we know, if not checked can destroy a higher and higher percentage of society and even eliminate the posterity. Therefore, sex pleasure needs to be enjoyed in a healthy and responsible manner for one's own sake, if not for any other reason.

Hearing or perceiving a sound with the help of ears (one of the sense-organs) is one of the five human faculties. In conjunction with speech, the hearing faculty helps in communication and conversation. The nature has designed this sense-organ—ear—for a certain range of sounds. The ear cannot pick up a sound below the minimum or beyond the maximum of the range. Even within the range, certain sounds are pleasing, a source of pleasure, others jarring, noisy and still others neutral. One type of sound is popularly called music. But music too may be described as a noise produced in a disciplined, calculated or regular manner. Sweetness or pleasure of music, therefore, is attributable to the discipline and controls involved in its creation. According to one's perception, what is music to one may be noise to the other and vice-verse. That is why one is advised to convert noise of life into music of life. However, to the credit of music, Dr. Samual Johnson has said: *"It is the only sensual pleasure without vice."*

Probably the reason is that music takes self-control and discipline to produce it although some of the ingredients of sense pleasures, e.g. contact with outside objects; having a beginning and an end, are present in it too. It is pleasing, enhancing and enticing. It attracts a person and even makes him dependent in as much as he may need it regularly as a diet. On balance, one may say that sound music is a pleasure but not as devastating in effect.

Music as a pleasure is not only the least of vices but is being discovered as a means of mental poise. People use it, with advantage perhaps while driving and of course, while studying. Since it calms the nerves, it helps free flow of serene energy in the body. Some claim that music increases the yield of milk in cows. Lure of music attracts animals too. The legendary flute of Lord Kṛṣṇa would attract cows from a distance.

Music by itself may be devoid of vices but in combination with dance and more so in combination with wine it does not remain a harmless activity. The Mughal Emperor Aurangzeb, had banned all music and dance as he was against all types of laxity and frivolity. That might be going too far and branded as violative of individual freedom and contra-culture. But gesticulations of the body, gyration of the pelvic region, particularly accompanied by sexually suggesting or inviting words of the song is no fine art—either of music or of dance. It is a corrupted music for the pleasure-seeking mind.

Of course, to enjoy the music of nature or to listen to the sound of silence, one has to tune up internally without recourse to physical ears.

Scent or smell is registered by nostrils and conveyed to the mind. Its effect can be powerful. It can have a pleasing or a repulsive effect on the recipient mind. It is considered as one of the pleasures. It has all the ingredients of a pleasure present in it. It attracts and has its own spell. There is a multi-billion business of perfumes in the world. In the feminine world particularly, one's taste and status are judged by the perfumes one wears in the same way as one judges the other by the clothes he or she wears. It has been known to have been used for winning over the opposite sex and that makes it to an exquisite pleasure. In the field of alternative medicine, there are advocates of the power of smell. They believe that different types of smells can be used to cure some ailment and restore balance of the human body. That apart, regular use may lead to dependence, addiction and at a later stage, to craving which needs to be controlled and avoided.

In conclusion, one must know the price one might have to pay for pleasure. No wise person would like to pay an unduly high price for a fleeting sense of pleasure and in the process become its victim also. The *mantra for the modern man is moderation.*

We know from previous discussion that pleasures are born out of desires and desires arise from the inter-action of sense-organs (taste, touch, sight, sound and smell) with worldly objects. We search for Happiness but get lost in the world of pleasures and desires. Further, our narrow, selfish desires follow wrong leads and cross limits of decency, reasonableness, honesty, morality and thus become selfish. Such a desire, when fulfilled is followed by another desire. The process continues endlessly till one's own end comes.

As against this an attitude of selflessness towards work or undertaking one's work without any selfish desire implies living and working in the world, in a balanced manner, enjoying in moderation and working according to one's capacity with the right state of mind for the society. Selfishness leads to corruption, degeneration and eventually to fall. *Selflessness elevates and leads to experience of bliss.* It is all within the reach of the modern man, an executive, a professional or a business man as all are *Karma Yogīs*. A *Karma Yogī* can act righteously with mastery over desires, enjoy, fulfil his duties in different roles. The puzzle of life is solved for him with all the pieces falling in their respective places.

Be a master not a slave of desires.

CHAPTER 11

Work as Sacrifice

Verse 9 of Chapter III of the Gītā says :

yajñārthāt karmaṇo'nyatra loko'yaṃ karma bandhanaḥ tadartham karma kaunteya mukta saṅgaḥ samācara

Meaning: Except work done as and for a sacrifice this world is in bondage to work. Therefore, Arjuna (son of Kuntī) do your work as a sacrifice, free from all attachment to fruits of work.

'Work as sacrifice' is a preparation for selfless work. One does not expect any reward out of his action of sacrifice. He makes the sacrifice (or offering) with reverence, modesty, humility to God. Once one makes an offering of any object it implies quite a few things. First, one is not expected to make an unclean offering, which in turn means that no wrong methods or unclean practices have been employed in obtaining the objects offered. The stipulation that an offering should be clean by itself has a very

---

यज्ञार्थात् कर्मणोऽन्यत्र लोकोऽयं कर्मबन्धनः ।
तदर्थं कर्म कौन्तेय मुक्तसङ्गः समाचर ॥ III (9)

important message for society. One cannot be a pious person, a worshipper of God or deities and still engage in malpractices in life, in business or otherwise. Generally, people care for superficial or physical cleanliness but not the innate cleanliness of mind and soul rather than that of body alone. In support, we have a story from the celebrated Indian epic, *Rāmāyaṇa*. Lord *Rāma* (with wife *Sītā* and brother *Lakṣmaṇa*) during his years of exile in the forest was to visit an old and poor lady of a lower caste. This woman searched and found some wild berries to offer to Lord Rāma whom she loved and worshipped. In order to make sure that the berries being offered were sweet, she herself tasted each berry eating a bit of that. Berries part-eaten by a low-caste woman were not unclean because of the cleanliness of the mind and soul, informing the act.

Secondly, the offerer has disclaimed ownership of the offering, once the offering has been made. He has left it to the Lord to do what HE wishes to do with the offering. As is the common practice, only a small portion of the offering is given back to the offerer as *Prasādam*, while the bulk is kept back for distribution among the congregation or the devotees. Sometimes *Prasādam* is from someone else's offering so that the identities of the offerings and the offerers are dissolved.

If one expands this idea further, the scenario becomes very interesting. In addition to one's own effort, as per one's capacities of different faculties, society at large and God's creation in various forms e.g., earth, sun, water, air as also men and animals, in gross form or in subtle energy form have contributed to the fruit or physical object produced. Therefore, the offering (any physical object) belongs to all, in a way.

The fruit or credit for the fruit cannot belong to a single individual. So, the Gītā requires of us all individuals that we surrender or willingly offer it to God. For sure, God being devoid of physical attributes, does not have physical needs and, therefore, does not need physical objects to satisfy them. What HE does with the offerings made to HIM is to distribute these offerings to all, the offerer included. Propitiation of God, of *devas* through Yajña in the Gītā is only symbolic and need not be taken literally. It is sharing with God, *devas* and others i.e. with higher beings, equals, and lower ones albeit symbolically.

A commonplace example is a family where there are more than one earning members. Each earning member contributes or in other words, offers his or her earning to the seniormost member of the family or in the modern days, adds to the family kitty. The seniormost member gives out money from the kitty to meet family and social obligations. Of course, the other members have to have faith in his fairness and judgement.

It is also observed that even in a small family, the earning member gives his/her income to either the widowed mother or the wife—the most respected and loved one. By analogy, the most respected and loved one is God, how much better that would be?

Here is an interesting real-life story. There was a couple who would make a living by peddling their wares on a motorbike throughout the week. The couple would visit the Church every Sunday donating ten per cent of their earnings and managing their life with the remaining, ninety percent. They got settled in life, prospered in business, reached an income level far beyond their needs. Their visits to the Church continued and they gradually raised God's share from ten to twenty, then to thirty per cent and so on. The couple called God as their partner in business.

A stage arrived when the couple owned an industrial empire and did not know what to do with the income. They went to the Church and declared that God owned his business. They would only be HIS employees like so many others, offering everything and receiving back only their salaries from God's business. The couple started the business giving God—a small share of ten percent, increased HIS share step-by-step and eventually, God became the Owner and the couple became HIS employees, getting reasonable salaries to meet their needs. Hence the title of the story—God Owns My Business. This is exactly the spirit in which the Gītā's message of *Yajña,* sacrifice or offering of all one earns is to be understood and appreciated. Give HIM all, and He will give you what you do need for *Jīvan-Yātrā*—Journey of life. Gradually, with right attitude, one reduces oneself to the level of an employee. It is difficult to figure out how much knowledge of the Gītā, the hero and heroine of the story had. They, indeed, however understood the real meaning of the Gītā and shaped their lives accordingly.

If one goes deeply into the import of the verses 11, 12, 13, 16 of Chapter III of the Gītā, with an open mind, it becomes clear that the whole life is to be looked upon as a continuing *Yajña,* Wherein all the fruits of one's labor and work are offered as a sacrifice. The field of activity or household is an *Agni-Kuṇḍa* a fire-place for performing *Yajña,* offering sacrifices wherein actions are regularly poured as sacrifice. Rather strong words such as 'thief' and 'eater of sin' have been used in the Gītā for those who are selfish and do not see beyond themselves and are oblivious of the rest of mankind. This highlights the social angle or the social message in the Gītā. Nobody is overly useful and nobody is utterly useless in society.

Verse 11 of Chapter III of the Gītā says:

devān bhāvayatānena te devā bhāvayantu vaḥ
parasparaṃ bhāvayantaḥ śreyaḥ param avāpsyatha

Meaning: By this you nourish the gods and let the gods nourish you. Thus, nourishing one another you shall attain to the supreme good.

The above verse underlines the inter-dependence in society. The smallest cog in the biggest wheel or machine also matters. A

देवान् भावयतानेन ते देवा भावयन्तु वः ।
परस्परं भावयन्तः श्रेयः परम् अवाप्स्यथ ।। III (11)

factory can not be run by managers alone. Laborers are no less necessary. If brain is the top, brawn is the base or foundation. The latter's strength determines the strength of the structure. The verse can also be interpreted to imply that loyalty and sincerity in family or in business is a two-way street. The wise with a deeper view of life see in the service of others or doing good to them as serving and doing good to their own selves. All can share in the supreme good.

Verse 12 of Chapter III of the Gītā says:

iṣṭān bhogān hi vo devā dāsyante yajñabhāvitāḥ
tair dattān apradāyaibhyo yo bhuṅkte stena eva saḥ

Meaning: The devas nourished by sacrifice, will give you the desired objects. One who enjoys the gift (received from) of the devas without offering anything is indeed a thief.

The phrase 'devas' may be amplified to mean the various manifestations of nature in different forms including land, water, trees, animals etc. which contribute to life on earth.

If man only depletes natural resources without doing anything or offering anything in return to replenish these, it will be suicidal for the world and the action of those who are responsible for causing such depletion is like that of a thief. In other words, message of the verse can relate to all exploitative human relationships, and activities.

For example, a Landlord who fattens himself and lets the poor tillers of land famish and starve is no better than a thief. He is pilfering someone's hard labor. Bonded labor or slave labor in different parts of the world is the worst example. There are other examples of exploitation of one individual by another or of one social class by another social class. Different forms of unearned income are different forms of thievery. It transcends caste and class because there are parasites in all castes and classes.

इष्टान् भोगान् हि वो देवा दास्यन्ते यज्ञभाविताः ।
तैर दत्तान अप्रदायैभ्यो यो भुङ्क्ते स्तेन एव सः ॥ III (12)

Verse 13 of Chapter III of the Gītā says:

yajñaśiṣṭaśinaḥ santo mucyante sarvakilbiṣaiḥ
bhuñjate te tv aghaṃ pāpā ye pacanty ātmakāraṇāt

Meaning: The righteous people who eat what is left from the sacrifice are released from all sins but those wicked people who prepare (or cook) food for themselves only, indeed they eat sin.

The emphasis is on placing others in the first place and oneself in the last. As a responsible member of society you should ensure that others have eaten or atleast there is enough for everyone else before you yourself eat. This is still the tradition in society that all guests eat first and the host eats last of all. This can become part of one's character for all time. Contrary to this there are people who jump at the food or anything for that matter without bothering about others. Such are obviously selfish people. Their character shows both in peace and in crisis. The former type attain release from sins while the latter type incur and accumulate more sins. One only eats sin when the neighbour remains hungry. One cannot revel in joy when others nearby suffer in agony. In essence, the verse is against usurping, accumulation, hoarding by depriving others of their needs. Though society cannot be entirely even-handed in the distribution of resources among different individuals, yet a situation wherein some eat and live in luxury while others go through dire deprivation is a wicked society.

Verse 16 of Chapter III of the Gītā says:

evam pravartitaṃ cakraṃ nānuvartayatīha yaḥ
aghāyur indriyārāmo moghaṃ pārtha sa jīvati

यज्ञशिष्टाशिनः सन्तो मुच्यन्ते सर्वकिल्बिषैः ।
भुञ्जते ते त्व् अघं पापा ये पचन्त्यात्मकारणात् ॥ III (13)

एवं प्रवर्तितं चक्रं नानुवर्तयतीह यः ।
अघायुर् इन्द्रियारामो मोघं पार्थ स जीवति ॥ III (16)

Meaning: He who does not, in this world, keep on turning the wheel (of creation) set in motion is malignant (evil) in nature, delights in senses and he O Pārtha (Arjuna) lives invain.

The above verse brings out the most essential fact of life and creation. It is a give and take. There is a constant interchange *inter-se* among humans and between human life and worldly life. If humans stop returning to nature, nature will stop giving to or providing for humans. It is an integrated whole. Those who help you some way must be helped in some other way. It applies to individual life, family life, business life, social life and so on. Man feeds the cow, cow gives milk to man. Man plants a tree, the tree gives fruit. In other words, in nature's wheel or cycle of cause and effect, there is a constant movement, constant action. There is no scope for stoppage of the wheel i.e. inaction. It is everyone's duty to be giving a shoulder to the wheel so that it does not come to rest marking end of creation. Those who are evil in nature and enjoy sense-delights are actionless parasites. They do not contribute anything to society but fulfil all their needs from the labor of society, their lives are meaningless or nugatory. Such people do get spotted and earn no respect. They must whip themselves into positive action.

Many types of sacrifices are described in different verses of Chapter IV of the Gītā. These encompass all actions of body, mind and senses. Some offer sacrifices to *devas* while others do it to the Brahma. It seems puzzling when verses 26, 27, 28, 29 and 30 of Chapter IV of the Gītā give examples of persons of different levels of achievement or realization sacrificing physical objects, and even their senses like hearing etc. Study of scriptures; knowledge; *prāṇa* itself are offered as sacrifice into the fire of *yajña*. At a still higher level, the *yajña* itself is offered in the fire of Brahma, performing the Yajña of self-knowledge. Therefore the puzzle seems to suggest that sacrifice and Yajña are a symbolic practice (not a mere ritual) requiring persons of different categories or types in the society-householders to offer objects (acquired as a result of action of physical senses or faculties), *yogīs* who have acquired control of their senses to offer self-restraint, intellectuals to offer their knowledge of scriptures and other subjects. Whatever attainment or accomplishment one has got is not meant to benefit him alone. He should part with it by making a sacrifice of it for the overall good of society.

The beneficiary should be the entire society because society has contributed to his attainment in many ways. The Gītā encourages the give and take; this inter-dependence in society. Even those who have contributed more than others, need not and must not claim a bigger share. A really great man generates but keeps nothing or very little for himself, like the hero and heroine of the story.

While discussing the sacrifice of all objects—physical and non-physical, it may also be relevant to comment briefly on the animal sacrifice. This is an undesirable and a loathsome practice to say the least. A true religion does not teach deluging of temples of gods with the blood of beasts, least of all, human blood. The beginning of this practice could be based, in essence, on one's willingness to part with a prized possession—a goat or a sheep or other animal to appease a god, goddess for individual or even collective gain or avoidance of catastrophe or evil. There are mythological stories about sacrificing human beings to appease a demon or an evil spirit to save a village or a community. These underline the spirit of sacrifice for a greater social or community cause but must not be interpreted literally and practised in modern times. In some societies even now a marriage, birth of a child, or recovery of an ailing friend or relative is celebrated with sacrifice of an animal. Meat from the sacrificed animal or meal prepared from it is distributed among relatives and friends. It might have made some sense in tribal societies in the past, man can find better method of thanksgiving now-a-days.

Verse 23 of Chapter IV of the Gītā says:

gatasaṅgasya muktasya jñānāvasthita cetasaḥ
yajñāyā carataḥ karma samagraṃ pravilīyate

गतसङ्गस्य मुक्तस्य ज्ञानावस्थितचेतसः ।
यज्ञायाचरतः कर्म समग्रं प्रविलीयते ॥ IV (23)

Meaning: Those who are devoid of attachment, whose mind is established in knowledge, who work as a sacrifice to Lord, all karma of such liberated persons dissolve away.

The logic of the above verse is simple. A person who is not attached to fruit of action, who has self-knowledge and who, in that state of mind, can only be acting as if performing a yajña for the larger social or universal good, can not be bound by such actions. One is giving back through sacrifice or service of humanity to HIM what he has received from HIM through the medium of HIS creation—objects, faculties both mental and physical in the form of sense perceptions, intellect, knowledge viz. both means and ends. Since one is not the sole creator, one can not be sole user of resources also. One is only one of the many mediums of flow in the creation. If one tries to hold back or block the flow by possessing too much, the flow will find an alternative route. Holding back, too much accumulation, possession, cause problems, as too much of food intake, causes to the individual's body system.

The Gītā tries to evolve a man into a more responsible man, a higher being where his responsibilities include not merely himself, or his family but the entire community. An erudite reader of the Gītā may discern that the thought underneath the edifice of socialistic and welfare societies is the concept of sacrifice or offering one's achievements to a higher power. Perhaps it is more so in the case of communist ideology wherein everything belongs to the state. God or the higher power is the institution of state. There is no concept of individual, private or personal ownership of any form of property. One lives and works for the state. All his faculties of body and mind function for the benefit of the state. Even intellectuals, writers, artists, musicians, poets *et al* contribute fruits of action of their faculties to the state. They generate but do not possess. The state in its wisdom distributes, the fruits garnered from all its subjects or citizenry, equitably, not in the same proportion in which these have been contributed to the kitty of the state.

Thus the ideal form of communism is a mega and a centralized form of joint family system of India in olden times. Conversely, the joint family system is a decentralized form of communism or socialism on a mini-scale. The important difference however, is that in the philosophy of the Gītā offering or sacrifice is voluntary (though those who do not make sacrifices are castigated) and of one's own volition, while in the socialistic or communist society, it is demanded as per the state law and is given as such. It does not have the spirit of reverence for the recipient or the detachment by the giver for what is given. Instead of a sense of reverence or duty, fear fills the mind of the giver.

A welfare state may be considered closer to the philosophy of the Gītā as the elements of fear and force are missing. The individuals evolve themselves to a higher level with higher responsibilities, transcending their own needs to encompass the needs of a much larger section of society. Such higher self-realized souls contribute whatever is feasible, their wealth, time, energy, accomplishments of body, mind and intellect. They feed the hungry, provide shelter to the needy, provide free education, medical attention and most of all, love to the destitute—all as an offering of sacrifice to the higher power. It takes the sacrificer a notch or two higher on the path of self-growth.

The Vedic cult of sacrifices and rituals connected with such physical sacrifices are really not relevant in the context of *Karma Yoga* or Yoga of action wherein works done as sacrifice are in the nature of selfless works and benefits flowing therefrom are for all to share. In the Vedic cult the sacrifice as a part of the ritual may be symbolic to appease or propitiate certain gods whereas in the *Karma Yoga*, it is the attitude or state of mind behind actions. Recipient of the benefit is not a god or goddess but the creation of God.

Symbolic offerings e.g. of flowers, fruit, food etc. may have some purpose for some such as remembering the God occasionally but not much. Generally, speaking man tends to worship and make a token offering to all manifestations of nature which can give him something or take away something. In other words, it is either out of desire or fear. That is to say, the worship is of the power of nature. Man worships rivers, mountains, clouds, winds, trees, animals even tools of trade. A farmer worships his plough, an engineer (*Viśvakarmā*) his tools, a trader his balance and weights, a warrior his weapons, a student his books and so on.

It may be a good idea to start one's day with remembering God but the important thing is that godliness should pervade man's actions beyond morning, throughout the day. These must be selfless and fruit thereof should be shared not only with gods, and devas but the lesser lot viz. humans and those who depend upon humans.

Symbolic offering or sharing should translate into actual sharing. Till recently, the householders would keep some food away for different persons dependent on that house, and some animals e.g. cow and dog which are exceptionally useful to the man. In the changed social milieu, the concept of sacrifice has not changed basically or in essence but only in form. Instead of giving to the needy individuals direct, one may now give to the institutions who help and look after, for example, handicapped (physically challenged), blind, orphans and Gauśālās where cows are looked after. The attitude of sacrifice is the attitude of sharing rather than monopolizing. Happiness manifests itself best when shared. To be happy, make others happy. To be contented, make others contented. Mere tokenism or symbolism attended by show and publicity, as a result of social competition rather than faith in its necessity or efficacy, is not desirable.

Sacrificing and sharing is growing.

CHAPTER 12

Work as Duty

Lord Kṛṣṇa upbraids Arjuna for signs of cowardice, self-pity and shrinking from his duty, in the field of battle viz. Kurukṣetra. However to be fair to Arjuna, one may argue that his concern was that of a genuine peace lover, a person who was being bothered by qualms of conscience. It was not lack of personal courage but destruction as a result of war which caused a wavering of his mind. Arjuna, with sense of foresight visualised that war would imply killing of cousin Kauravas, other close relatives and honored *gurus* for whom he had immense regard. He pondered over other side effects of war, also.

Quite importantly, he is concerned about the mixing of blood in the family as a result of menfolk being killed in the war and their wives getting corrupted. It is a destruction of moral values in the family. It is a truth that war brings about disasters of several kinds. It causes shortage of resources. Marching armies cause a lot of destruction and indulge in atrocities on the populace, including rape of women. Arjuna's state of mind takes him to the wasteland of destruction. Therefore, he prefers to be killed to killing. He prefers to be begging and living on alms to having the pleasures which victory in the war would bring to him. He considers such pleasures stained with blood of his relatives and gurus. He argues that even if Kauravas have stooped so low (as to take up arms against their kith and kin etc.), why should Pāṇḍavas too act similarly. His doubts prevail and he lays down his arms. He is showing signs of renunciation (*Karma Saṃnyāsa*) rather than action and *Karma Yoga*.

At this juncture, Lord Kṛṣṇa commences his important task of teaching Arjuna and through him, the entire mankind, the correct philosophy of life in its various aspects. The Lord studies Arjuna's mind and prepares him to fight. Arjuna's wavering mind needs to be compared with the perpetually recurring predicament of an ordinary man. Another point is also relevant in practical terms. The decision to fight had been taken already after due consideration of all the factors. All efforts which could have averted recourse to war having exhausted, attempts were made to physically eliminate the Pāṇḍavas by burning them in *Lakṣāgṛha* (house made of lacquer). The Pāṇḍavas went out of the way to meet the conditions imposed by Kauravas, after the former lost in the chess game of gambling. Kauravas, refused, point blank, to accommodate Pāṇḍavas in the matter of division of the kingdom which rightfully belonged to the latter. Hence the decision for war. Armies had been raised. Just at the point when the war was to begin, the despondency of Arjuna was not justified. This war was not of Pāṇḍavas' choosing. It was a war of the last resort and a righteous one—to protect good against evil. He was not to fight for his lower selfish interest but for a higher purpose or in the larger interest of society, for victory of good over evil as a duty.

Thus it was not a mere physical act of fighting. There was a higher purpose behind it. That is how, the messages of the Gītā bring out metaphysical truths and explain as to how these can be made applicable to day-do-day life. The Gītā is not a mere philosophy of life-physical and metaphysical, secular and spiritual for the leisurely scholars with contemplative dispositions but marries it to a practical programme for self—growth and social betterment.

Lord Kṛṣṇa employs different methods to encourage Arjuna to fight. If one may say with due respect, He (Lord Kṛṣṇa) approached the problem of Arjuna's inaction on two different planes—lower as well as higher. He tells Arjuna that if he retreats from battle, other warriors would think that he had retreated out of fear and they would lose respect for him. They will associate him with disgrace and there is nothing worse than disgrace or dishonor. Further, enemies (i.e. Kauravas) will use unspeakable words about him and what could be more painful than that. As against such a scenario, he has a far better option, Lord Kṛṣṇa tells Arjuna. In case of getting killed in the battle, he will go to heaven. In case of victory, he will enjoy the kingdom on earth itself. Warning of disrepute, dishonor and temptations of kingdom on earth or abode in heaven are arguments on a physical-lower-plane to motivate Arjuna to put up a determined fight. [Incidentally, one may compare the above temptation with the temptation built in the concept of 'Holy war' in some religions. Participation in such a war is rewarded with pleasures in this world in case of victory and martydom in case of defeat.

These do not seem to work on the intelligent, sacrificing and peace loving mind of Arjuna. Lord Kṛṣṇa then invokes the concept of duty of a Kṣatriya.

Verse 31 of Chapter II of the Gītā says:

svadharmam api cāvekṣya na vikampitum arhasi
dharmyāddhi yuddhāc chreyo'nyat kṣatriyasya na vidyate

Meaning: Further, having regard for your own duty, you should not falter as there exists no greater good for a Kṣatriya than a battle enjoined by duty.

In the context of modern society, we may note two important aspects of this verse. Firstly, the emphasis is on duty. Duty implies not what I or you wish to do but what I or you ought to do. It is a *svadharma* not *Svecchā*-own duty not own desire or sweet will. The

---

स्वधर्मम् अपि चावेक्ष्य न विकम्पितुम् अर्हसि ।
धर्म्याद्धि युद्धाच्छ्रेयोऽन्यत् क्षत्रियस्य न विद्यते ॥ II (31)

Gītā is a document for life where emphasis is on duty/obligation, rather than right/claim. Duties and obligations in various aspects of life of different persons in different roles at different stations and circumstances of life are enjoined upon whereas rights and claims come by the way, so to say. Secondly, the battle as a duty is enjoined for Arjuna as a Kṣatriya.

As some religions have the concept of defender of the faith; Arjuna as a Kṣatriya prince, should be taken to represent, in the context of battle, defender of the good against evil in society. In modern age, Arjuna's equivalent could be the defence forces of a country. Defence forces are not expected to prevaricate whether or not to fight a war. As in the case of the war in the Gītā, a decision has already been made to fight after careful consideration of all relevant factors, Arjuna as a Kṣatriya or a fighter or as the armed wing of the society meant to protect it has no choice but to fight.

Armed forces or defence forces of a country cannot brood over the killings or bloodshed and decide, as Arjuna was trying to, that they would prefer to surrender. These considerations against the war were taken into account duly but consideration of greater good of society or national interests as these are called now-a-days, in favor of war far outweighed these and hence the decision to fight the war. Arjuna's dilemma was inopportune and untimely caused by selfish, narrow and even wrong considerations and perceptions.

If one can discern the representative character of Arjuna as a defender or protector of the good in society, one would not worry about the *Varṇa* 'Kṣatriya' mentioned in different verses of the Gītā. Doubt and confusion about the caste system would also dissolve.

Protection of good with the help of battle, if necessary, not renunciation was the professional duty of a Kṣatriya in the time of Mahābhārata or its equivalent viz. defence forces, in the present times. He was not to turn to asceticism but to fight the righteous battle for social good.

From arguments to turn Arjuna's mind from desisting to engage in war, Lord Kṛṣṇa moves on and transports Arjuna to a metaphysical plane to explain the true nature of soul and death. He had given an insight showing that death was but a stage in the long journey of the soul whereas the body was cast away like old gar-ments or like a vehicle which no longer remained usable for further journey. It explained the insignificance of death of which Arjuna was and all of us remain mortally afraid. To enable the inexhaustible soul to continue on its journey and to arrive at its destination of *Brahma*, different modes of life or disciplines mainly *Karma Yoga; Jñāna Yoga, Bhakti Yoga* have been described in the Gītā. All take one to the destination or to the top of the mountain as if by different routes. All paths and travellers meet and merge at the destination. The most popular and pragmatic is Karma Yoga—Yoga of action. Though the discipline to generate a right state of mind for betterment of self is necessary here too, it comparatively gives the practitioner or the follower a greater degree of elbow room.

In verse (1) of Chapter V of the Gītā, Arjuna, based on his doubt, poses a question as to which is better between the renunciation of works and their unselfish performance.

The verse (1) of Chapter V, the Gītā says:

Arjuna uvāca
saṃnyāsaṃ karmaṇāṃ kṛṣṇa punar yogaṃ ca śaṃsasi yac
chreya etayor ekaṃ tan me brūhi suniścitam

Meaning: You praise, O Kṛṣṇa, the renunciation of works and again their unselfish performance. Tell me definitely which one is better of these two.

Responding to the question, Lord Kṛṣṇa, clarifies, in verse (2) of Chapter V, that like two routes leading to the same destination, both renunciation i.e. *Karma saṃnyāsa* and unselfish performance of actions i.e. *Karma Yoga* lead to the soul's salvation. But of the two, the unselfish performance of works is better than their renunciation.

अर्जुन उवाच
संन्यासं कर्मणां कृष्ण पुनर् योगं च शंससि ।
यच्छ्रेय एतयोर् एकं तन् मे ब्रूहि सुनिश्चितम् ॥ V (1)

The verse (2) of Chapter V, the Gītā says:

śrībhagavānuvāca
saṃnyāsaḥ karmayogaśca niḥśreyasakarāv ubhau
tayos tu karmasaṃnyāsāt karmayogo viśiṣyate

Meaning: The renunciation of works and their unselfish performance both lead to soul's salvation (or Brahma). But (if one has to make a choice) the unselfish performance of works is better than their renunciation.

It comes out that the route of renunciation is not in the interest of an active society. It is commonly said that only those who stir out and act are likely to make mistakes. With guidance, discipline, training and practice they will learn and improve in their endeavor. The Gītā is not for a microscopic minority of renunciates or ascetics but for the large majority of active members of society. It is their conduct or way of life which is more relevant for the health of the society. A minority can guide but cannot replace the majority in society. The latter has to engage in action both in peace and in war. Thus it is their mental makeup or state of mind and their motivation which will determine the nature of their action. Nature of work, in turn, will impact society accordingly. Work performed as duty is righteous and, therefore, required of members of a healthy society. Such work does not bind but releases one from the bondage of cause and effect.

Duty in peace or normal times takes various forms depending upon the role one is playing or the hat one is wearing. One has duty to elders, family, friends and society. Duty must be performed earnestly and not be merely for show as a formality. The fact is one actually takes it as a burden. No doubt, in the context of modern society, it is a delicate balancing act like that of a dancing girl adjusting and dancing to different tunes. Attitude of duty would make the task easy and the performer cheerful.

श्रीभगवानुवाच
संन्यासः कर्मयोगश्च निःश्रेयसकराव् उभौ।
तयोस तु कर्मसंन्यासात् कर्मयोगो विशिष्यते ॥ V (2)

Now let us discuss the duty in abnormal situations. Most Hindu gods are depicted as carrying weapons along with other objects in their hands. The concept behind the practice seems to underline the fact that gods too have many roles as their worshippers do and they may have to resort to violence, sometimes, to save good against evil, in the larger interest of society. To have peace, one has to be ostensibly prepared for war, without cowardice and selfish concern for result creeping in. Even in the day-to-day life, when one's life, life of family members or their honor is threatened, the first reaction is to put up one's own defence and fight. One may even injure or even kill the aggressor in the process. The law gives the right of self-defence even with use of weapons. The American constitution gives rights to U.S. citizens to bear arms.

Extending the argument to the battle of Kurukṣetra, (in the epic of Mahābhārata), it was amply justified, it being a battle in defence of good which was under constant attack by evil, in various ways. Arjuna was required to act not to sulk. Fighting, in the context of a righteous war was his duty. It was not mad violence but a calculated decision, taken in the interest of society, to fight to protect good in society, as a surgeon, in his calm judgement decides to remove a cancerous growth from a patient's body with the help of a surgical operation to restore the patient to health and help him to lead a normal life. But the surgeon is not rejoicing carrying out the surgery. Nor does a soldier rejoice in the killings in the battle. Both are doing their respective duties. In case of operation being unsuccessful, the surgeon does not get any punishment because he did his duty efficiently. Similarly, the soldier or the general-in-charge does not get punishment if the war is lost.

The example of an executioner carrying out the sentence of capital punishment by hanging or electrocution makes the point more clear. He is just carrying out or discharging his duty attached to his job. He does not enjoy or rejoice in it at all. He is not punished for it. On the contrary, he may be punished if he does not do it properly. No one ever has heard the executioner being blamed by the relatives of the executed for the sentence although in purely physical terms it is he who has for sure, 'killed' the prisoner.

Work as duty is one form of *Karma Yoga* which leads to the destination and whereby one is delivered from the bondage of cause and effect or life and death. Death in the battlefield of Kurukṣetra or in the larger righteous battle of life, can ensure attainment of Brahma.

Verse 7 of Chapter VIII of the Gītā says:

tasmāt sarveṣu kāleṣu mām anusmara yuddha ca
mayy arpitamanobuddhir mām evai'ṣyasy asaṃśayam

> **Meaning:** Therefore at all times, remember ME and fight. When your mind and understanding are set on ME to ME alone shall you come without doubt.

One can remember Him at the time of death in the field of one's respective duty, only if one models and lives a life in His image.

Only disciplined and genuine devotion devoid of material desires, rather His reflection in all activities of life, can make one capable of remembering Him at the time of death and thus getting release from bondage. It cannot be the short-term practice merely out of pragmatism, that can deliver. Last minute or death-bed repentance is far less potent for the purpose.

The word 'fight' in this verse in chapter VIII cannot be taken literally. The chapter VIII deals with cosmic evolution and, therefore, the fight should also have a cosmic dimension. Whatever separates a person from the cosmic whole is ignorance and has to be fought and gotten over.

As man's existence is on different planes—physical, mental, spiritual and metaphysical, so is his duty. One has a multitude of duties and an intelligent and responsible man responds to them all. That makes him a complete man. The Arena or field of duty or Dharma kṣetra is all-encompassing. It can take care of one's duties in all aspects of life and all roles one is required to perform. The message of the Gītā is to treat all actions (karma) as duty (dharma) so that the field of action—*Karma kṣetra* becomes the field of duty—*Dharma kṣetra*.

Perform actions as your duty, reward is self-fulfilment.

तस्मात् सर्वेषु कालेषु माम् अनुस्मर युद्ध च ।
मय्य् अर्पितमनोबुद्धिर् माम् एवैष्यस्य् असंशयम् ॥ VIII (7)

CHAPTER 13

Pairs of Opposites

In order to remove the confusion and conflict in the mind of Arjuna, who is hesitant to fight in the battlefield of Kurukṣetra, Lord Kṛṣṇa, tackles in different Chapters of the Gītā, various basic reasons—ignorance, wrong assumptions, illusions etc. which are at the root of confusion and conflict. What affects the mind of Arjuna, indeed, affects the minds of one and all. One of the reasons for confusion and conflict which make life unpleasant, even miserable, is our misunderstanding of the pairs of opposites in the phenomenal world. Thc Gītā commands us to rise above the pairs of opposites and acquire an attitude of even-mindedness or equanimity towards all aspects of life even though they may appear to be opposing in nature.

Verse 14 of Chapter II of the Gītā says:

mātrāsparśās tu kaunteya śītoṣṇa sukha duḥkhadāḥ
āgamāpāyino'nityās tāṃs titikṣasva bhārata

Meaning: The contacts of the senses with the sense-objects give rise to the feelings of heat and cold and pain and pleasure.

मात्रास्पर्शास् तु कौन्तेय शीतोष्णसुखदुःखदाः।
आगमापायिनोऽनित्यास् तांस तितिक्षस्व भारत॥ II (14)

They are transitory and impermanent. Therefore, learn to endure them—O Arjuna.

Verse 15 of Chapter II of the Gītā says:

yaṃ hi na vyathantyete puruṣaṃ puruṣarṣabha
sama duḥkha sukhaṃ dhīraṃ so'mṛta tvāya kalpate

Meaning: Because the calm person who is not afflicted by these feelings and is steady in pain and pleasure, becomes fit for immortality, O Arjuna.

The context is hesitancy on the part of Arjuna to fight in the war-theatre of Kurukṣetra, Lord Kṛṣṇa has earlier explained the fallacy of the phenomenon of death and now He is explaining the fallacy of the phenomenon of the pairs of opposites in the world.

This thought is developed in subsequent Chapters of the Gītā taking it to higher and still higher planes of human personality and embracing all of its relationships with humans, animals and even the inanimate part of the world.

Two rather basic facts or realities about the pairs of opposites– may it be on a physical-body plane or emotional plane or intellectual plane—must be clearly understood. First, that Mother Nature's Womb is incapable of producing or generating anything without simultaneously generating or bringing into being its opposite. *It is a two-some game nature has invented for us to play.* Secondly, it is the transitory or impermanent nature of all phenomena. *One phenomenon yields to another—its opposite,* in the course of time. All are subject to cyclical changes. One cycle may have a particular duration that may vary from that of others. It may also undergo a variation in its own duration, over a period of time.

यं हि न व्यथन्त्येते पुरुषं पुरुषर्षभ।
समदुखःसुखं धीरं सोऽमृतत्वाय कल्पते॥ II (15)

The famous Chinese Philosopher Lao Tzu expresses the thought somewhat as follows :

"A whirlwind does not last a whole morning."
"A downpour of rain does not last a whole day."

The English Poet Shelly in his immortal poem "Ode to the West Wind" says: *"If winter comes, can spring be far behind?"*

In other words, one yields place to the other on a continuing basis. Thus, it may not be wrong to compare the opposites to the two sides of the same coin. When we see or experience one side, the other side is also right there behind it. It is also said that the obverse of a Great Truth is not a Great Lie but another Great Truth. Either both exist or neither has an existence.

Rudyard Kipling has beautifully brought out the concept of equanimity in the following verses of his poem:

"If you can dream – and not make dreams your master;
If you can think – and not make thoughts your aim;
If you can meet with Triumph and Disaster
And treat those two impostors just the same.
If you can make one heap of all your winnings
And risk it on one turn of pitch-and-toes,
And lose, and start again at your beginnings
And never breathe a word about your loss."

Some of the popularly known pairs of opposites, mentioned in the Gītā, or referred to elsewhere are : like and dislike; pleasure and pain; joy and sorrow; victory and defeat; heat and cold; honor and dishonor; love and hate; attraction and aversion. The list can go on endlessly. The pain of child-birth is quickly replaced by the pleasure of having a child. Happiness in meeting one's dear ones is replaced by the sadness at the prospect of their departure, as if it were waiting in the wings, so to say, to take over. Bright faces change into sad and serious ones. Pleasure has pain in its womb and vice-versa. The same applies to prosperity and adversity.

Again the Chinese philosopher, Lao Tzu says:

> "that if every one in the world calls the beautiful as beautiful, thereby the ugly is already generated." Similarly, Lao Tzu says:

> "If every one in the world regards the good as good, as a result, the non-good is already brought into existence."

Create one, the opposite is created automatically. More significantly, erase or eliminate one, its opposite too is eliminated automatically without any effort.

In preaching to Arjuna and indeed to us all, Lord Kṛṣṇa is trying to transport us and expose us to the laws of a higher planes of existence—from the world of attributes to the world where attributes are absent; from the *Saguṇa* to *Nirguṇa* God and His World. It is a part of a step by step, upward journey through which the Gītā takes the reader.

The above-quoted Chinese philosopher, Lao Tzu also points out the complementary nature of the pairs of opposites. He says:

> "Heavy and light complete each other. Long and short share each other. High and deep convert each other. Before and after follow each other."

Neither has any existence or meaning without the other. As the Gītā says, there is death because there is life and conversely there is life because there is death. Why celebrate one and grieve over the other. All existence is generated or comes out of non-existence and vice-versa. From unmanifest to manifest and from manifest back to unmanifest—a cycle though with duration of some billion years.

Pairs of opposites also serve to educate man in their own peculiar way. One would not appreciate happiness if one has not experienced unhappiness or appreciate sufficiency if one has not gone through deficiency. In a way, the existence of one phenomenon should make one aware, appreciative and prepared to face the existence of its opposite.

Einstein said: "*Opportunities lie in the middle of difficulties.*" Similarly, prosperity has in it the seed of adversity and vice-versa. It has also been said that "*some defeats are more important than victories*". In a wise man, this gives rise to a desire to move beyond and above the world of opposites. Since, the way the world is, one cannot simply wish away the opposites in the world but may succeed, with effort, to a higher mental plane where one's mind is not deceived or deluded by the presence of opposites even though these are present merely as appearances.

In verse 22 of Chap. IV of the Gītā, a person though engaged in action is advised to remain unaffected by dualities viz. pairs of opposites e.g. success and failure.

Verse 22 of Chapter IV, the Gītā says:

yadṛcchā lābha saṃtuṣṭo dvandvātīto vimatsaraḥ
samaḥ siddhāv asiddhau ca kṛtvāpi na nibadhyate

Meaning: Content with whatever gain comes his way by grace of God, remaining unaffected by dualities, free from jealousy and even-minded towards success and failure, though engaged in work, such a person is not bound by (i.e. is free) from the cycle of cause and effect.

Verse 3 of Chap. V of the Gītā elevates a person who has risen above dualities, to the level of a true renunciate or a *Saṃnyāsī* and qualified to be free from bondage, which otherwise would result from actions performed.

It (Verse 3 of Chapter V) says:

jñeyaḥ sa nityasaṃnyāsī yo na dveṣṭi na kāṅkṣati
nirdvandvo hi mahāabāho sukhaṃ bandhāt pramucyate

Meaning: A person is to be considered to have qualified as a true *Saṃnyāsī* (or renunciate – renouncer of actions) who neither

---

यदृच्छालाभसंतुष्टो द्वन्द्वातीतो विमत्सरः।
समः सिद्धाव् असिद्धौ च कृत्वापि न निबध्यते॥ IV (22)

ज्ञेयः स नित्यसंन्यासी यो न द्वेष्टि न काङ्क्षति।
निर्द्वन्द्वो हि महाबाहो सुखं बन्धात् प्रमुच्यते॥ V (3)

hates nor loves. Because, having become free from dualities, O'mighty armed-one (Arjuna), one is freed from bondage (otherwise caused by action).

Verse 18 of Chap. V of the Gītā, takes the concept of non-duality and the attitude of equanimity to a larger field and to a higher level by including the animals into the field of vision of the mind of an equanimous person.

The verse 18 of Chapter V, the Gītā says:

vidyāvinayasaṃpanne brāhmaṇe gavi hastini
śuni caivaśvapāke ca paṇḍitāḥ samadarśinaḥ

Meaning: A learned and cultured Brahmin; a cow; an elephant; a dog and an outcast are viewed even-mindedly by the wise.

This lofty thought in the verse implies that one should rise high enough to a level in the world wherefrom he sees the entire creation—humans of all classes and categories with different or no endowments, *Sāttvika, Rājasika* or *Tāmasika* by nature, as also the animals of various species, useful, not useful, harmful, clean or dirty—as if on an equal plane of existence. Reason is simple. But this simple reason is of a very high order. The accomplished, the wise, see unity behind diversity and oneness in the multitudinous variety of creation. The same mother nature or God is responsible or is the cause for the entire creation. It cannot be likeable in part only. In the mother, all children though differently endowed and different in appearance, arouse similar emotions of love and affection.

A poet, through his poetic humour, also comes to the rescue of the ignorant and ugly, blaming the creator for the fault, not the creation. One of the Rubaiyat of the famous Persian poet, Omar Khayyam, translates roughly as: *None answered this. After silence, however, a pot of not-so-good a shape, spoke thus, "They sneer at me for leaning awkwardly; What ! did the Hand of the Potter then shake?"*

विद्याविनयसंपन्ने ब्राह्मणे गवि हस्तिनि।
शुनि चैव श्वपाके च पण्डिताः समदर्शिनः॥ V (18)

The attitude of equanimity is not only useful but is a pre-requisite for all routes of spiritual journey. It may be the route of *Karma Yoga* (Yoga of Action); *Jñāna Yoga* (Yoga of Knowledge); *Saṃnyāsa Yoga* (Yoga of Renunciation) or *Dhyāna Yoga* (Yoga of Meditation). That is why, one finds discussion on equanimity of mind in all the relevant Chapters of the Gītā.

While selfless action qualifies a person to be a *Karma Yogī*, one must additionally imbibe the attitude of equanimity to proceed further on the spiritual journey.

The thought is further developed in verse 7 of Chapter VI.

Verse 7 of Chapter VI, the Gītā says:

jitātmanaḥ praśāntasya paramātmā samāhitaḥ
śītoṣṇasukhaduḥkheṣu tathā mānāpamānayoḥ

Meaning: When one has conquered one's self (i.e. lower self, lower nature or senses) and has attained to the state of self-mastery (i.e. self-control) and is steadfast in the supreme self, he is at peace in cold and heat, in pleasure and pain, in honor and dishonor.

This particular verse is of special significance and is full of deep meaning. It brings out that in order to acquire an attitude of even-mindedness, one needs to attain peace through control of senses (lower-self) and become steadfast in the supreme. Peace and equanimity have their roots in self-control. The three specific pairs of opposites viz. cold and heat; pleasure and pain; honor and dishonor mentioned in the verse 7 of Chapter of VI are not chosen at random. These have been selected and used very intelligently, to bring home the point that the heat and cold pertain to the plane of physical body or person, pleasure and pain pertain to the emotional plane of a person and honor and dishonor pertain to the intellectual plane of a person. The verse, therefore, implies that a person is truly equanimous in his attitude when

---

जितात्मनः प्रशान्तस्य परमात्मा समाहितः।
शीतोष्णसुखदुःखेषु तथा मानापमानयोः॥ VI (7)

he is not affected by pairs of opposites on any plane. It is a steady upward movement from lower to higher levels. In the process of getting over the pairs of opposites, operating at the physical level is easier as compared to those operating at the emotional level. Overcoming the pairs of opposites at the emotional level is easier than those at the intellectual level. Conquering the pairs of opposites at the intellectual plane is the most difficult task.

It is more difficult to overcome the temptation of being concerned about the suffering of those whom one loves than about one's food and clothing. For example, people with an unselfish attitude towards life sacrifice willingly good food and clothing, undergo other physical discomforts, (i.e. become even-minded towards tasty and insipid food and towards good and ordinary clothes) for a good cause but would not be willing to abandon attachment to their families. However, as a result of steady self-growth one may reach the stage where attachment to the family also vanishes and its happiness or opposite i.e. unhappiness ceases to bother him unduly. Even such a person—who is out of the ordinary—would care about name, fame, praise and censure; honor and dishonor. Great personalities, in the material and spiritual world are not only unable to overcome the weakness for fame, they consciously work towards that end. They want a following and fame in their lifetime and statues, memorials and monuments built even when they are gone. A Roman Statesman said, "*I would much rather have men ask why I have no statue than why I have one*?" A truly wise person is put off by glorification as by condemnation or vilification. Fortune and fame are impermanent. Worse still, they, like flirts, are insincere and do not stay with one person howsoever one may love them. On the contrary, the more one loves them, the greater are the chances of their desertion.

Swami Vivekanand said: "*Fortune is like a flirt. She will run away from you when you want her, but if you are not interested in her, she will come chasing you.*". Only when one has risen above the pairs of opposites on all the three levels, may one qualify to be called equanimous in attitude.

Verse 9 of the same Chapter VI, extends the scope of equanimity to a much larger circle of human relationships. It says: "*A person is considered superior, who is impartial towards companions, friends, enemies, neutrals, haters, relatives, saints and sinners.*" The verse seeks to demolish barriers/dividers or distinction between different categories of human relationships. In the world of the even-minded, friends and foes; saints and sinners are on the same pedestal. None is loved and none is hated. None is lofty and none is low. It is not a mere empty statement of philosophy but is backed by strong logic. All religious disciplines, supported by scientific knowledge and enquiry, agree that the entire creation is one and that there is only one creator. If so the same creation cannot be partly good and partly bad. All beings are images of the same supreme being. In other words, the multitude of forms has sprung from the single formless or in other words, the multitude of manifestations is born out of the one and the same unmanifest. Guru Nanak emphatically said that in the world entirely created out of the same energy source or energy ("*noor* literally" meaning 'light'), how can there be some creation which is good or noble and the other bad or evil.

Further, because equanimity generates peace of mind for the one who is able to adopt and practise such an attitude, it pays rich dividends to him. Therefore, an attitude of equanimity in life is righteous in terms of religion, logical and scientific in terms of metaphysics and beneficial also to the individual himself and to those around him.

Even in modern society—both in the East as well as in the West, there is a rethinking about the methods of tackling the sin and sinner viz. crime and criminal. The emphasis is upon removal of the causes which prompted or forced a person to commit crime and improvement in the state of mind of the criminal by the process of reformation—education etc. The effort is to win him over to bring him back to the right path. Sheer hatred towards him would make him a harder criminal always following the wrong path. That is why Mahatma Gandhi said "*Hate the sin, not the sinner.*" Treat the mind without punishing the physical body, least of all, with capital punishment. The physical body has only followed the command of the mind. The motive behind imprisonment should ideally be a temporary physical isolation to minimize the risk of repetition of crime till the mind has been reformed.

There is still another approach to sin or crime which too is very logical. Swami Ram Tirtha says; "*We are punished by the sin and not for it (sin).*" Punishment for the sin presumes a role of an outside agency e.g. society or state or both. One may escape punishment by an outside agency as we commonly observe with the help of money, influence etc. Further, the definition of crime and the corresponding punishment by the state depend upon the law at a particular time as to when and in what particular place the crime was committed. What is crime in some Arab countries may not be a crime in other countries. For example, stepping out of the house without a veil (burqa) by a woman is a crime in Saudi Arabia but not elsewhere. Similarly, what might have been a crime in the Twentieth Century or earlier may no longer be a crime in the Twenty-first Century and vice-versa. Practices like slavery, bonded labour, early marriage etc. which were practised freely are now banned. Hence, the wise saying that one may escape man's punishment but not that by God (or Nature). One's indulgence in such simple things as eating, drinking, sex etc. (even committed in the privacy of one's home) are going to punish him in the form of ill-health and related diseases. To err is human but persisting in erring is devilish. Leniency is available only to first offenders, not to hardened criminals. This is punishment by the sin of indulgence without any role by an outside agency. Persistence in indulgence may be followed by a deadly disease. Drug addicts and victims of AIDS are two examples. Therefore, society or state, both being outside agencies need not hate the sinner or criminal. His (sinner's) misunderstanding or ignorance has led him up the wrong path. Don't cut him asunder by hatred but win and bring him back with love which an even-minded Yogī has in abundance for one and all.

In verse 8 of Chap. VI, Lord Kṛṣṇa, extends the scope of equanimity to the inanimate world of creation.

The verse 8 of Chapter VI says:

jñāna vijñāna tṛptātmā kūṭastho vijitendriyaḥ
yukta ity ucyate yogī sama loṣṭāśma kāñcanaḥ

> **Meaning:** A yogī is called self-realised who is satisfied with knowledge and understanding (realization) of Brahma who is equanimous (unchanging), who has control over and is master of senses, and to whom a clod, a stone and gold are the same.

The message is that in order to qualify as a self-realized person, one has to abandon the worldly value-system and rise to a higher plane where, to him, the three very different physical materials—clod, stone and gold are the same. It is not easy even for those who spend a life-time leading a life of total renunciation, meditation and devotion. One may argue that a science student does know that there is no basic difference between coal and diamond as diamond is the purest form of carbon and that coal is nothing but carbon. The argument can extend further. Science also informs us that the physical, chemical and other properties of matter, e.g. color, texture, hardness, chemical reaction etc. depend on the molecular arrangement within that particular matter. Further, that in the ultimate analysis forms of matter are composed of atoms. Atoms are composed of nuclei and electrons and so on. The million-dollar question is whether such a student or scientist with the knowledge of basic unity or sameness of all forms of matter, can be considered to have attained to Brahma? The answer is 'No.' It is not mere knowledge of books, scientific or scriptural that can qualify one to be equanimous in attitude or to have attained to Brahma or Nirvāṇa. The knowledge is

---

ज्ञानविज्ञानतृप्तात्मा कूटस्थो विजितेन्द्रियः।
युक्त इत्युच्यते योगी समलोष्टाश्मकाञ्चनः॥ VI (8)

perhaps the first essential step but the last step which is realization still remains a distant goal. Knowledge loses in status further, if it is not used as a necessary first step or a requisite or an equipment for furtherance of self-improvement and self-growth. It only becomes another tool of trade if its use is restricted to earning livelihood or collecting wealth. One graduates and qualifies to the level of self-realization, when with the help of self-control (of senses and mind) and true understanding (oneness is nature) when in day-to-day life, one would not lock up gold to guard it better and part with it with the same ease as in the case of clod or a stone. That is the height of the mental level of the self-realized. Ordinary humans set on the path of knowledge, righteous action or renunciation and even those with scientific knowledge about the essential unity of all matter are way behind though they too deserve respect and encouragement because all of them are seekers of truth (not self-servers) at different stages in their respective journeys towards truth. They are a lot better than the ignorant and the selfish lost in the material world. This latter lot has not even commenced the journey to the supreme goal.

Looking further deep into nature, we can discover pairs of opposites operating in the field of energy. It is common knowledge that electric current, such a significant part of our life and indeed of the contemporary civilization, has two opposite charges—positive and negative. This common knowledge and a common-place phenomenon has an uncommon truth behind it—the *inevitability of the coexistence of opposites*. The same is true of another form of energy—magnetism. A magnet of any size or shape must have two poles namely North and South—opposite of each other. One may split a long magnet into a smaller and still smaller-sized magnets, but the beauty is that each piece, howsoever, small, will still have the two poles. We also know and observe that circular motion generates centripetal and centrifugal forces each working in a direction opposite to the other—centripetal towards the center and centrifugal away from the center. In the cosmos, there is force of gravity and anti-gravity. This is how, through balance and counter-balance, cosmic existence maintains its stability.

To cap it all, after Newton's discovery that to every action there is an equal and opposite reaction, scientists have lately confirmed existence of anti-matter. They believe, on the basis of scientific research in different countries, that *matter and anti-matter are created out of pure energy but always in pairs.* Physicists use positrons and anti-protons in accelerator experiments that recreate a flash of energy similar to the condition at the origin of the universe, the beginning of time. This is what Stephen Hawking, a great scientist of our time, is devoting his life to. The quest of both scientists and saints is to get to the singularity as it was or the way it appeared before it expressed itself in multiplicity. As a first step, the scientist is trying to know what the universe is like. Next and perhaps the final step would be to understand why, it (Universe) is, but only if the first step is completed. For centuries, man has been in the first phase of knowing and realising the singularity. However, in the process, resolution of one mystery only leads to still another. Chances are that the Universe will get into the mode of contraction (as against the presently expanding mode) and disappear. We would not know into what and where, leave aside 'why'.

Despite human limitations of various kinds, it may be best to be content with the important enough finding, agreed to both by saints and scientists that there is a basic unity in nature even in the apparent opposites. In Hindu belief, unity behind male and female—Puruṣa and Prakṛti has also been acknowledged. In the 8th century Śiva temple in Elephanta caves near Bombay and other places, e.g. Vṛndāvan, unity of male and female has been deified and depicted through a figure which is half-male and half-female. In the Hindu mythology, the deity or god so symbolized is called Ardhanāriśwara—god who is half-male and half-female.

Having acknowledged the existence of pairs of opposites and also the basic unity in nature, despite opposites, one needs to move higher to the level of realization, to benefit from this knowledge of basic unity. Mere knowledge is not going to make much difference in life. It is as good as reading a road map or a guide book but not undertaking the journey to the destination applying the knowledge in real life. One must rise to the level of calmness above the reach of opposing forces pulling in opposite directions which may rock or toss your craft and even cause its destruction. Sea farers when caught in a storm seek the safety of calm waters. Pilots of aircraft, when the craft is tossed up and down due to turbulent weather, moves to higher altitude where the atmosphere is calm and his craft becomes steady and the journey smooth. Human beings too must move themselves to a level higher than normal level at which opposites operate and rock the human mind. We can not change the way nature is — full of opposites. We can only make ourselves impervious or immune to their operation by changing ourselves i.e. our attitude to life by self-growth, self-improvement and move to the plane where instead of opposites, the basic unity prevails. Even if one is not able to succeed completely, the undertaking itself is worthy, joyful and rewarding. No effort in the right path is ever lost. No further promotion does not mean demotion to a lower class as a punishment. The Gītā guarantees it and our experience supports it, too.

The messages of the Gītā are in the nature of an applied philosophy of life. They assure that though journey towards higher plane of life is long and slow, no sincere effort is ever wasted. Having left the camp at the base, and having commenced the journey, one has started putting in the sincere effort. Even if one is not able to make it to the top for whatever reason, one has moved higher in comparison to the previous position. Not making the final grade does not in any way take away the knowledge gained or improvement achieved thus far. No action is extinguished till it has produced its corresponding result sooner or later.

The attitude of equanimity is not only for the saintly or for the elderly. It is not exclusively for the greying or the balding. In fact, it may be more useful for the young executives and corporate leaders. For them, the equanimous attitude may imply treating members of their teams or employees equally and equitably. We often hear about industrialists asking the Government to ensure a level playing field against foreign companies. In the same spirit, they too should ensure a level playing field for their competitors and their employees *inter-se. They should not play favorites.* It is neither business ethics nor practical wisdom. Uneven treatment to employees by the executives or owners creates divisions, rivalry and disloyalty in the ranks of employees. Sycophants should not be allowed to have an upper hand over others.

The other aspect of equanimity for executives is to plan for profit but to be prepared to take a loss. Work to rise higher but not to give up or run away from the field of activity when economic downturn or recession sets in. Despite fluctuations in business, mind must not fluctuate. The rougher the weather the more composed the captain needs to be. After all, it does not rain all day long. Every phenomenon is temporary and transient. Impermanence is the law of nature. One cannot change this: A wise man learns, endures and benefits without trying to change it unsuccessfully.

Rise above pairs of opposites
enjoy a calm mind and a clear vision.

CHAPTER 14

Death and Life after Death

The only thing which is certain about life is death. But still man rejoices at birth and grieves at death. Rejoicing at birth may be all right but grieving at death is not.

Verse 27 of Chapter II of the Gītā says:

jātasya hi dhruvo mṛtyur dhruvaṃ janma mṛtasya ca
tasmād aparihārye'rthe na tvaṃ śocitum arhasi

Meaning: Because death is certain for the one who is born and birth is certain for the one who dies, therefore, you should not lament over the inevitable.

Famous British writer, Sir Francis Bacon (1561-1626), said:

"It is as natural to die as to be born; and to a little infant, perhaps, the one is as painful as the other."

Why then have such widely different attitudes to the two ? The saint-poet Kabir, sees the nature's cycle of birth, death and rebirth on a much wider scale in the entire creation and expresses it as follows :

जातस्य हि ध्रुवो मृत्युर् ध्रुवं जन्म मृतस्य च।
तस्माद् अपरिहार्येऽर्थे न त्वं शोचितुम् अर्हसि॥ II (27)

"Whatever is born (rises) must have an end. Whatever blooms must wither. Whatever is built must crumble. Whoever enters must exit."

What dies is the physical body and what does not ever die is the eternal soul. To live meaningfully, peacefully, harmoniously, we must understand the reality of death. In Sanskrit, death is called "*dehānta*", meaning end of the body but has nothing to do with Ā*tman* or soul. After discussing the irrevocability of death of all physical beings, the Gītā proceeds to set apart the soul as immortal and unaffected by different physical forces of nature.

Verse 23 of Chapter II of the Gītā says:

nainaṃ chindanti śastrāṇi nainaṃ dahati pāvakaḥ
na cainaṃ kledayanty āpo na śoṣayati mārutaḥ.

Meaning: Weapons do not cut this self, fire does not burn it; water does not wet it, nor does the wind make it dry.

Verse 24 of Chapter II of the Gītā says:

acchedyo'yam adāhyo'yam akledyo'śoṣya eva ca
nityaḥ sarvagataḥ sthāṇur acalo'yaṃ sanātanaḥ

Meaning: It cannot be cut, it can not be burnt. It can be neither wetted nor dried. It is eternal, all-pervading, unchanging and immovable. It is the same forever.

Self is the causation of creation. While creation can be destroyed, cause may not be.

Men have been as afraid of death as children are afraid of darkness. This unfounded fear has been compounded by fantasies of heaven and hell and rewards and punishment to be awarded there. Such fantasies might have been created for the ordinary members of society so that they do not commit religious or social wrongs. Even though non-existent, these fantasies do serve as

---

नैनं छिन्दन्ति शस्त्राणि नैनं दहति पावकः।
न चैनं क्लेदयन्त्यापो न शोषयति मारुतः॥ II (23)

अच्छेद्योऽयम् अदाह्योऽयम् अक्लेद्योऽशोष्य एव च।
नित्यः सर्वगतः स्थाणुर् अचलोऽयं सनातनः॥ II (24)

deterrent for the ordinary folk and may thus serve a social purpose but do not find a place in the rational thought process.

A fruit-yielding tree or plant acquires the flower [seed-flower] first and fruit later. At a certain stage, growth of the seed-flower stops and the baby fruit appears. The fruit grows in size and ripens. In a way, fruit has replaced the flower.

The flower is dead but only in the limited sense. Flower-seed has given birth to the fruit. The fruit, having served its purpose of providing food to the human beings, dies but the seed within the fruit has taken over the task of giving birth to another tree. Thus the cycle of birth, death and rebirth continues in the botanical world too.

The figure of dancing Śiva-Natarāj symbolizing both creation and destruction or birth and death, with an attitude of holy indifference, conveys, working of this cycle in nature. We see nature all around us, going through the cycle of birth, death and rebirth but do not shed tears or grieve about it. We also take a matter-of-fact view of deaths in the animal world. But death of a pet dog or cat upsets the householder, particularly the young kids, who used to play with the pet. They even grieve at the death of their fond pet for days and days together. The reason is one's attachment to the pet which is no more. Similarly grieving is caused by the feeling of attachment with the deceased person and the sort of vacuum left behind. In the cycle of seed, flower and fruit, we do not see them as separate identities but as a chain of continuity. We do not even know the time of change with any exactitude. Similarly, we may not know exact time of death or birth, but only a mere approximation. There is a whole lot of controversies about time of birth and death. There is biological birth, medical birth and legal birth. Similarly, there is biological death, medical death and legal death. Each event may have a different time, albeit slightly, according to criteria applicable. The basic reason is that the man wants to divide and define exactly, without any overlapping, which is not possible. It is a continuum. There are no full stops, only commas. Even commas are fuzzed and blurred.

Verse 22 of Chap. II of the Gītā, makes a rather simple statement as to the true nature of death.

It says:

vāsāṃsi jīrṇāni yathā vihāya
navāni gṛhṇāti naro'parāṇi
tathā sarīrāṇi vihāya jīrṇāny
anyāni saṃyāti navāni dehī

Meaning: Just as a person puts on new garments after discarding the old worn out ones, similarly embodied soul (Jīvātmā) takes on a new body (form) after discarding the old worn out ones.

The Gītā's reader may wonder why Lord Kṛṣṇa or the author of the Gītā chose the metaphor of changing clothes or garments to explain the events of death and rebirth. The answer is that discarding the worn-out garments takes place several times and so does the soul take on new forms several times. Further, life has been compared with an assignment or role as ordained by God. The actor while performing his assigned role, uses garments suitable for the role as a king, fighter, teacher, trader or a servant. The same actor may perform different roles on the stage, using different costumes and makeup.

In Western literature, William Shakespeare has compared man with an actor who comes (is born) to the stage (in the world), plays his role (lives the life) and leaves the stage (dies in the world). Different roles necessarily require different types of costumes.

Sir Francis Bacon, in his essay 'Of Clothes', has brought out how a man's occupation (say role) in life can be known by his clothes. A doctor is recognized by his white coat, a lawyer by a black coat, a judge by his black robe and the list goes on. Thus, the author of the Gītā could not have been wrong in using the metaphor of changing of clothes (rather than a vehicle etc.) to suit

---

वासांसि जीर्णानि यथा विहाय
नवानि गृहणाति नरोऽपराणि।
तथा शरीराणि विहाय जीर्णान्य्
अन्यानि संयाति नवानि देही।। II (22)

changing of roles through different lives. Clothes are also an outer covering for the body but close to the body.

The statement made in verse 22 of Chapter II of the Gītā is indeed true and draws a distinction between permanence of soul and temporary nature of physical elements, out of which the human body is made. Ordinary persons do not like to be told or reminded of the above truth, particularly when in prime of life and in the midst of enjoyment. They do not want to think of death, until perhaps the hour of death. However to the wise, and great men, life and death seem no different as both are physical phenomena. They are ever ready to go.

Socrates (469-399 B.C) said:

> "The hour of departure has arrived, and we go our ways— I to die and you to live, which is the better, only God knows."

When Crito asked:

> "In what way shall we bury you"?

Socrates answered:

> "In any way you like, but first, you must catch me, the real me. Be of good cheer, my dear Crito, and say that you are burying my body only, and do with that whatever is usual and what you think best."

Some compare death with long sleep, others call it a great equalizer, a steam-rolling agency of nature. However this is what the rich and the powerful (but not the wise in the same measure) are scared of. The Bible tells the rich that they would not get entry into the gates of heaven. The Gītā informs them that all their wealth and belongings would not go with them. With transfer of soul from one body to another, transfer of residence and of personal effects is not a part of nature's scheme.

William Shakespeare, the English poet-dramatist, brings out the tragedy which attends the death of kings, as against the peace and calm in the case of the wise who see it as an inevitable and essential part in the cycle of nature.

In his play Richard II, William Shakespeare says:

"...How some have been deposed: some slain in war; some haunted by the ghosts they have deposed; some poisoned by their wives; some sleeping killed; all murdered: For within the hollow crown that rounds the mortal temples (Cheeks) of a king, keeps death his court."

Even as man recognizes the inevitability of death and birth the mystery and questions about life and death have baffled mankind since time immemorial. Death is perhaps more baffling because man believes that while he is more privy to birth and life that follows, experience of death itself and what happens thereafter is beyond the realm of his knowledge. A person who goes through the experience of death, has already crossed the threshold and does not return to recount his experience. A chemistry student might have learnt that nobody knows the taste of potassium cyanide because the effect of merely tasting it is instantaneous death. In a somewhat, similar manner one may be able to describe the suffering, one undergoes, before the death knocks but never the actual meeting with death or whatever happens thereafter. It is a one-way street. Or as Shakespeare said: *"It is a passage to an unknown, undiscovered country."*

Apart from the Bhagavad-Gītā, in the matter of death and life thereafter, let us see how different persons look at the phenomenon of death and prepare themselves to face it. Certainly, a wise man does not see it as anything unnatural and is ready to meet it whenever it comes.

Jean De La Fontaine, the French poet, said: *"Death never takes the wise man by surprise, he is always ready to go"*.

Sir Winston Churchill, on the eve of his 75th birthday, said:

"I am prepared to meet my Maker, Whether my Maker is prepared for the great ordeal of meeting me is another matter".

Thus, death is as good as redemption by the Lord. As the Gītā has it, death, is like changing one's garments. When the old garments are worn-out, one replaces them with new ones but the journey of the soul, in the new garments, viz. new body goes on. This is the lesson given by Lord Kṛṣṇa right in the beginning of the Gītā to Arjuna so that his mistaken concept of death or ignorance about its true nature does not come in the way of his performing his duty. Apart from the Gītā and Hinduism in general, all great religions of the world are in agreement that death is not the end of the long eternal journey of the soul.

H.G. Wells an internationally acknowledged science fiction writer (who lived between 1866-1946) expressed his belief in the continuity of life from the past, to the present and into the future. His novel—Time Machine—foresees the possibility of man traveling into past—witnessing state of life in the past and into future—witnessing state of life to be in the future.

He also said:

> "I am a temporary enclosure for a temporary purpose; that served, my skull and teeth, my idiosyncrasy and desire, will disperse, I believe, like the timbers of booth after the fair."

Even after extinguishing the fear in the mind, a person may still have the curiosity as to how the death may impact him or what may happen thereafter. Different religions and races handle the dead bodies of their followers in different manners. Hindus invariably burn their dead while Christians and some others bury their dead. Hindus believe that dead bodies comprising of five elements (*Pañcabhūtas*) return to five elements through the process of burning. Souls leave the body and endeavor to find new bodies for their new material or manifest existence. Only a few can manage a merger with the energy source viz. *Paramātmā*. Other religions believe that the souls acquire a separate existence outside the dead body but the separation is only temporary. On the Day-of-Judgement these separately existing souls will re-enter their respective dead bodies. Further, on such an Appointed Day, rewards or punishments will be awarded by God. In some countries, like Egypt, the dead bodies have been preserved to the extent possible using mummification as one of the methods. To take care of the needs e.g. food, water etc. of their dead these are kept by the side of the dead body in the belief that soul would return to the dead body and would need material objects and comforts. There are instances, or atleast stories, that servants were buried alive by the side of dead prince or princess in the belief that services of the servant would be available to the prince or princes as and when needed. According to the Gītā, however, the new journey for the departed soul begins right after death. In a lighter vein, one may say that on death, the soul reports to the Head Quarters i.e. God and awaits to receive fresh orders as to the next assignment. We believe that all of us are in this world on different allotted assignments. Therefore, fresh assignments become necessary on the completion of one. Naturally, one would like to think that such an important decision is to be made by no less an authority than God Himself. One may compare death with a stage or station in the long journey in which one has to change train or vehicle to get to his destination. The Gītā has used the much simpler metaphor of garments bringing down the insignificance of the body still further and to emphasise the fact that body is an outer covering like garments or clothes.

Even agreeing that death is but a stage in the long journey to change clothes i.e. to acquire a new body the important questions, as to what type of new body, what type of next assignment or destination it would be, who would decide upon it and what method or criteria, if any, would be followed, remain. Will 'I' be a party to it ? Will 'I' be consulted at all ? What if 'I' have some unfinished task ? May be, with greater determination, harder efforts, 'I' will perform better, this time. Will 'I' be given another chance as they do here—in schools, colleges, and elsewhere in life ? Happily the answer is Yes. The Gītā vividly describes the technique involved. It is not arbitrary or partial in its operation. According to the Gītā, the dying person decides the new assignment by himself. It may sound quite strange but interesting all the same that a person who is approaching death in a short-while is expected to make such an important decision. It is not certain whether medical science would support this view or not but it is believed that the memory of a dying person becomes photographically clear. The entire life revolves before his mental eye like a film with a faithful record of all deeds—good not so good and bad, as well. The dying person is able to strike a balance, be it positive showing good deeds to his credit or negative, showing bad deeds to his debit It also leads one to believe that a dying person generally speaks the truth. That is why "dying declaration" or the statement of a dying person is of special significance and has a lot of weightage in law, though the person making the statement is physically not available to be cross examined. It is presumed that a dying person has no motive or inclination to tell a lie. Another way, possibly more reliable and supported by the Gītā, to look at the decision making capacity of the dying man, is to contemplate the role of desires in ones life. It seems logical in the case of an ordinary person, that there are some desires of selfish or unselfish nature—of lower nature or higher nature, which are left unfulfilled at the end of his life. It may also sound equally logical that the ordinary dying man would wish that he could satisfy such desires somehow. If he has been overtaken by death and there is life thereafter, he would like to satisfy those unfulfilled desires in the new life. The Gītā says that this stock of unfulfilled desires becomes, the *raison' d'etre* or the rationale, for the future birth in a body and environment where fulfilment of the unfulfilled desires of the dying person becomes possible. Though physical stores are left behind but the spiritual store—your traits—goes with you in the new assignment In other words, man himself is an arbiter of his new assignment that is a new life in a new body. Work on what you can take with you or can pass on to the progeny—values or *saṃskāras*. More so because the time available is limited.

The Gītā has embodied this rationale in the verse 6 of Chapter VIII. It says:

yaṃ yaṃ vā'pi smaran bhāvaṃ tyajaty ante kalevaram
taṃ taṃ evaiti kaunteya sadā tadbhāvabhāvitaḥ

Meaning: Whosoever, at the end, leaves the body, in thinking of any object, to that object only he goes, O Kaunteya (O son of Kuntī), because of his constant thought of that object.

For those who wish to attain to God. i.e. not wishing to be reborn to fulfil any desires, there is an assurance that one can achieve the supreme desire while doing one's duty with mind on God i.e. performing righteous actions.

In verse 7 of Chapter VIII, Lord Kṛṣṇa advises:

tasmāt sarveṣu kāleṣu mām anusmara yoddha ca
mayy arpitamanobuddhir mām evai'ṣyasy asaṃśayam

Meaning: Therefore, at all times, remember Me, and fight (do your duty) with mind and intellect fixed (or absorbed) in Me; you shall doubtless come to Me alone.

Fighting may be seen in the context of Arjuna in the battle field of Kurukṣetra whereas doing one's duty has a general connotation and applies to all.

The two verses 6 and 7 of Chapter VIII. read together imply that to attain to God, a dying person must have his mind and intellect fixed on God. But fixing one's mind on anything, particularly as high, as subtle and as abstract as God, cannot be achieved with the push of a button. Fixing one's mind on God and concentrating on Him alone cannot be achieved instantaneously as a result of a sudden decision but as a result of constant practice over a long period i.e. throughout life before the stage of death arrives. It is the quality of deeds performed, the type of life led which creates such a state of mind where God

---

यं यं वापि स्मरन् भावं त्यजत्य् अन्ते कलेवरम्।
तं तं एवैति कौन्तेय सदा तद्भावभावितः॥ VIII (6)

तस्मात् सर्वेषु कालेषु माम् अनुस्मर युध्य च।
मय्य् अर्पितमनोबुद्धिर् माम् एवैष्यस्य् असंशयम्॥ VIII (7)

and godliness would govern your thoughts and your actions. Therefore, the practical implication of the message of the above cited verses is to lead a life of righteousness, getting rid of all desires except the desire to merge with God. No doubt, such a person, at the time of his death, would only wish to be one with God and the Gītā guarantees that he would succeed in it. No more births and deaths for such a person. From the manifest he has transcended into the unmanifest. The microcosm has merged with the macrocosm losing the previous separate identity. Some scriptures and saints describe death as an instance of dust returning to dust, earth to earth or ashes to ashes. However, it implies disposal of body or the elements after death. The Gītā tackles the ticklish question of what happens to life which was contained in that body which has returned to dust. The Gītā tells us additionally about *Ātmā* returning to *Paramātmā*—a single atom merging with the ocean of atoms or *in other words, a speck of energy returning to the source of energy*. The Gītā, on the one hand talks of the cyclical nature of birth, death and rebirth; on the other, it also tells us the technique as to how the cycle can be broken. The above cycle of birth, death and rebirth, in fact, implies in turn, appearing in the manifest world, leaving the manifest world and reappearing in the manifest world. In the scientific world also it is believed that the sum total of matter remains constant. The matter may change from one form to another through chemical action or otherwise but if the science man could manage to arrive at the aggregate of the entire matter in the universe, it would remain constant. Later on, however, this scientific theory was modified to include energy together with matter. It was established scientifically and is open to everyday experience of a scientific mind that energy can be converted into matter and matter into energy. Burning of wood or coal produces heat—a form of energy. Radium and Plutonium through the mechanism of nuclear devices are notoriously capable of releasing enormous energy, enough to destroy a whole continent. Now, the scientists believe that the sum total of matter plus energy remains constant i.e. the sum total of manifest (matter) and unmanifest (energy) should be constant. Both matter and energy have co-existed and will continue to co-exist forever changing into one and the other but, continuing the cycle without any real addition or loss. Similarly, birth and death are following each other in a cycle from the unmanifest to manifest, then to unmanifest again. Therefore, birth is not production of anything new but only reassociation or re-manifestation. While death is not destruction of anything but only separation. Death is by no means, an enemy. Such an enlightened attitude removes cowardice, and fear and prepares you for the new assignment.

With such a change of attitude, a journey between life, death and new life appears like transferring your residence from one town to another town or from one country to another country.

That town or country remains unknown or undiscovered only till one gets there. This truth was stated by Cornelius Nepos—Roman historian and biographer of 1st Century (B.C.) in the following words: *"So that he seemed not to relinquish life, but to leave one home for another."*

As death is not an end of the journey, birth is also not the beginning of a journey. Male sperm (over 50 million sperm per millilitre) and female egg, both of which have their respective lives, combine to fertilise the egg and create another life. Thus, there is no ending and no beginning. It is only changing of form of life. Although as per the Gītā too *Prāṇa* (primal energy) and *Ātmā* (Soul) enter the body of a child at some point of time, before the birth in the biological sense of the word viz. the child coming out of the mother's womb or being taken out of the mother's womb as in the case of a caesarian birth. Till that point of time, it is a body within a body. All the same both bodies—of mother and child—have independent lives.

The above-mentioned two mysterious ingredients viz. *Prāṇa* and *Ātmā* supposedly leave the body at the time, we call death in the normal terms and transition point in the continuing journey in religious or philosophical terms.

While the Gītā teaches one to be prepared to die in the course of doing one's duty and not to lament over the death of even kith and kin, it lays a lot of emphasis on the state of mind of a dying person. It promises that whatever is in one's mind at the time of death, one will attain to that. As stated before, verse 6 of Chapter VIII brings out that an object of thought at the time one leaves the body at the end of life, is attainable because of the constant thought of that object.

While verse 6 talks of attaining 'any object.' Verse 5 of Chapter VIII talks of attaining the abode of God by remembering the Lord at the hour of death.

It says:

antakāle ca mām eva smaran muktvā kalevaram
yaḥ prayāti sa madbhāvaṃ yāti nā sty atra saṃśayaḥ

Meaning: Whosoever at the hour of death leaves the body and goes forth remembering ME alone, without doubt he attains to my being.

Even if one does not believe the contents of the above two verses literally, it is a very intelligent way to encourage and make people live a righteous life throughout. Only when a person is righteous throughout life, can he be so at the hour of death. How a person lives would determine how he would die. The right state of mind is an evolving process, over a long period of time. To earn the reputation of an honest man, one must be always honest. One can not be celibate by practicing celibacy for a fraction of lifetime. One cannot claim to be *Brahmacārī* for the entire period of twenty-five prescribed years, by observing *Brahmacarya* in the last year only.

There is another way of looking at the concept of life after death. It is easier to comprehend and accept as compared to the one wherein soul, having been released at the time of death, finds a suitable environment in the form of a womb to facilitate birth in a family and environment whereby it will be able to carry forward its mission of pursuing its unfinished agenda from previous birth(s).

However, before coming to the other way of looking at the

अन्तकाले च माम् एव स्मरन् मुक्त्वा कलेवरम्।
यः प्रयाति स मद्भावं याति नास्त्य् अत्र संशयः॥ VIII (5)

concept of life after death, it may be added that some thinkers suggest that in the event of death, genes return to what may be called cosmic genomic pool. From the pool, genes find way into individual new suitable wombs.

Verse 41 of Chapter VI of the Gītā says:

prāpya puṇyakṛtāṃ lokān uṣitvā śāśvatīḥ samāḥ
śucīnāṃ śrīmatāṃ gehe yogabhraṣṭo'bhijāyate

Meaning: Having attained to the world of the righteous and having lived there for many years he who has fallen from yoga (i.e. could not make it to the top-Brahman) is born in the house of the pure and illustrious.

Verse 43 of Chapter VI, says further:

tatra taṃ buddhi saṃyogaṃ labhate paurva dehikam
yatate ca tato bhūyaḥ saṃsiddhau kuru nandana

Meaning: There he comes to be associated with knowledge (or mentality or traits) of his former body (life) and he strives from that point of time onward into perfection, son of Kuru.

The message of the above two verses is very significant. First, the man himself ordered or decided upon, in the past life, his present environment. In other words, he is an arbiter of his own destiny though in the following birth it becomes a part of pre-destiny or *Prārabdha*. Secondly, that no effort ever goes waste. The effect is cumulative. Efforts of previous births will add up to the effort of the following birth in the conducive or suitable circumstances. A study carried out by William T. Dickens of the Brookings Institution in Washington D.C. (and his colleague James R. Flynn of the university of Otago in New Zealand) showed that a whole lot of traits—including IQ—have been shown to be highly heritable, much of the effect of genes may come from the way genes

---

प्राप्य पुण्यकृतां लोकान् उषित्वा शाश्वतीः समाः।
शुचीनां श्रीमतां गेहे योगभ्रष्टोऽभिजायते॥ VI (41)

तत्र तं बुद्धिसंयोगं लभते पौर्वदेहिकम्।
यतते च ततो भूयः संसिद्धौ कुरुनन्दन॥ VI (43)

seek out good environments. Further, that a relatively small change in the environment can have a very large and quick impact on IQ. They found that seemingly small environmental triggers play a large role in influencing an individual's IQ. Researchers suggest a snow-balling effect on a person who is only slightly more genetically gifted than average. He may have easier access to situations with higher than average degree of intellectual stimulation.

Such a person will be motivated to seek out more of the same, which in turn will put him in contact with like-minded people. The simple result is an upward spiral of IQ driven by genes and circumstances as in the case of a geometrical angle, the gap between the two arms of the angle-average and above average-keeps on increasing as the two arms extend further and further.

Genetic predisposition is not disputed or denied. Right environment (sum total of all other influences) having been sought and achieved have a snow-balling effect. In mathematical language genetic superiority increases in geometrical progression rather than in arithmetical progression.

This is the logic behind the Gītā's assurance of continuance and completion of the journey of the righteous one even if it takes more than one birth. Thus, death is not the end but a new beginning, without a full stop.

How else could one explain certain childrens' extraordinary IQ or proficiency in a particular field at a comparatively young age. Almost unconsciously we refer to such children as born scientists or born singers, musicians, actors etc.

Now, coming to the alternative concept of life after death, it roughly means, living through your progeny/posterity who carry your genes. In addition to progeny carrying one's genes, in the scientific sense, the progeny is generally looked upon as a medium or a vehicle for fulfilling one's desires and dreams. Whatever part of one's life-agenda a person—father or mother could not fulfill, he or she wishes that to be fulfilled by the offspring. The offspring is an extension of one's own personality and rightly so. Through the union of male and female (i.e. father and mother) both types of attributes of the couple—'person' (physical) and persona (non-physical) become available for transfer into the new body, created and born as a result. That is why it is correct to see in the offspring an extension of one's own personality or image, as they say.

Thus, the progeny provides an aspiration as well as a means, a vehicle, to fulfil one's own unfinished agenda.

In course of time, the progeny builds up its own agenda or charter of life. The life which started as one's own extension may be considered to have become eventually one's life, after one's death. In real terms it amounts to living after death. Further weight may be added to this approach if we take into account the probability that the two persons joining to procreate have shared values which in a certain measure arc likely to be passed on into the new life. Both in love and arranged marriages and even in coming together for sexual union only, there is a reasonable presumption that the two partners do share some values of life. Minds must meet before the bodies do.

Lastly, life after death may be seen as living through one's deeds, the result of one's actions. Ordinary persons live in the memory of their dear ones only, while those who have accomplishments of some sort to their credit are remembered by far too many and for much longer. Death is not their end. They continue to live through their deeds, even if the memorials and mausoleums are not built for them. THEIR DEEDS, THEIR ACHIEVEMENTS INSPIRE PEOPLE, GENERATION AFTER GENERATION. Some write about them, more read about them and a few follow them also.

This is the life after death that one should aim at living.

Let good deeds live long after your death.

Glossary

Abhyāsa	:	Regular practice.
Adharma	:	Contrary to Dharma i.e. righteous duty.
Agni-Kuṇḍa	:	Pot wherein the Sacrificial fire is lit.
AIDS	:	Acquired Immuno-Deficiency Syndrome.
Ajantā	:	A place with Indo-Aryan sculpture.
Akbar	:	Famous Mughal King of India.
Alexander	:	Greek King.
Ardhanārīśwara	:	A concept of God who is half female and half male implying singularity in duality.
Arjuna	:	The Pāṇḍava Prince and hero of the battle of war representing the struggle between good and evil and wherein Lord Kṛṣṇa gives him the teaching which came to be known as the Gītā.
Āsana	:	Literally—seat, meditation.
Aśānti	:	Lack of peace.
Ātmā	:	Soul or spirit—pure consciousness.
Aurangzeb	:	Mughal King.
Āyurveda	:	Ancient Indian system of medicine.
Bhakti Yoga	:	Yoga of Devotion.
Bhautika	:	Elemental form.

Birbal	:	Minister of King Akbar, honoured for his wisdom.
Brahma	:	The supreme God—ultimate reality or energy source.
Brahmacarya	:	Regular fruit of balanced diets and emancipating ritual.
Buddhism	:	A religion of India, which spread world-wide
Cakras	:	Spanish energy wheels at nodal points in human spine and brain.
Cervantes	:	author of "Adventures of Don Quixote".
Chariot	:	A vehicle driven by horses.
Cornelius Nepos	:	Roman historian—Ist Century B.C.
Daihika	:	Bodily—physical form .
Daivika	:	Pertaining to the spirit form.
Dehānta	:	Literally meaning end of body.
Deja Vu	:	Already seen implying something experienced in distant past but forgotten till now.
Devas	:	Male Gods or Goddesses.
Devis	:	Female gods.
Dharma	:	Loosely comparable to righteous duty.
Dharma Kṣetra	:	Field of right action.
Dharma Yuddha	:	Battle of Righteousness.
Dhyāna Yoga	:	Yoga of meditation/contemplation.
Don Quixote	:	Main character in the work—Adventures of Don Quixote.
Draupadī	:	Common wife of the five Pāṇḍava brothers whom Duryodhana tried to disrobe in an assembly when Pāṇḍavas lost her in a betting game.
Duryodhana	:	Elder of Kaurava brothers respresenting evil, who resorted to all cunning and foul means to usurp the kingdom.

Edmund Burges	:	Irish philosopher and statesman.
Elephanta Caves	:	Cave with stone figures, near Bombay.
Ellora	:	Cave sculptures near Bombay.
Francis Bacon	:	English writer of 16th Century.
Friends of Earth	:	A band of people espousing protection of the planet from degradation.
Gandhi	:	M.K. Gandhi, spiritual and political leader of India.
Gauśālā	:	A place where cows are kept and looked after.
Gītā	:	Celestial song, the dialogue between Lord Kṛṣṇa and Arjuna stretching into 700 verses in the Indian epic Mahābhārata.
Gītāñjalī	:	A famous poetry book by Rabindra Nath Tagore.
Guṇas	:	Behavior traits.
Guru	:	Spiritual master and teacher.
Hastināpur	:	Capital of the kingdom in North India, a cause for dispute between Pāṇḍavas and Kauravas.
H.G. Wells	:	English Writer. His 'Time Machine' explores the 4th dimension i.e., time.
Jainism	:	A religion of India, which promotes non-violence, renunciation, non-attachement.
Jal	:	Water
Janaka	:	Father of Sītā—wife of Lord Rāma and king of Mithila.
Jean De La Fontain	:	French Poet 469-399 B.C.
Jīvan-Yātrā	:	Journey of life.
Jīvātmā	:	Embodied soul i.e. individual soul in any living organisation.
Jñāna	:	Knowledge.
Jñāna Yoga	:	Yoga of knowledge.

Jñānendriya	:	Sense-organs.
Jñānī	:	Knowledgable.
Kabir	:	A Sufi poet and Saint.
Kalidasa	:	A famous Indian Poet.
Kāmasūtra	:	A famous Hindu treatise on aspects of sex.
Karma Bhūmi	:	Field of action in the form of duty.
Karma Kṣetra	:	Field of Action.
Karma yoga	:	Yoga of action.
Karma Yuddha	:	Battle of Action.
Karmendriyas	:	Organs of Action.
Khajuraho	:	A town in Uttar Pradesh in North India famous for temples with exotic engravings.
Kṛṣṇa	:	Incarnation of God, who is the guide, philosopher of Arjuna.
Kṣatriyas	:	The warrior caste.
Kurukṣetra	:	An area identified in North India. 100 miles from Delhi—which was the battlefield in the epic Mahābhārta.
Lakṣāgṛha	:	House of Lacquer that is easily comb - ustible.
Lakṣmaṇa	:	Brother of Lord Rāma.
Lakṣmaṇa Rekhā	:	Implying a limit one must not cross in one's actions.
Lakṣhmī	:	Goddess of wealth, prosperity.
Leo Tolstoy	:	A Russian writer of repute.
Lokasaṃgraha	:	Maintenance of welfare of society at large.
Mahābhārata	:	Epic of India of which the Gītā is a part.
Mantra	:	Sacred verse or specific syllable mantra may be for specific goal or purpose.
Manu	:	Hindu law giver and author of Hindu caste system.

Mūrti	:	Idol—a god depicted in a physical medium to facilitate concentration in one's spiritual pursuit. Mūrti Pūjā-or idol worship is very popular among humans.
Nirguṇa	:	Absence of attributes.
Nirvāṇa	:	Literally extinction, a state of liberation, release from the cycle of birth and death.
Niṣkām	:	Without selfish desire.
Niyama	:	Ethical observance for prayer.
Noor	:	Dynamic energy.
Pañcabhūtas	:	Five elements in nature viz. earth, air, fire, water and space.
Pañcāyata	:	A body of justice givers used by people at grass-roots level in rural India.
Pāṇi	:	The power to grasp.
Paramātmā	:	Supreme soul.
Paśupati	:	A popular Hindu God 'Lord Śiva' meaning deity of animals.
Prakṛti	:	Nature.
Prāṇāyāma	:	Regulated inhaling, retention and exhaling of breathing.
Prārabdha	:	Actions which have not produced their fruit and are carried forward in the next life.
Prasādam	:	A small portion of the offering to a God, received by the offerer.
Pravṛtti	:	Same as *guṇa* or trait.
Pṛthvī	:	Earth.
Rājasika	:	One of the three primal qualities or strands of human nature.
Rāma	:	Hero of the epic Rāmāyaṇa.
Ramakrishna	:	A 19th Century saint and a spiritual leader, founder of Ramakrishna movement.
Rāmāyaṇa	:	Indian epic.
Reiki	:	A concept of healing by correcting the flow of 'life force' in the body.

Ronald Reagan	:	One of the Presidents of U.S.A.
Saguṇa	:	With attributes or qualities.
Śakti	:	Goddess of Power.
Samādhi	:	A state of higher consciousness.
Samāndṛṣṭi	:	Attitude of equanimity and evenmindedness.
Saṃkalpa	:	Will or determination.
Saṁnyāsī	:	Renunciate.
Sancho Panza	:	Attendant of Don Quixote.
Śānti	:	Peace and quiet calmness.
Saraswatī	:	Goddess of Learning associated with fine arts.
Sāttvika	:	One of the three primal qualities or standards of human being, characterised by peace, righteouness, harmony and wisdom, also appends to that which promote these standards.
'Satyameva Jayate'	:	Ultimately Truth Shall Prevail.
Sewādāras	:	Men and women engaged in works of charity.
Sītā	:	Wife of Lord Rāma.
Spinoza	:	Writer and philosopher.
Stephen Hawking	:	A famous contemporary scientist who studied the formation of Black Hole or the planet of heavy matter.
Sūtras	:	Ancient Hindu proverbs designed to help understand nature.
Svabhāva	:	Natural trait, tendency
Svaddhmi	:	Going by one's own desire.
Swayambar	:	A royal ceremony in which the princess selects husband from amongst the gathered princes.
Talisman	:	Name of the main character in the story 'How Much Does a Man Need' by Leo Tolstoy.

Tāmasika	:	One of the three primal qualities or strands of human nature characteristed by dullness ignorance depending on the nature of food we consume.
Upaniṣads	:	Ancient Hindu Scriptures.
Urdu	:	One of the languages spoken in North-West India and parts of Pakistan.
Vanaspati	:	Vegetable world.
Varṇa	:	Caste
Vāsanā	:	Basic desires.
Vedas	:	Plural of Veda—four most ancient Hindu scriptures.
Vega	:	Literally speed implying intensity of impact.
Viśwakarmā	:	Diety of those engaged in mechanical work.
Vivekananda	:	Swami Vivekanand (1863-1902) founder of Ramkrishna Matha, learned internationally renowned philosopher of India.
Vṛndāvana	:	Forest birthplace of Lord Kṛṣṇa
Winston Churcill	:	English Prime Minister during the World War II period.
Yādavas	:	A clan of North India in which Lord Kṛṣṇa was born.
Yajñas	:	A ritual of sacrificial fire accompanied by worship, chanting of hymns.
Yajur Veda	:	One of the four Vedas.
Yama	:	Control of one's ethical and moral nature.
Yudhiṣṭhira	:	The eldest of five Pāṇḍava princes known for truthfulness and righteouness.

Bibliography

Agarwal, Staya P., *The Social Role of the Gita How and Why,* Motilal Banarsidass, Delhi, 1st Edition, 1997.

Bacon, Francis, *Essays,* J.M. Dent & Sons Ltd. London, 1st Edition, 1906.

Boslough, John, *Stephen Hawking's Universe,* Avon Books, U.S.A. Ist Avon Books, 1989.

Cassirer, Ernst, *Determinis and Interdeterminism in Modern Physics.*

Chakraborty, Aparna, Karma, *Freedom and Responsibility,* Kaveri Books, Ist Edition, Delhi, 1998.

Chinmayananda, Swami, *The Holy Geeta,* Central Chinmaya Mission Trust, Mumbai, New Edition, 1996.

The Dalai Lama, *An Open Heart,* Little Brown and Company, First Published in Great Britain, 2001.

Dayananda, Swami, *The Teaching of the Bhagavad Gita,* Vision Books, New Delhi, 1st Edition, 1989.

Desai, Mahadev, *The Gospel of Selfless Action or the Gita According to Gandhi Jivanjidahyabhai Desai,* Navajivan Press, Ahmedabad, 1st Edition, 1946.

Edgerton, Franklin, *The Bhagavad Gita,* Motilal Banarsidass, Ist Indian Edition, Delhi, 1994.

Einstein, Albert, *Ideas and Opinions,* Rupa & Co. India, First Rupa Paperback, 1979.

Fritjof Capra, *The Tao of Physics,* Fontana Paperbacks & Reprint of 1st Edition, Great Britain, 1989.

Miguel De Cervantes, *The Adventures of Don Quixote,* Penguin Books, London, first Published, 1950.

Munshi, K.M., *Bhagavad Gita and Modern Life,* Bharatiya Vidya Bhavan, Bombay, 5th Edition, 1960.

Prasad, Ramanand, *The Bhagavad-Gītā,* Motilal Banarsidass, Delhi, 2nd Edition, 1996.

Radhakrishnan, S.(Dr.), *Eastern Religion and Western Thoughts;* Oxford University Press, 2nd Edition, Oxford, 1940.

Radhakrishnan, S. (Dr.), *The Bhagavadgita,* George Allen and Unwin Ltd. Great Britain, 2nd Edition, Oxford, 1970.

Russell, Bertrand, *The Impact of Science on Society,* First Published by Unwin Hyman, 1976.

Sagan, Carl, *Cosmos,* Ballantin Books, U.S.A. 1st Ballentin Books Edition, 1980.

Skolimowski, Henryk , *Dancing Shiva in the Ecological Age, Great* Clarion Books, 1st Edition, New Delhi, 1991.

Zukav, Gary, *The Dancing Wu Li Masters,* Bantam Books, U.S.A. & Canada, 1980.

Index

BOOKS OF RELATED INTEREST FROM NAB

THE GITA FOR 21st CENTURY— *S.P. Agarwal*
This latest version of Bhagavad-Gita (with shlokas in Sanskrit and commentary in English) explains how the message of social service has been derived from this universal scripture. Written in a simple style, *The Gita for the 21st Century* will enable common people (including high school students) to obtain a clear understanding of the teachings of the Gita so that they can work efficiently for the good of the society (and for their own good too).

ISBN: 81-7822-153-5

BHAGAVAD-GITA —*William Quan Judge*
The Gita offers a succinct summary of ancient Indian philosophy, with particular emphasis on the Supreme Spirit as both immanent and transcendent. Since its introduction into the Western world some two hundred years ago, the poem has been translated into practically every modern tongue, and is today the most widely read and discussed of all Eastern scriptures. Its emphasis is on two aspects of selflessness.

ISBN: 81-7822-096-2

REALIZATION OF THE SUPREME SELF—*T. Leggett*
The special contribution of the Gita is yoga, practical methods for expanding individual consciousness to realize the supreme Self. This book presents the Gita yoga in the light of explanations by Sankara. Also the Gita is directed at the vigorously active, with responsibilities in the world. The whole basis of Gita yoga is confirmation through experiment, not mere exhortation. This book presents the Gita as a training manual for spiritual practice.

ISBN: 81-7822-071-7

THE HINDU MIND — *Bansi Pandit*
This is a remarkable and highly rewarding book. It is rational, objective, interesting, relevant, and meaningful. In his philosophical discussions, enhanced by a rational, scientific, and truly moral sensibility that is distinctly unique to Hinduism, Mr. Pandit unravels the genius and vision of Hinduism. This book lucidly explains Hinduism in a nutshell. The handy volume has answers to a number of questions on wide-ranging issues.

ISBN: 81-7822-007-5

THE BOOK OF HINDU IMAGERY: Gods, Manifestations and Their Meaning—*Eva Rudy Jansen*
Hinduism is more than a religion; it is a way of life. This volume is a compilation of important deities and their divine manifestations, to help the reader understand the significance of the Hindu pantheon. Over 100 illustrations and several photographs make this book an important reference, both to the student of Hindu art and the interested amateur.

ISBN: 81-7822-056-3

TEN UPANISHADS OF FOUR VEDAS—*R. K. Piparaiya*
Upanishads are a record of human mind's earliest contemplative flights to the Unknown. Many of the anonymous seekers preceded great Masters and Prophets like Lao-Tzu, Confucius, Socrates, Zoroaster, Buddha, Mahavira, Abraham and Jesus, by at least a few centuries. Physicists' concept of Ultimate Reality has progressed from atoms to sub-atomic particles to vibrating strings; and search for a Theory of Everything continues.

ISBN: 81-7822-159-4

NOBODY HOME: From Belief to Clarity—*J. Kersschot*
This book can be used as an initiation into a new way of seeing, into the recognition that there is another possibility, which simply transforms everything. Nobody can tell you what to do or where to go. You may discover that your true nature is so much more than you always imagined it to be and that your awareness is not limited to the function of your brain, but that it goes beyond the limitations of your body and mind.

ISBN: 81-7822-192-6

KAILASH MANSAROVAR — *Nilesh D. Nathwani*
This profusely illustrated travelogue is a tale about fancies and fears, adventures and aspirations, expectations and disillusions, escapes and retreats experienced by the adventurous pilgrimage team. This travelogue takes us on a journey to the wild, seldom travelled northern route visiting the remote cities, towns and monasteries of Tibet. This is an engrossing, touching and remarkable account of a picturesque travel with nice imagery.

ISBN: 81-7822-054-7